RIPLEY'S Believe It or Not!®

2026

Ryan DeSear Vice President, Attraction Operations and Technology
Suzanne Smagala-Potts Senior Manager

Editor Jordie R. Orlando
Project Manager Yaneisy Contreras
Text Geoff Tibballs
Feature Contributors Amanda Askew, Emily Harriss, Allyson Iovino, Jordan Neese, Jordie R. Orlando, Kyra Wojdyla
Copy Editors Amanda Askew, Jordie R. Orlando, Kyra Wojdyla
Fact-checkers Amanda Askew, Engrid Barnett
Proofreader Amanda Askew
Indexer Amanda Askew

Designers Rose Audette, Ekechi Pitt
Reprographics Bob Prohaska, Michael Smagala
Cover Designer Rose Audette

Special Thanks Gabby Barela, Tacita Barrera, Steve Campbell, Kieran Castaño, John Corcoran, Denis Diaz, Barbara Faurot, Jeff Goldman, Chris Graham, Caleb Hagood, Axel Jimenez, Amanda Joiner, Colton Kruse, Matt Mamula, Julia Moellmann, Bobby Orlando, Andrew Petersen, Bretta Sejas, Sabrina Sieck, Emmanuel Tarantino, Alejandra Vidal

Copyright © 2025 by Ripley Entertainment Inc.

All rights reserved. Ripley's, Believe It or Not!, and Ripley's Believe It or Not! are registered trademarks of Ripley Entertainment Inc.

ISBN 978-1-529-96102-7

First published in Great Britain in 2025 by Century

Century
Penguin Random House UK
One Embassy Gardens
8 Viaduct Gardens
London SW11 7BW

www.penguin.co.uk

Century is part of the Penguin Random House group of companies whose addresses can be found at global.penguinrandomhouse.com

ISBN 978-1-529-96102-7
10 9 8 7 6 5 4 3 2 1

No part of this publication may be reproduced in whole or in part, or stored in a retrieval system, or transmitted in any form or by any means, electronic, mechanical, photocopying, recording, or otherwise, without written permission from the publisher. For information regarding permission, write to:

Vice President, Creative Solutions
Ripley Entertainment Inc.
9545 S. John Young Parkway, Suite 222
Orlando, Florida 32819
publishing@ripleys.com

A CIP catalogue record for this book is available from the British Library.

Printed in China by Leo Paper

PUBLISHER'S NOTE
While every effort has been made to verify the accuracy of the entries in this book, the Publishers cannot be held responsible for any errors contained in the work. They would be glad to receive any information from readers.

WARNING
Some of the stunts and activities in this book are undertaken by experts and should not be attempted by anyone without adequate training and supervision.

Ripley's Believe It or Not!

2026

a Jim Pattison Company

SEEK THE STRANGE

The world is full of the unexpected, the bizarre, and the unbelievable—you just have to know where to look!

From mind-bending marvels to nature's oddest wonders, there's no shortage of extraordinary things waiting to be uncovered. Every twist of history, every jaw-dropping feat, and every bizarre creature in this book goes to show that truth is often stranger than fiction. So, open your mind, question the impossible, and follow your curiosity to the strangest corners of reality. The unbelievable awaits—are you ready to find it?

SHARE YOUR THOUGHTS

Throughout this book, you'll find thought-provoking and interactive questions inspired by the stories inside. Let your creativity run wild, then share your thoughts and discover what other readers have to say!

RIPLEY'S RAMBLES

Robert Ripley set off for his first trip around the world in 1922—long before you could use the internet to research and book a vacation! Ripley sought out the bizarre, the unbelievable, and the extraordinary. He collected artifacts, told stories, and unraveled mysteries. He took what he found and shared it in his *Ripley's Believe It or Not!* newspaper cartoon, radio program, and TV show. All in all, he visited more than 200 countries in his lifetime. With every trip, he proved that truth is often stranger than fiction. Ripley's legacy continues today, inspiring the curious to seek the strange wherever they go!

THE ORIGINAL TRAVEL INFLUENCER!

Ripley decorated his suitcase with stickers from places he visited, including Tokyo, Rotterdam, Chicago, Shanghai, and New York City!

❝ I have traveled in 201 countries and the strangest thing I saw was man. —Robert Ripley

CHECK OUT THESE THROWBACK PHOTOS FROM ROBERT RIPLEY'S TRAVELS!

SEE PAGE 70 FOR SOME "GREAT" FACTS!

Robert Ripley at the Great Wall of China in the early 1930s.

GREAT WALL OF CHINA

Ripley's favorite country to visit was China. He preferred to stray off the beaten path, beyond tourist traps. Throughout the years, he watched as the influence of war transformed his peaceful trips into tense, stressful journeys. Nevertheless, he continued to go and bring back stories to tell, as well as souvenirs to fill his home.

UNDERGROUND FAIRYLAND

In 1932, Ripley explored the South Pacific on a cruise. Over the course of three months, he visited over a dozen countries and performed transoceanic radio broadcasts along the way. During this trip, he explored New Zealand's Waitomo Cave. He called it an "underground fairyland!"

SEE A COLOSSEUM MADE OF CHOCOLATE ON PAGE 160!

CHECK OUT PAGE 190 TO SEE THE CAVES IN FULL COLOR!

ART APPRECIATION

Ripley found himself "breathless and bewildered" by what he saw in Rome, Italy. As an artist himself, he was blown away by the work of Michelangelo. Ripley also enjoyed seeing the Colosseum in person for the first time, calling it a "stupendously impressive" and "profound" structure.

> " The principal delight in my Believe It or Not work is the pleasure of traveling. —Robert Ripley

SEEK THE STRANGE

WHAT'S NEW?

OUR NEW HEADQUARTERS IN ORLANDO, FLORIDA!

WELCOME HOME

Ripley's Believe It or Not! World Entertainment has moved to new headquarters in Orlando, Florida! The colorful space features a jaw-dropping lobby filled with oddities, a robust art department, and upgraded facilities to house the Ripley's Collection—including a state-of-the-art archival vault to preserve rare and valuable artifacts. Our new home ensures Ripley's legacy of sharing the strange and extraordinary continues for years to come!

BIGGER AND BETTER THAN EVER!

TALLEST LIVING MAN WAX FIGURE

SHORTEST LIVING WOMAN WAX FIGURE

HIGHS AND LOWS

Ripley's Art Department has been hard at work crafting incredible new wax figures! Among them is Sultan Kösen, the world's tallest living man, towering at an astonishing 8 feet 2.8 inches (2.5 meters). Our costume designer needed a ladder to get his measurements! The team also made a figure of Jyoti Amge, the world's shortest living woman, standing at just 24.7 inches (62.8 cm) tall!

CHEERS TO BRANSON!

In 2024, Ripley's Believe It or Not! Branson celebrated 30 years of the unbelievable! Since 1994, this iconic Missouri attraction has wowed visitors with over 500 oddities, interactive exhibits, and mind-bending displays. Here's to another 30 great years!

30 YEARS STRANGE!

TURTLE MOBILITY AID!

MEET BANDIT!

Say "*Shell*-o" to Bandit, the newest *sea*-lebrity at Ripley's Aquarium of Myrtle Beach! She was found stranded on a Georgia beach in 2021 after a boat propeller injury left her partially paralyzed. She was rescued by the Georgia Sea Turtle Center, and in 2024, Bandit joined the Ripley's family! Visit the Marine Science Research Center to see Bandit in action and learn her incredible story!

Bandit has a special weight pouch attached to her shell that lets her glide effortlessly through the water.

SEEK THE STRANGE

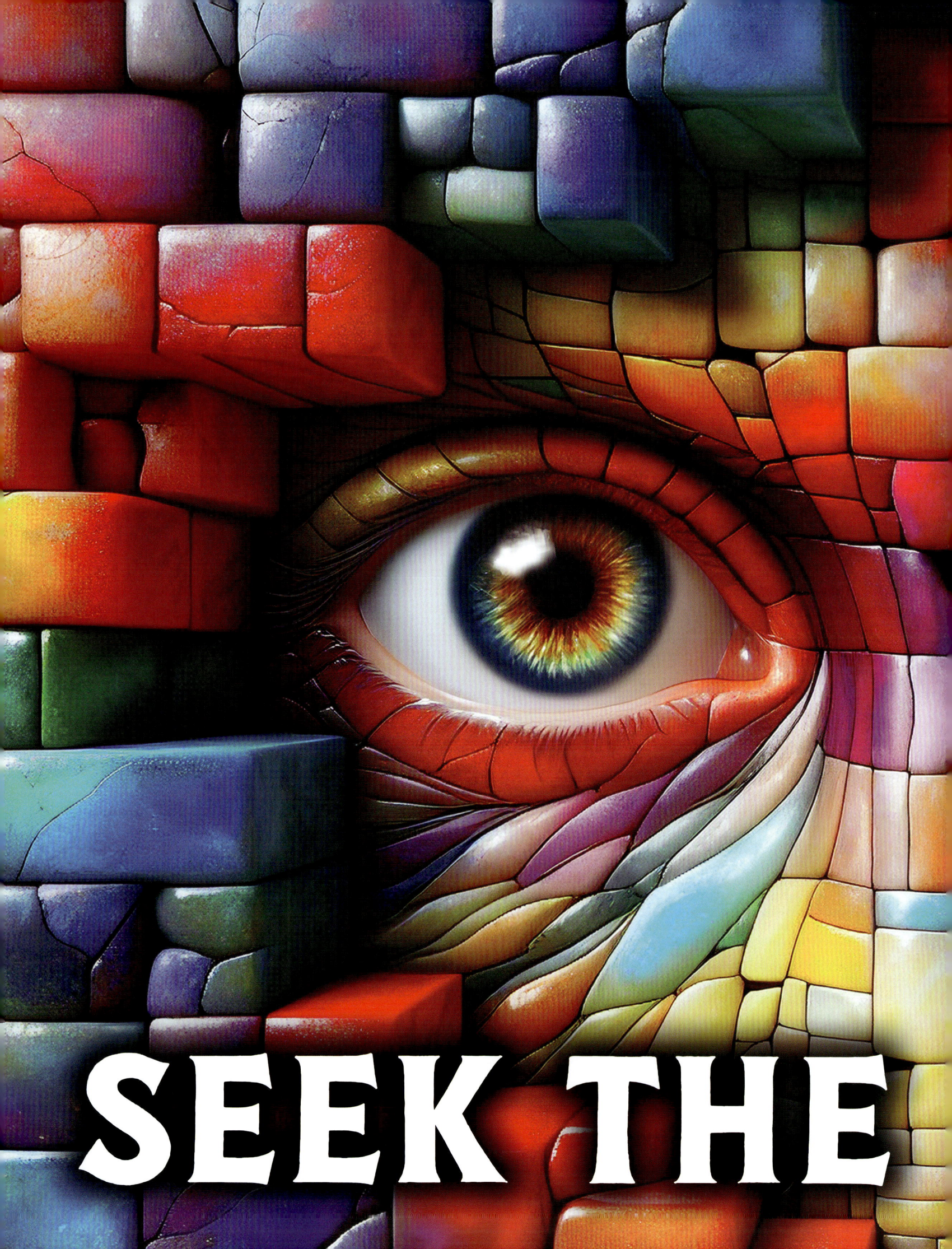

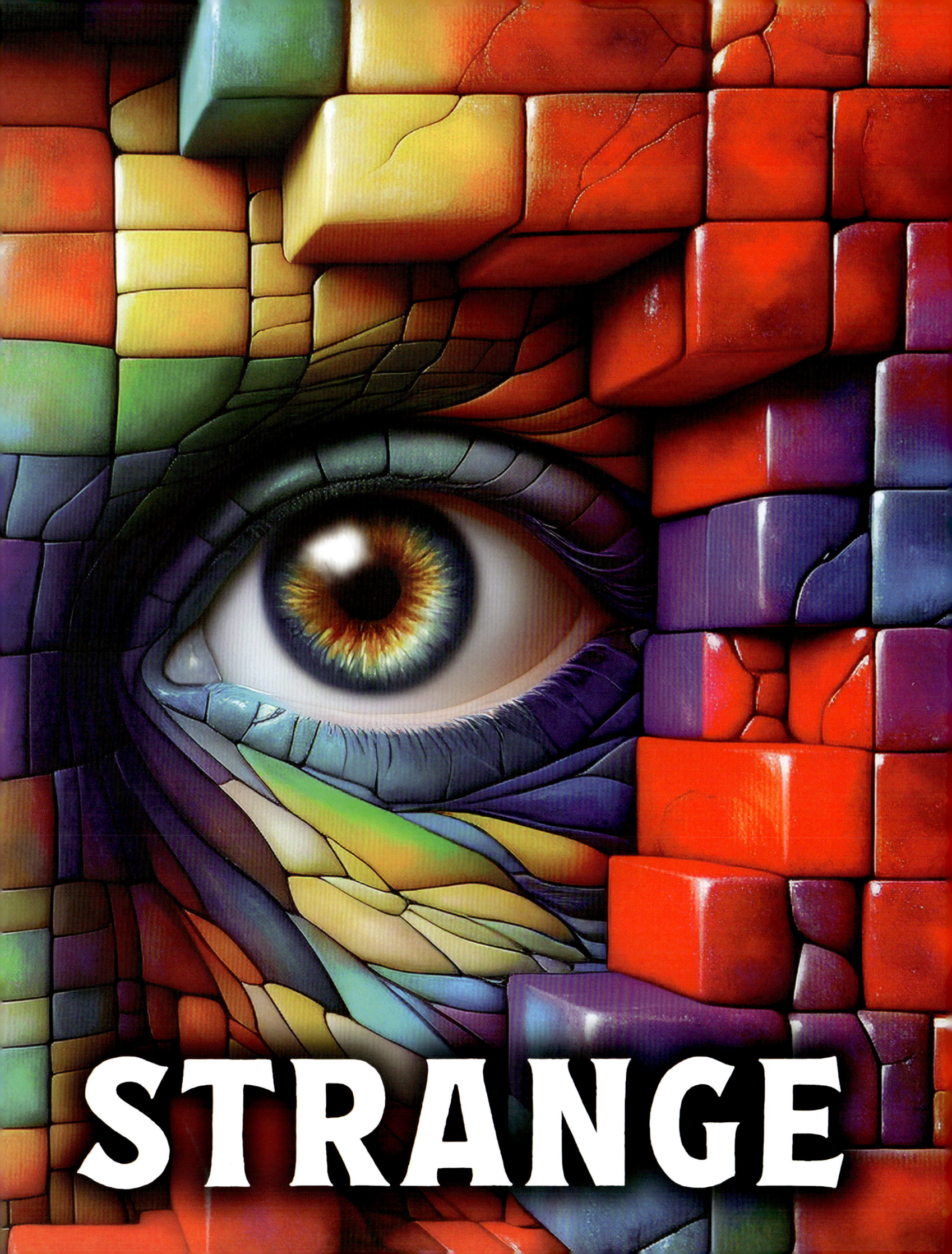

RIPLEY'S Believe It or Not!®

em🙂ji ART

New York artist Lauren Edelstein makes celebrity portraits on her phone by layering thousands of emojis!

You thought your emoji game was next level? Think again. Lauren's use of emojis is totally out of the box. From turning peppers into nails to using crickets for eyelashes, her creativity knows no end! Lauren places the emojis one at a time. It takes many hours, and a lot of screen time, to get it all just right! For example, Dolly Parton's eye makeup was made from emojis like the spider, crystal ball, and pink flower. She used 1,258 emojis in total to create the portrait! Talk about using your *emoji*-nation.

SNOOP DOGG

BRITNEY SPEARS

AFGHANISTAN ▶ As of 2016, there is only pig in the entire country of Afghanistan—Khanzir at Kabul Zoo. **ALBANIA ▶** The most driven car brand in Albania

PICTURE *Perfect*

The Dubai Frame is a massive building that offers views of both the old and new parts of the city.

It's the largest frame in the world and helps people see how the city has changed from its past to its modern present. The design of the Dubai Frame was created by architect Fernando Donis. The frame is 492 feet (150 m) tall and has glass elevators to take visitors to the top. There, they can walk on a clear glass pathway that stretches across the entire 312-foot (95-m) width.

CRANE IN THE CLOUDS!

season to prevent students from cheating. **ANDORRA** ▶ The principality of Andorra, located between Spain and France, has no airports, trains, or seaports!

SPORTS STADIUM ▶ With a capacity of 16,360, Monaco's main sports stadium, Stade Louis II, can hold 45 percent of the principality's population.

COLOR QUESTION ▶ Since 1996, New Mexico has had its own official state question—"Red or green?"—referring to the choice of red or green chile sauce, a question frequently heard in the state's restaurants.

FORBIDDEN FOODSTUFF ▶ Chewing gum has been banned for sale in Singapore since 1992, except for medical reasons.

GRAB A GOAT ▶ On the island of Alicudi, located off the coast of Italy, there are about 100 residents and 600 wild goats. With the animals damaging gardens and even wandering into homes, in 2024 the mayor announced an "adopt-a-goat" program, allowing island visitors to take away up to 50 goats each by boat.

POPULAR PAIRS ▶ At the height of its popularity, the Tokyo Spectacles Museum store displayed 120,000 pairs of eyeglasses and sunglasses on its walls.

TASTY TREAT ▶ Mexican company Mazapán de la Rosa created a 1,429-pound (648-kg) marshmallow in Guadalajara. It took a team of about 100 people 53 hours to prepare the tasty treat.

DIVE DETECTOR
Using a metal detector, Darick Langos, a scuba diver from Port Barrington, Illinois, has recovered more than 200 Apple watches from the water at the Chain O'Lakes State Park.

MANY MENUS ▶ Henry Voigt of Delaware has a collection of about 10,000 vintage American menus, some dating back to the 1840s. One menu, from Taylor's Saloon in New York, has 58 pages.

BEER BIRTHPLACE ▶ Adolph Coors, who founded Coors beer in 1873, was born in the German town of *Bar*men!

STICK AIRSHIP ▶ New Jersey's Naval Air Engineering Station, Lakehurst, was the location of the 1937 *Hindenburg* disaster. Hanging from the ceiling of its museum is a 12-foot-long (3.6-m) model of the ill-fated airship, built from 6,000 popsicle sticks.

COFFIN CAR ▶ A custom dragster car shaped like a casket sold at auction in 2024 for $28,750. The bodywork is an 8-foot-long (2.4-m) fiberglass casket, at the rear of which is a seat for the driver. It is street-legal and is registered in New York as a 1928 Ford. It was inspired by the Drag-U-La coffin car in an episode of *The Munsters*.

UNKNOWN STONE ▶ There are at least 255 ancient granite and sandstone pyramids in Sudan, more than double the number in Egypt. The first was constructed around 751 BC.

WARCRAFT WOW ▶ Hungarian video gamer Barnabás Vujity-Zsolnay played *World of Warcraft* for 59 hours 20 minutes straight.

LOOPY LIFT
There is a type of elevator with no buttons, no doors, and no stops! Called paternoster elevators, they move in a constant loop on a chain up and down a building. People can step in or out of the open stall as it passes by. Safety concerns have made paternoster elevators rare, but there are a few hundred still used in Europe today.

ANGOLA ▶ A Boeing 727 was stolen from an airport in Luanda, Angola, on May 25, 2003, and it

THE RIPLEY'S COLLECTION

PIGCASSO PAINTING

The artist behind this abstract piece is Pigcasso—a painting pig! She was rescued from a South African slaughterhouse by Joanne Lefson, who helped nurture Pigcasso's hidden talent. This piece is titled *Amazone*.

CATALOG NO. 175866

Signed with a noseprint!

SPEED PAINTING

This landscape painting was completed in less than one minute! Art instructor Conni Gordon painted this lush green landscape with a lake and snow-capped mountains in just 40 seconds.

CATALOG NO. 13716

Masterpiece in a minute!

GARLIC ART

Garlic isn't just for eating—in the hands of Lauren Mark Libunao from the Philippines, it's used to make art! He painted this quetzal bird with garlic extract.

CATALOG NO. 167635

Painted with garlic!

SEEK THE STRANGE

Ripley's Believe It or Not!

PRETTY IN PINK!

THINK PINK

The Amazon river dolphin has pink skin! Also known as "botos," these dolphins aren't born pink. Their skin starts gray and turns pink as they get older. Male botos are usually a brighter pink than females. The pinker their skin, the more attractive they are to a female! The pink color is thought to be scar tissue from rough games or fighting over mates. Diet, sun exposure, and behavior also play roles in how pink the dolphin appears—from mostly gray all the way to bubblegum pink!

SUSPECTED SPY ▶ A pigeon suspected of being a Chinese spy was detained by Indian police for eight months before finally being released in January 2024. The bird was captured near Mumbai with two rings tied to its legs, carrying what appeared to be a message in Chinese writing. However, it turned out to be an escaped racing pigeon from Taiwan.

TALL TRIP ▶ Benito, a four-year-old giraffe, made a 40-hour, 1,200-mile (1,930-km) road trip from a zoo in hot, arid Northern Mexico to the cooler Africam Safari park in Puebla, Central Mexico. He traveled in a 16-foot-tall (5-m) crate on the back of a flatbed truck. The roof of his crate could be lowered to pass under low bridges.

MISTAKEN MEAL ▶ When highly stressed, snakes will sometimes eat themselves. If they get too hot, they can become confused and will start to eat their tail and work their way along their own body. If not stopped soon enough, they can draw blood and end up killing themselves.

SWIFT SLEEP

To protect their eggs and newborn chicks, chinstrap penguins in Antarctica sleep for only four seconds at a time. They take thousands of quick naps every day so they can be constantly alert.

TERMITE TERMINATOR

The aardwolf is neither an aardvark nor a wolf! A distant cousin of the hyena, the aardwolf lives in the African wilderness. Oddly, it feasts almost entirely on termites! Its super long, sticky tongue helps it scoop up the insects without destroying the termite mound. This nocturnal mammal can eat up to 300,000 termites in one night! Because it doesn't eat meat, most of the aardwolf's teeth are flat, little nubs. But it still has sharp canines that it uses for self-defense!

SPEEDY SPIT ▶ Spitting spiders can trap their prey by firing streams of poisonous, sticky silk from their fangs at speeds of more than 98 feet (30 m) per second.

CARING CROCS ▶ A young dog that was being chased by a pack of feral dogs sought refuge in the shallow waters of the Savitri River in India's Maharashtra State—unaware that three adult mugger crocodiles were lurking nearby. But instead of snatching the dog as prey, the crocs gently steered the dog to a safe area of the riverbank, allowing it to make its escape.

EEL EVICTION ▶ When a 34-year-old man went to a hospital in Quang Ninh Province, Vietnam, with severe stomach cramps, doctors saved his life by removing a live, 12-inch-long (30-cm) eel from his abdomen. They believe the eel somehow entered through his anus, moved to his colon, bit through the intestine, and then slithered into his abdomen.

has never been found! **ANTIGUA & BARBUDA** ▶ Boggy Peak, the highest point on the island nation of Antigua and Barbuda, was renamed Mount Obama

Larger than LIFE

When animals roam the Miniature Park in Crimea, they look like movie monsters!

Animals from the park's zoo sometimes walk through the outdoor display. When they do, they look huge! That's because the buildings are tiny copies of real places. The park has 86 miniature models of famous landmarks from around Crimea. They're built 25 times smaller than the real places! Many of the buildings have tiny people and cars parked around them that also look real.

from 2009 to 2016. **ARGENTINA** ▸ Paleontologists in Argentina discovered a new carnivorous

SEEK THE STRANGE

RIPLEY'S Believe It or Not!

BRICK BEASTS

There was a wild twist at Scotland's Edinburgh Zoo in 2024—some animals were made of toy bricks! The exhibit featured 25 life-size animals made of about 1.5 million bricks. It took nearly 400 hours to build all of them! Some of the brick animals weighed almost the same as their real counterparts. The brick gorilla weighed 348 pounds (158 kg), the size of an average male gorilla! One of the largest models was an African elephant and its baby calf, which took five people 1,600 hours and 149,071 bricks to build.

SPRINTING SAVIOR ▶ Running in the 2023 Chicago Marathon, athlete Sarah Bohan from Massachusetts was on course for a personal best time until she stopped 5 miles (8 km) from the finish to rescue a tiny, cowering stray kitten. She carried the kitten for the next mile before handing it to some spectators who offered to give it a home.

RAINFOREST REPTILE ▶ Scientists in the Amazon rainforest discovered a northern green anaconda that measured 26 feet (8 m) long and weighed 440 pounds (200 kg). The snake's body was the thickness of a car tire and its head was as big as an adult human's.

COIN COLLECTION ▶ Thibodaux, a rare, 36-year-old white alligator living at the Henry Doorly Zoo in Omaha, Nebraska, underwent surgery to remove 70 coins from his stomach.

FIRECRACKER FISH ▶ A tiny 0.4-inch-long (10-mm) fish native to Myanmar, *Danionella cerebrum*, drums out a rhythm on its swim bladder that can reach 140 decibels—as loud as a firecracker. The drumming sound may be used as a means of underwater communication.

Cucumber Couture

Xandiloquence "Xandi" Bizarre makes hats out of dried cucumbers!

To make a hat, Xandi peels cucumbers into very thin strips. He spends about 20 minutes putting the strips in a hat shape. He then dries it for about 12 hours. Sometimes he coats the hat in resin. This makes the hat hard and helps it last up to a few months. Without resin, the hats only last for about a day! Xandi has tried making hats from other fruits and vegetables like apples, pears, and radishes, but cucumbers are his favorite!

Xandiloquence "Xandi" Bizarre

dinosaur species, *Guemesia ochoai*, that was essentially armless thanks to its super short front limbs. **ARMENIA** ▶ Armenia's public school curriculum includes

DOGGY DETECTOR ▶ Kobe, a four-year-old husky dog, saved an entire neighborhood from a possible gas explosion. When Kobe dug a hole twice in the front yard—something he had never done before—his owner Chanell Bell became suspicious, especially as there had recently been a gas leak in her home. She used a gas detection device near the hole and discovered a major new leak that could have devastated the neighborhood.

DOUBLE TROUBLE ▶ Peggy Jones was mowing the lawn of her home in Silsbee, Texas, when a snake suddenly fell from the sky and wrapped itself around her arm. As she was trying to free herself, a hawk swooped down and clawed at her to get the meal it had dropped. Eventually the hawk tore the snake from her arm and flew off with it, leaving her arm covered in blood.

ACCIDENT-PRONE STONE ▶ Unlucky American actress Emma Stone suffered seven broken bones before she turned 30. In 2019, she broke her shoulder in two places after slipping on the floor while celebrating a David Blaine stunt. She even had a black eye on her wedding day in 2020 after the handle of a fridge door broke off and hit her in the face.

Trimming off the excess yarn.

CRAFTY CAKE

Heather Rios makes cake out of yarn! While her creations look good enough to eat, they're made using punch needle embroidery, acrylic paint, clay, and foam. She uses a needle to poke yarn through fabric to make the cake pieces and sprinkles. At first, it looks like little loops of yarn. But then Heather trims off the excess, and the cake is revealed! For the frosting, she uses acrylic paint.

EACH HAT IS A ONE-OF-A-KIND VEGGIE CREATION!

The hats are dried for 12 hours in a dehydrator machine.

mandatory chess lessons! **AUSTRALIA** ▶ Mount Disappointment in Australia earned its name

SEEK THE STRANGE

BANG-UP JOB

Vin Wardman, from Craven Arms, England, turned his mobility scooter into a replica of the *Chitty Chitty Bang Bang* car!

To build it, the 92-year-old repurposed things like an old trash can, a cake tin, stroller wheels, and a picture frame. The project took him around three months to finish. Vin has made model scooters for years. His previous creations include Thomas the Tank Engine and royal-themed trains for British monarchs. But Vin believes the *Chitty Chitty Bang Bang* scooter is his best yet!

The 1968 musical Chitty Chitty Bang Bang was based on a children's book by Ian Fleming—better known as the creator of James Bond.

NAILED IT

California artist Vivian Xue Rahey paints hyperrealistic images on a very small canvas: press-on nails! She hand-paints each one with a thin brush. A full set takes many hours to complete. Most are themed after movies or celebrities. Vivian loves taking her nails to the next level. Some glow in the dark or are covered in crystals. Some even have details that only show under UV light!

This James Bond nail set took Vivian more than 65 hours to paint!

TOILET TABOO ▸ The family bathroom in *The Brady Bunch* did not have a toilet because when the show first aired in 1969, U.S. networks were still wary of showing a toilet on TV.

POTTER PROGRESS ▸ It took J.K. Rowling five years to write the first Harry Potter book, *Harry Potter and the Sorcerer's Stone*.

FELINE FRAGRANCE ▸ In the 1690s, English novelist Daniel Defoe, author of *Robinson Crusoe*, tried to sell a perfume made from the anal gland secretions of civet cats.

TWO ROLES ▸ In adaptations of *Peter Pan*, Mr. Darling and Captain Hook are traditionally played by the same actor.

SMALL SANDWICH ▸ British miniatures artist Nadia Michaux created a realistic clay model of a fish stick sandwich. It is less than 0.3 inches (8 mm) tall and weighs about the same as a single pea. The sandwich even has a tiny splash of ketchup.

MISSED ROLE ▸ Frank Sinatra wanted to play the Joker in the 1960's *Batman* TV series, but he lost out because the part had already been awarded to Cesar Romero.

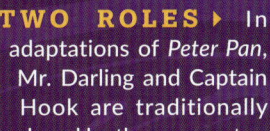

THE RIPLEY'S COLLECTION

CHITTY CHAIR

This rocking chair, featured in the 1968 movie *Chitty Chitty Bang Bang*, was designed by Rowland Emett. A cartoonist and kinetic sculptor, he created many props for the film—including the title car!

CATALOG NO. 11889

This chair rocks!

ODD BODS

RIPLEY'S Believe It or Not!®

Have you ever wondered how rare your body might be? From special muscles to unique toes, everyone has something that makes them one-of-a-kind. This list looks at some cool, uncommon body features. Whether you have them or not, remember that every body is awesome just the way it is!

1. HAIR SWIRLS

About 5 percent of people have a double crown, where hair spirals out in two spots on the scalp. It doesn't affect how hair grows, but it's a rare trait! Scientists don't know exactly why some people have it, but it seems to occur evenly across different populations.

2. EAR HOLE

A preauricular pit is a tiny hole near the ear that happens in about 1 out of 100 people. These pits are usually harmless and are present at birth. They can occur on both ears, but it is more common to just have a pit on one side.

What's one thing you love about your body?
Share your thoughts...

---

volcanoes are found in Azerbaijan. **BAHAMAS ▶** The pink sand found on the beaches of Harbour Island in the Bahamas gets its color from millions of

3. HAND LINE

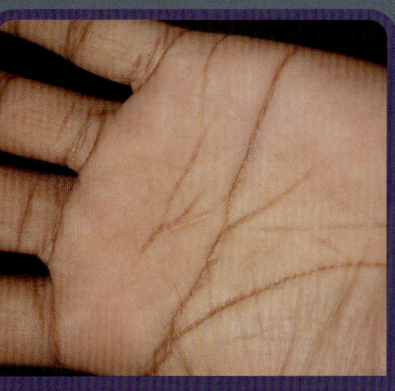

About 1 in 30 people have a single line across their palm instead of the usual two or three. It's rare, but it doesn't affect how your hand works. Called palmar creases, the lines form on the hand before birth.

5. NEAT NAVEL

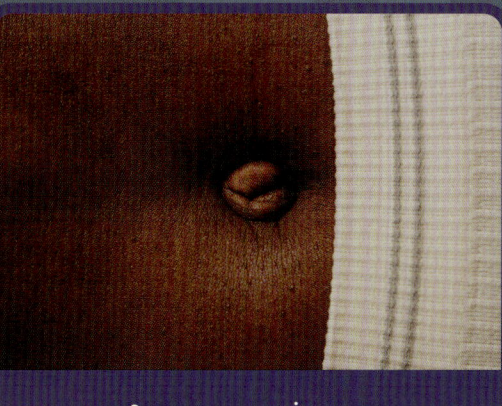

Most people have an "innie," but about 10 percent of people have an "outie" belly button! Outies happen when the skin around the belly button bulges outward. It's a simple difference in how the belly button forms after birth. Though rare, outies are perfectly normal and don't impact a person's health.

4. MISSING MUSCLE

This palmaris longus muscle is missing in up to 26 percent of people. Bring your pinky and thumb together, and bend your wrist so your hand moves up. If a long, thin line pops out on your wrist, you've got it. If you don't have it, don't worry—it's not needed for normal movement. Some people even have it removed during surgery and used elsewhere!

6. TOP TOE

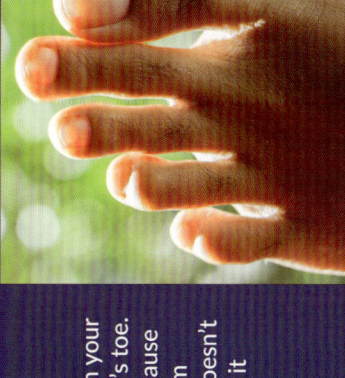

If your second toe is longer than your big toe, you might have Morton's toe. It's often called "Greek toe" because of its appearance in statues from ancient Greece. Morton's toe doesn't usually cause problems, though it can affect the way shoes fit.

SEEK THE STRANGE

RIPLEY'S Believe It or Not!®

MYSTERY MARATHON

The Barkley Marathons is one of the toughest footraces in the world—and possibly the most mysterious.

Held every year in Tennessee's Frozen Head State Park, the race is at least 100 miles (160 km) long. The exact distance is unknown because the course changes each year. The race has a 60-hour time limit and includes steep hills, thick forests, and very rough terrain. Runners can only use a map and compass to find their way—no GPS allowed. Just 40 people are permitted to compete each year. Since the first race in 1986, around 1,000 runners have started the Barkley Marathons. Fewer than 30 have finished.

In 2024, Jasmin Paris became the first woman to complete the Barkley Marathons, finishing with just 99 seconds to spare!

Runners must find books hidden along the route and tear out pages to prove they completed each section.

RUNNING WILD

- Athletes hoping to run the Barkley Marathons **must submit an essay** on why they should be allowed to compete.
- The race's **start time** is unknown until a **conch shell** is blown **one hour before it begins**.
- **Race bib number 1** is always given to the person deemed to be the least likely to finish—the **"human sacrifice."**
- The **entry fee** for first-time runners is a **license plate** from their home state or country.
- The amount of climbing in the entire race is equivalent to going up **Mount Everest—twice**.
- **Returning runners** are asked to give a pair of **dress socks** as their entry fee.

in Bahrain generates nearly 2,000 pounds (907 kg) of waste per year. **BANGLADESH** ▶ More people live in Bangladesh than in Russia, despite the former

HOW COAL IS THAT?

KEEPING IT COAL

Did Christmas come early? Not all these coal carriers are on the naughty list. Hundreds joined the World Coal Carrying Championships in Gawthorpe, a village in West Yorkshire, England. More than 400 people, including 200 kids, signed up to run 3,320 feet (1,012 m) while carrying heavy sacks of coal! Men carried around 110-pound (50-kg) sacks, and women carried 44-pound (20-kg) sacks. The World Coal Carrying Championships, held every Easter Monday, started in 1963 as a challenge between men in a local pub. It has since grown, attracting people from around the world.

PEOPLE POWER!

PLANE PULL

At the fifteenth annual Dorset Plane Pull, over 400 people helped move a 35-ton Boeing 737! Teams of 20 worked together to pull the plane 164 feet (50 m) down the Bournemouth Airport runway in England. That's like pulling the weight of nearly eight elephants! The event has been running since 2009 and helps raise money for charity. More than $400,000 has been raised so far. Talk about pulling your weight!

being 115 times smaller. **BARBADOS** ▶ Wearing camouflage clothing is illegal in Barbados.

SEEK THE STRANGE

THE RIPLEY'S COLLECTION

LIND LIMELIGHT

This lamp once lit the stage for famous opera singer Jenny Lind during her 1850–52 U.S. tour, organized by P.T. Barnum. The device created a bright light by burning calcium oxide, or quicklime. To this day, "the limelight" is understood to mean the center of attention.

CATALOG NO. 16933

Jenny Lind, the Swedish Nightingale

THRILLING PROP

This is an original mold of Michael Jackson's werewolf fangs for the legendary 1983 *Thriller* music video. They were crafted by Oscar-winning makeup artist Rick Baker.

CATALOG NO. 168167

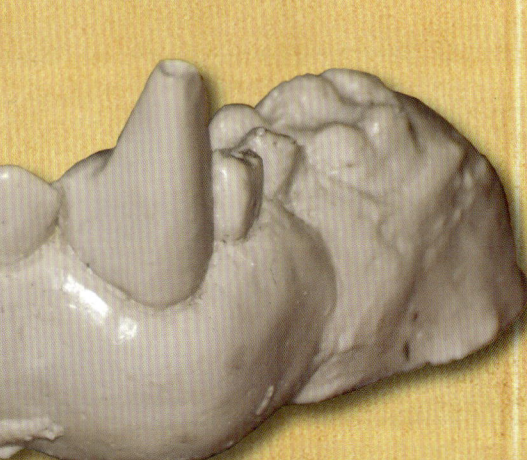

POPULAR PUPPET

This doll is a replica of Charlie McCarthy, a famous dummy used by ventriloquist Edgar Bergen. The duo was one of the most popular acts in the 1930s. Oddly enough, the height of their career was a radio show—when listeners couldn't even see the dummy talking!

CATALOG NO. 172712

Even celebrities like Marilyn Monroe were fans of Charlie McCarthy!

Ripley's Believe It or Not!

SWORD GLOWS FROM WITHIN!

YOU GLOW GIRL!

Sideshow artist Carmen G. takes the spotlight when it comes to sword swallowing—literally!

In addition to blades, Carmen can also swallow a special light tube. The sword, designed by Carmen and her husband, can be seen glowing from inside her! But it's not all fun and games. Carmen must be careful and time her act perfectly so she does not burn her throat! With her unique skill, she amazes audiences and shows just how daring a sword swallower can be.

BELARUS ▸ You can be fined for driving a dirty car in Belarus. **BELGIUM** ▸ A Belgian farmer accidentally moved the border between his country and France

RIPPED FROM HISTORY

LIGHT LADY

Carmen G. isn't the first person to swallow light! Edna Price was one of the remarkable "human rarities and oddities" who performed at the first Ripley's Believe It or Not! at the Chicago World's Fair in May 1933. She swallowed 2-foot-long (0.6-m) neon tubes that glowed through her throat! Edna could also swallow 12 swords at a time, removing the blades one by one. Robert Ripley dubbed her the "Queen of Sword Swallowers."

SWORD STUNT ▶ Erin Hunter, of Minnesota, can balance 30 swords on her legs simultaneously. She first learned how to balance swords on her body in 2004 when she started taking Middle Eastern dance classes.

BIRTHDAY BASH ▶ Malcolm Metcalf completed 90 new challenges in the nine months leading up to his 90th birthday—including riding a horse, flying a plane, shearing a sheep, and hosting his own radio show.

DIGGING DANCING ▶ After working as a farmer and a street cleaner, Liu Ziqing decided to learn ballet at age 53—and a decade later he was a professional dancer.

SALVAGED SWORD ▶ Magnet fisherman Trevor Penny pulled an 1,100-year-old Viking sword from the River Cherwell in Oxfordshire, England, in 2023. He had cast a powerful magnet into the water in the hope of finding metal objects.

WINNING WHOOPS ▶ Miriam Long from Virginia accidentally hit the wrong button on a lottery vending machine, but her mistake won her a $1 million Powerball prize.

CHICKEN CELEBRATION ▶ Bride Liang Le Wong and groom Xie Peng had a KFC-themed wedding in Singapore, with the bride's bouquet made up of chicken drumsticks. The couple had their first date at a KFC restaurant.

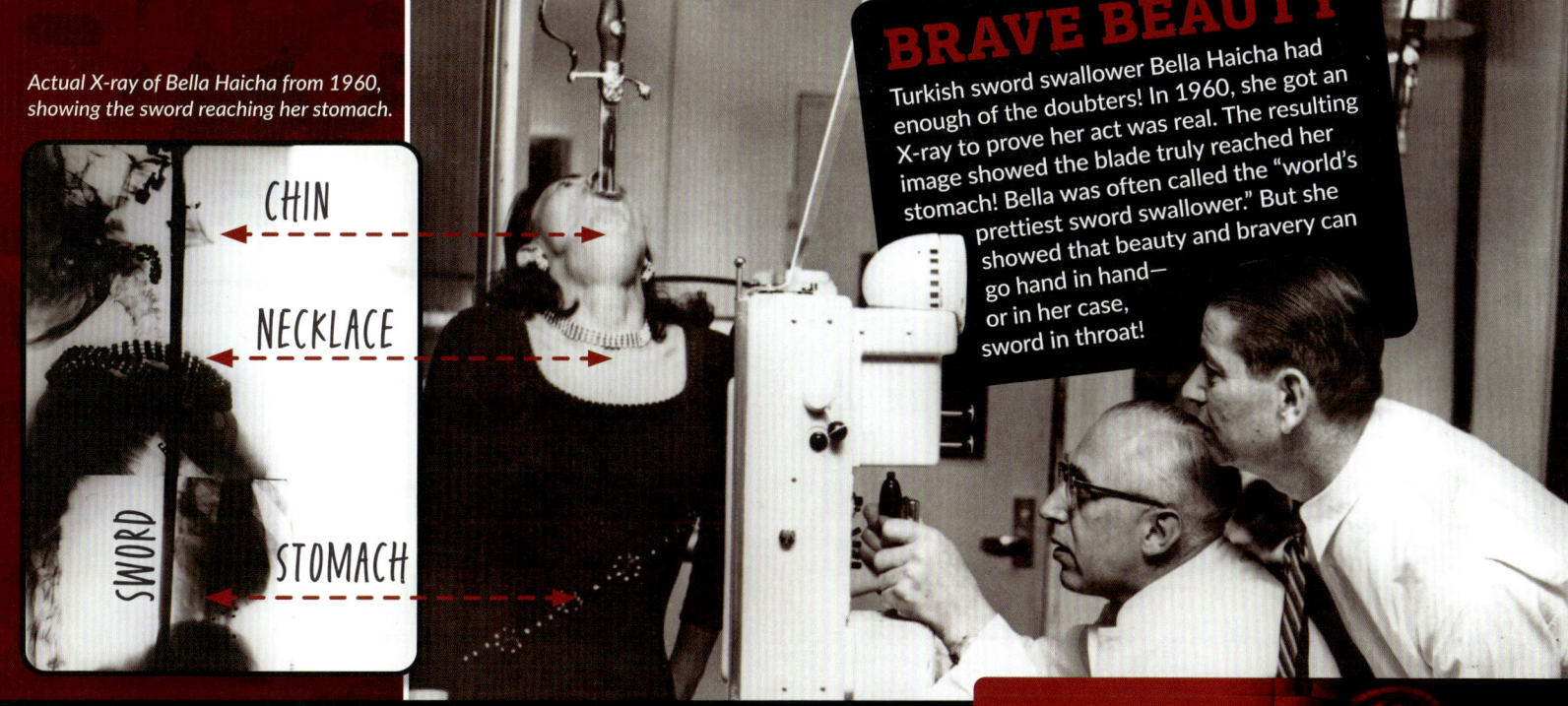

Actual X-ray of Bella Haicha from 1960, showing the sword reaching her stomach.

BRAVE BEAUTY

Turkish sword swallower Bella Haicha had enough of the doubters! In 1960, she got an X-ray to prove her act was real. The resulting image showed the blade truly reached her stomach! Bella was often called the "world's prettiest sword swallower." But she showed that beauty and bravery can go hand in hand—or in her case, sword in throat!

when he relocated one of the boundary stones that had been placed in 1819 by 7.5 feet (2.3 m)

SEEK THE STRANGE

RIPLEY'S Believe It or Not!®

OH, THAT STINGS!

ALL FOR ONE

The Portuguese man o' war looks like a jelly, but don't be fooled! It's actually a siphonophore—a colony of tiny zooids, or clones, working together as one. It has a colorful float that sticks up to 6 inches (15 cm) out of the water and long tentacles that can grow more than 100 feet (30.5 m). Man o' wars live in warm oceans and drift with the wind and currents, sometimes in groups of more than 1,000! Even after washing ashore, they can still sting for weeks. So be careful!

HAZARDOUS HUNGER ▶ A species of Australian mosquito, *Mimomyia elegans*, sucks blood from frogs' nostrils. The insect lands on the frog's back and then crawls to the nostril to start feeding, its thirst for food overcoming the very real risk of being eaten by the frog.

COUNTLESS CATS ▶ U.S. horror author Shirley Jackson always kept at least six black or dark-gray cats. This was to fool her husband, who was very short-sighted and didn't like cats. So because they all looked the same, he never knew exactly how many she had.

SLEEPY SNACKS ▶ Arctic reindeer have changed their behavior to sleep and chew cud at the same time. Cud chewing is when tough plant matter is broken down by being chewed, swallowed, regurgitated, and chewed again. When food is plentiful in summer, reindeer need to eat as much as possible to gain enough weight to survive the long, cold winter—this adaptation means they can feed for longer, even while they are sleeping.

CLEVER CHIMPS ▶ Chimpanzees and bonobos can recognize photos of friends in their group that they haven't seen for over 20 years.

NOXIOUS NEWT ▶ The skin of the California newt produces tetrodotoxin, a potent poison for which there is no known antidote.

MUSICAL MUTT ▶ Storm, a German shepherd dog belonging to Kathy Villa and Aribeth Hurtado, snuck out of her home in California and made her way to a Metallica concert at the nearby SoFi Stadium. She was found sitting in a seat watching the concert, having somehow passed through security.

LEGS FOR DAYS

This bird dad has a leg up on the rest! Despite how it appears, it truly has only two legs. The African jacana is a unique bird that lives in sub-Saharan wetlands. The male will take care of his chicks by himself. To keep them safe, he hides them under his wings. All that is exposed is their little feet, making it look like the feathered father has many legs!

HOW MANY LEGS DO YOU COUNT?

because it was in the way of his tractor, making Belgium temporarily bigger. **BELIZE** ▶ In 2014, divers searching for Mayan artifacts in a sinkhole in Belize

Ssnack ATTACK!

A hungry rat snake needed surgery after eating a gear shift knob!

The reptile was found with a hole worn through its skin. It was taken to Second Chance Wildlife Center in Gaithersburg, Maryland. They performed surgery to remove the object, which shocked the vet when she saw it was a car part! Why did a snake try to eat such a strange item? Probably because the round, white knob looked like an egg—one of a rat snake's favorite snacks!

WORE RIGHT THROUGH SKIN!

CAR PART OR YUMMY EGG?

instead discovered the remains of a 27,000-year-old giant sloth! **BENIN** ▶ The town of Ganvié in

SEEK THE STRANGE

FLOAT FOR GOLD

Ballooning was once part of the Olympics! In 1900, the Games took place in Paris, France. Balloon pilots earned points by competing in events like distance, altitude, and duration. Frenchman Henry de La Vaulx won the most points. His long-distance flight lasted 1,194 miles (1,922 km)! His prize was a gold plate and 1,000 francs—about $13,000 today. It was the only year ballooning was in the Olympics. Motorized sports were banned after 1900.

BALLOON FLYING: AN OLYMPIC SPORT!

THE RIPLEY'S COLLECTION

1900 OLYMPIC MEDAL

Winner's medal for shooting from the 1900 Olympic Games in Paris, France. Held during the world's fair, or Exposition Universelle, it was the first modern Games in which women played.

CATALOG NO. 176053

Rare rectangular medal shape!

banned television until 1999. **BOLIVIA** ▸ Measuring over 4,000 square miles (10,360 sq km), the

SEEK THE STRANGE   35

Feathers and Fur

Australian besties Peggy, Ruby, and Molly prove that friendship has no limits!

Peggy the dog was on a walk with her owners, Juliette Wells and Reece Mortensen, in 2020 when they found a magpie chick. He was all alone and in need of care. So he was brought back to Peggy's home to receive help and named Molly. Peggy and Molly bonded quickly. When Peggy became pregnant a year later, Molly would even sing to the unborn puppies! One of the puppies, Ruby, joined the unlikely flock. Today, the trio are as close as can be and are truly best friends forever!

UNLIKELY TRIO!

Peggy's owners received special permission to care for Molly. You should always contact your local wildlife authorities before touching or trying to help an animal in need.

In what ways are you and your best friend different? Share your thoughts...

Salar de Uyuni salt pan in Bolivia is so flat that rain can't drain—creating the world's largest natural mirror. **BOSNIA & HERZEGOVINA** ▶ The historical

GNOME HOME

Welcome to Gnome Island! This mysterious rock, known as Swallow Craig, is located near Scotland's Inchcolm Island. Gnomes first appeared on the rock in 2010, and no one is sure why. Some think a local fisherman left them there. Others say they escaped from a garden center. Another story even tells the tale of a shipwreck. Gnomes show up on "Inchgnome Island" to this day. Their origins remain a mystery, and the lore only continues to grow!

HANGING WITH A SASSY SEAGULL!

SPITTING SNAKE ▶ The Mozambique spitting cobra can hit targets more than 8 feet (2.5 m) away and is 90 percent accurate from a distance of 5 feet (1.5 m), even when the target is moving. The snake achieves this remarkable aim by taking just one-fifth of a second to predict precisely where the moving target is going to be next. The snake usually aims for its victim's eyes.

ANGRY BIRD ▶ Alejandro Rios was attacked by the same magpie every day for over a week as he biked home from work in Brisbane, Australia. He realized it was personal when the angry bird swooped down to peck at his helmet, but ignored other cyclists. Magpies can remember human faces for long periods of time and are particularly aggressive when they have young chicks.

ELE-FURY ▶ After a man driving a car accidentally hit an elephant calf on a road in Malaysia, the four adult elephants in the herd rushed toward the car, trumpeting loudly, and began trampling it while the man and his family were still inside. The car's left-side doors were crushed and all the windows were smashed. Miraculously, no one was injured and the calf got back to its feet.

MADE BY A UFO?

MISSING PIECE

Is this hole in the clouds proof of alien visitors from another planet? Not quite! It's called a cavum cloud, also known as a hole-punch cloud or fallstreak hole. They form when an airplane flies through a cloud made of extremely cold water droplets. The plane's propellers and wings cause the water droplets to get even colder and turn into ice crystals. The crystals then fall from the cloud, leaving behind a big hole!

Sarajevo Clock Tower in Bosnia and Herzegovina is the only public clock in the world to measure

SEEK THE STRANGE

RIPLEY'S Believe It or Not!®

RIPLEY'S Exclusive

CHALLENGE ACCEPTED

Paralyzed from the waist down after an accident, circus artist Silke Pan redefines what's possible with her unique handstand routine!

In 2007, Silke fell from a trapeze. The injury left her unable to feel anything below her belly button. She had to leave the circus, but her love of performing never faded. Over time, she adapted to her new abilities. She even became a champion para-cyclist! Eventually, Silke relearned how to do handstands. After 14 years away, she returned to the circus. Her amazing strength and balance inspire audiences and prove that determination can overcome even the toughest challenges.

Since she is unable to move her legs, Silke keeps them in place by attaching a rod between her ankles.

lunar time. **BOTSWANA** ▶ There are truffle mines in Botswana's Kalahari Desert. **BRAZIL** ▶ Inmates at federal prisons in Brazil can reduce their sentences

Ripley's spoke with Silke and asked her some quesetions about her journey and approach to life. Check out what she had to say!

Q: What made you want to return to the circus after your accident?
A: One day, 13 long years after the accident, I was doing push-ups. My paralyzed side was strapped to a board to keep it in place, and my husband was holding my legs. Suddenly, my arms had the reflex to seek balance. My husband let go, and I balanced on my arms for a minute! That was my rebirth. I immediately understood that this was the beginning of the realization of a dream I hadn't dared believe in for so long.

Q: What dreams or goals do you hope to achieve next?
A: Since my accident, I consider each day a gift. Of course, I still have big goals in my art, but the fact that I've already overcome so many difficulties in my life and got to where I am now is more beautiful than I could have dreamed. When I balance on my hands, I forget about the handicap and feel like I'm flying.

Q: What do you wish more people knew about artists and athletes with disabilities?
A: We have to train hard like any other top-level athlete, but there are extra factors to consider. You have to constantly listen, adapt, and find new strategies to make progress. I'd say that being an artist or an athlete with a disability requires double the effort to achieve the same goal.

Q: What does your training routine look like?
A: My training includes aerobic exercises, stretching, muscle strengthening, and acrobatic technique. Mental preparation is a vital part of my training. I practice meditation to help me stay calm and focused in moments of great tension.

Q: What advice would you give to someone going through difficult changes?
A: Try to reflect on how you can turn the situation in your favor. Once you change your perspective in life, you'll see the world differently and start seeing opportunities, even if you're in a state of hopelessness. Persevere with faith and optimism until you achieve your goals!

"When I balance on my hands, I forget about the handicap and feel like I'm flying."

THE RIPLEY'S COLLECTION

SUPERMAN CAPE

Worn by actor Christopher Reeve in the walking scenes of 1978's *Superman* and 1980's *Superman II*. A wider cape was used for flying scenes!

CATALOG NO. 168400

RIPLEY'S Believe It or Not!®

WET WEB

Thought you were safe from spiders underwater? Think again. The diving bell spider spends most of its time below the surface!

Found in Europe and parts of Asia, it's the only spider that lives mostly underwater. To breathe, the spider makes an air bubble. First, it spins a silk web between underwater plants. Then, it uses tiny hairs on its body to bring air from the surface to its web. The air collects to make a bubble. The spider makes the air bubble big enough so it can fit inside. Female spiders make bubbles twice as large as males because they need room to care for their babies.

1,788 rooms, 257 toilets, and a garage for 110 cars. **BULGARIA** ▶ In Bulgaria, shaking your head from side-to-side means "yes," while nodding up and down

WACKY WASP

The cuckoo wasp is unlike any other. It has a shimmering, metallic exoskeleton that comes in colors like green and blue. Also unlike its yellow-and-black relatives, the cuckoo wasp has no stinger. Instead, it curls up into a ball to defend itself. Its exoskeleton is like armor. But don't be fooled by its pretty colors and lack of stinger. The cuckoo wasp can be brutal. It lays its eggs in the nests of other wasps. When its larvae hatch, they eat the food meant for nest owner's offspring. And then they eat the offspring!

BEAUTIFUL BUT DEADLY!

TAXI TRIP ▶ Gizmo the cat traveled more than 500 miles (800 km) over several days after becoming trapped in the grille of a taxi. Unaware that he had an extra passenger, driver Tom Hutchings made journeys all over Wales and into England. When he finally found her, he removed the front bumper and took Gizmo to a veterinarian who gave her a clean bill of health.

RUNAWAY RACEHORSE ▶ In April 2024, an escaped racehorse trotted onto a platform at Warwick Farm station in New South Wales, Australia! It walked up and down behind the yellow safety line, before leaving when a train arrived.

SICK STEALER ▶ The frigatebird steals regurgitated food from other birds by grabbing their tail feathers and shaking them until they vomit their most recent meal.

SUPER SENSITIVE ▶ Houseflies taste with their feet, which have taste buds 10 million times more sensitive to sugar than those on human tongues.

BIRD BEAT ▶ Male palm cockatoos from Australia attract females and mark their territory by rhythmically tapping twig drumsticks and seed pods that they craft into the ideal shape. Each male plays to his own beat, allowing other birds to recognize who is drumming from a long way away.

ANIMAL ART ▶ Welshman Craig Evans has 69 rabbit tattoos on his arms, legs, and chest. He got his first one in 2009 and has since spent about 125 hours in tattooist chairs as far afield as Japan, Spain, and the U.S. He estimates that he has spent over $12,000 on his body art.

HYENA HELPERS ▶ The Ethiopian walled city of Harar has special "hyena doors" fitted into the walls. This allows hyenas to act as a garbage disposal system by entering the city at night to eat any edible waste left on the streets.

SPIDER SMASH ▶ A tarantula crossing the road in Death Valley National Park, California, caused a collision that put a motorcyclist in the hospital. Two Swiss tourists in a camper van braked suddenly to avoid killing the spider, and a Canadian biker crashed into the back of their van. The tarantula walked away unharmed.

LONG LEGS ▶ An ostrich has such long legs that it can cover 16 feet (5 m) in a single stride.

BLOOD SUCKER

The Amazon giant leech can grow up to 18 inches (46 cm) long. To suck blood, it pierces deep into the skin of its victims with a needle-like appendage that can measure up to 4 inches (10 cm) in length.

EXTREME HOMEBODY

The purple frog lives most of its life underground. It only emerges once a year! The purple frog lives exclusively in the Western Ghats, a mountain range in India. It lives underground until early monsoon season, when it goes topside to mate. The purple frog stays above ground just long enough to breed, which can range from a few hours to a few days. Then, it goes back underground until the next mating season!

means "no!" **BURKINA FASO** ▶ The population of Burkina Faso is one of the youngest in the

SEEK THE STRANGE

POKE AROUND

For the festival of Thaipusam, some people carry heavy altars that are attached to their skin with sharp rods and hooks!

This is the *vel kavadi*. It is one of the many kinds of offerings made to honor the Hindu god Lord Murugan. Some devotees attach small pots of milk or fruit to their skin using hooks. Others pierce their cheeks and tongue with metal skewers. These extreme acts are to show devotion, seek blessings, and fulfill vows. Vel kavadi can be very tall and weigh over 100 pounds (45 kg)! They are often decorated with peacock feathers and flowers. The piercings are a powerful display of spiritual strength and dedication.

PENCIL PILE ▶ Aaron Bartholmey, of Iowa, has a collection of more than 70,000 wooden pencils, some of which are over 100 years old. Many have business advertisements along the body of the pencil, and one even displays a high school basketball team's schedule.

DETOUR DRIVE ▶ When heavy rain washed out an important bridge in Western Australia on the most direct route from Broome to his home in Kununurra, driver Chris English made a 3,000-mile (4,800-km), four-day detour to reach his destination. His detour was further than driving from Montreal to Mexico City.

COUNTRY CROSS ▶ Holden Ringer, from University Park, Texas, walked more than 4,500 miles (7,200 km) across the U.S. in 14 months. He set off from Washington State in March 2023 and eventually reached Washington, D.C., a year later before extending his walk up the Atlantic coast to New Haven, Connecticut. He arrived there in May 2024, having passed through a total of 20 states and worn out at least eight pairs of shoes.

BORROWING BODIES

At the Nature-to-You Loan Library inside the San Diego Natural History Museum, instead of borrowing books, customers can take home dead animals. More than 1,300 specimens are available, ranging from plant pressings and pinned insects to a box full of snake bones and a polar bear skull. The taxidermy turkey is often in great demand around Thanksgiving.

LOST LEGO ▶ A rare LEGO octopus, which fell into the sea from a cargo ship in 1997, was discovered washed up on a beach in Cornwall, England, in 2024 by 13-year-old Liutauras Cemolonskas. He has collected about 800 pieces of LEGO from the spill but had been searching for the elusive octopus for two years. The octopus was one of nearly five million pieces that were lost when a massive wave knocked 62 containers into the sea off Land's End.

NOSE NOISE ▶ Canadian LuLu Lotus can blow a 44-decibel whistle through her nose. She was only seven years old when she first discovered that she could whistle tunes with her nose. She does it by closing her mouth and using her throat muscles to control the flow of air through her nostrils.

SENIOR TRUCKER ▶ Doyle Archer, from Kansas, was still driving trucks in 2024—at 90 years old! The great-grandfather has been a truck driver for more than 60 years and has traveled an estimated 5.5 million miles (8.8 million km).

world—about 45 percent of its people are under the age of 15! **BURUNDI** ▶ Since March 2014, it has been illegal for joggers to run in groups in Burundi.

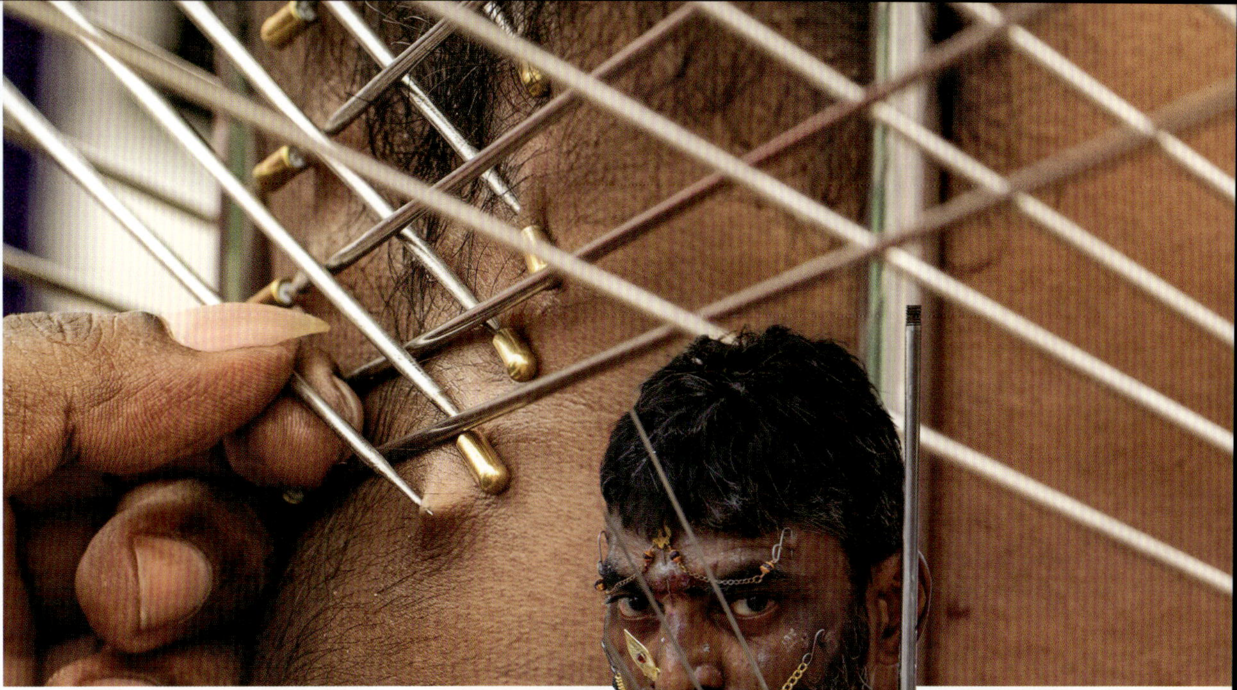

CROSS WITH CARE!

GET OVER IT
The Millau Viaduct in France is the tallest bridge in the world! It spans 8,070 feet (2,460 m) across the Tarn Valley and has seven large concrete supports. The tallest one reaches 804 feet (245 m) high. It can even be seen from space! Masts make the bridge's highest point 1,125 feet (343 m) above the valley. The bridge is often surrounded by mist, making it seem like you're traveling through the clouds!

CAMBODIA ▸ The Khmer alphabet of Cambodia includes 33 consonants and 37 vowels.

SEEK THE STRANGE

THE RIPLEY'S COLLECTION

MURDERER SKIN

This tanned strip of skin belonged to 18-year-old convicted murderer John Horwood, who was executed in Bristol in 1821. Under an eighteenth-century law, his body was dissected and skinned as an added punishment.

CATALOG NO. 13098

CRIMINAL MIND

This is a preserved cross-section of an eighteenth-century French criminal's head! It was dissected to determine if a criminal's brain differed from others. Used in a Paris medical hospital for over 200 years, it remains a historical specimen of early forensic science.

CATALOG NO. 17855

What's going on in there?

Killer or survivor?
We may never know!

CANNIBAL CRANIUM

This mummified head belonged to Alfred Packer, a.k.a. the Colorado Cannibal. He was a mountain guide accused of killing and eating five men in 1874. He claimed it was for survival, but his story kept changing. He was sentenced to 40 years in prison but was released on parole after about 15 years.

CATALOG NO. 18717

Ripley's Believe It or Not!®

FORBIDDEN FEAST

BANNED BITES

There is a food that some say is so shameful you have to hide your face while eating it!

The ortolan bunting is a small bird that's illegally eaten as a delicacy in France. The bird is caught alive, fattened, and then drowned in brandy before being roasted. Diners eat it whole in one bite, often covering their heads with a napkin. Some say this is to trap the smell, while others believe it's to hide from God while eating the forbidden dish! Even though it is against the law, some people still secretly enjoy this rare meal.

What is the most memorable meal you've ever eaten?
Share your thoughts...

CAMEROON ▶ In 1986, Lake Nyos in Cameroon burped a carbon dioxide gas cloud that killed more than 1,700 people and thousands of animals

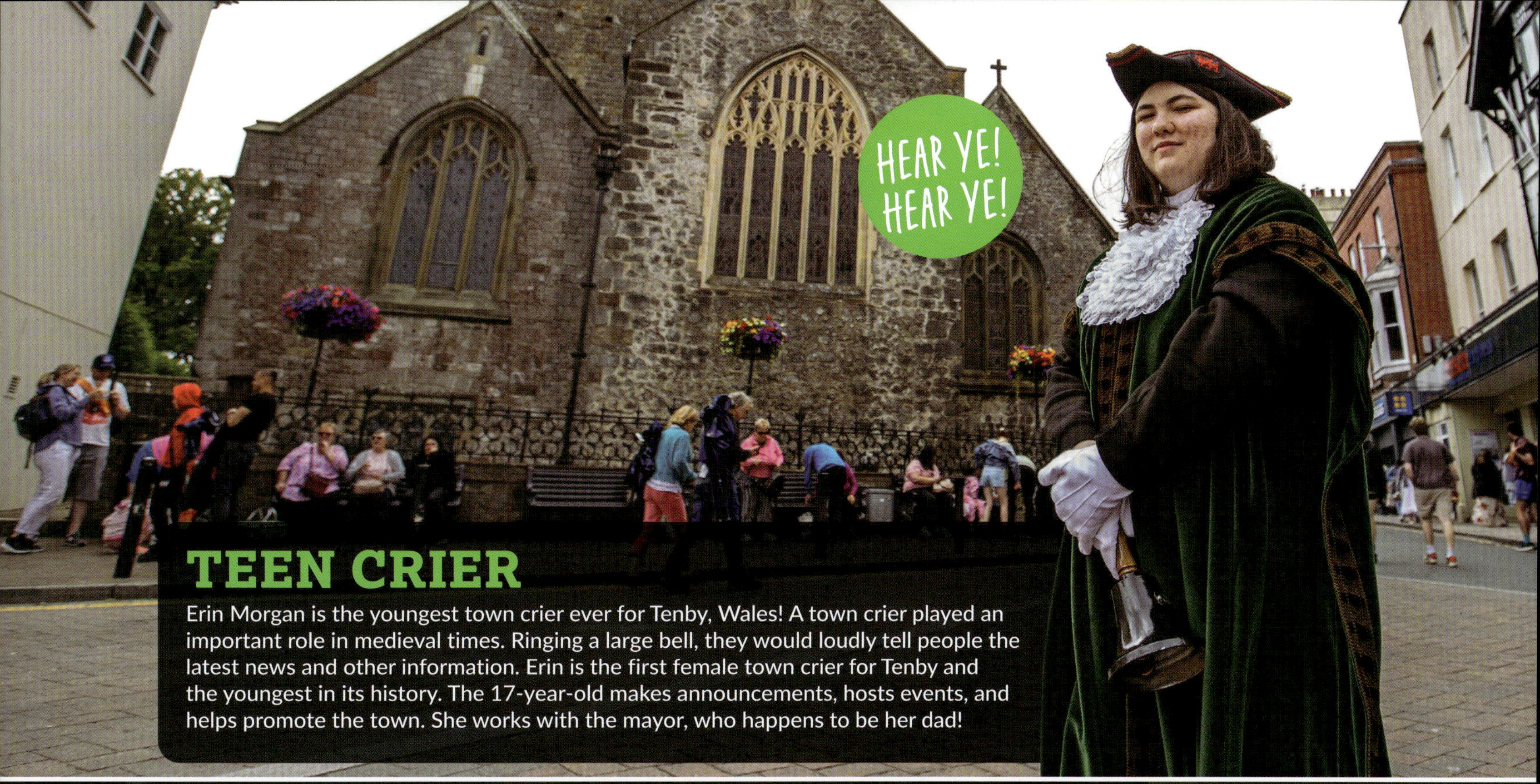

HEAR YE! HEAR YE!

TEEN CRIER

Erin Morgan is the youngest town crier ever for Tenby, Wales! A town crier played an important role in medieval times. Ringing a large bell, they would loudly tell people the latest news and other information. Erin is the first female town crier for Tenby and the youngest in its history. The 17-year-old makes announcements, hosts events, and helps promote the town. She works with the mayor, who happens to be her dad!

LOSING SHORTCUTS ▶ Out of the 30,000 runners who took part in the Mexico City Marathon on August 27, 2023, 11,000 were disqualified for taking shortcuts along sections of the course. Some competitors were spotted using cars, bikes, or public transport.

LOST LUGGAGE ▶ Items left behind in rooms by guests at European hotels in 2023 included witchcraft paraphernalia, prosthetic limbs, an inflatable boat, and a clown costume with wig and red nose.

MUSIC LOVERS
Tijan and Matthew Brown attended 135 concerts in a year, spending a total of $18,407.24 on tickets to see the likes of Beyoncé, Billy Joel, and Lizzo.

DOLL DELIVERY ▶ American Airlines pilot James Danen went more than the extra mile to reunite nine-year-old Valentina Dominguez with her lost doll, Beatrice. After the doll was accidentally left on a plane in Tokyo, Japan, Texas-based Danen located it and flew 5,880 miles (9,463 km) to deliver it to Valentina by hand.

KNOWN KNOT ▶ More than six billion different knots and links have been described in print or illustration since the nineteenth century, when knot theory began.

CURDS AND NEIGH

Cheese horses are toys made from cheese! A long time ago, Hutsul shepherds living in the Carpathian Mountains in Europe made these toys while watching their sheep. When they went back home after spending the summer in the mountains, they brought the toys as gifts for their kids and loved ones. The tradition is still around today in the villages of Brustury and Kosmach. The cheese is soft and stretchy, so it's easy to shape into horses, saddles, and harnesses.

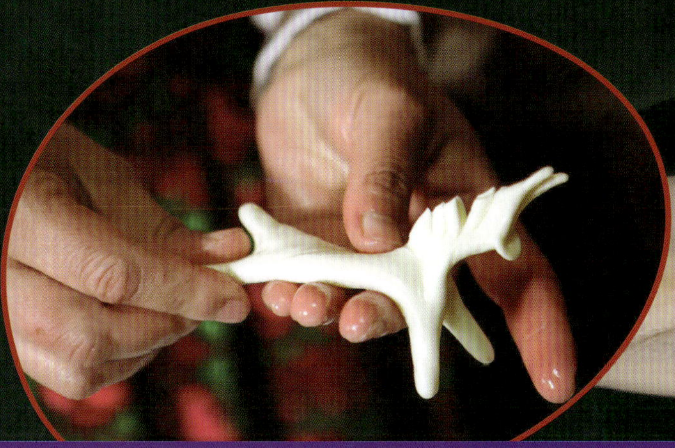

within minutes. **CANADA** ▶ Saint-Louis-du-Ha! Ha! in Quebec, Canada, is the only town in the

SEEK THE STRANGE

Ripley's Believe It or Not!

TRAM
Champs

Every year, tram drivers from across Europe gather to compete in events like tram bowling, tram billiards, and more!

At the TRAM-EM European TramDriver Championship, drivers must complete a course to earn points. Tasks test their reaction time, precision, and knowledge. In tram bowling, drivers must reach high speeds and perfectly time their braking to knock down 6.5-foot-tall (2-m) pins with a giant ball! While slower, tram billiards is just as exciting. It takes a lot of control to gently tap a pool cue with a 40-ton vehicle!

Trams are also known as streetcars or trolleys. They run on tracks and are often powered by an overhead wire.

world with two exclamation points in its name. **CAPE VERDE ▶** The giant baobab trees on Magdalen, in the Cape Verde islands, always extend their trunk

CITY MODELS ▶ The Musée des Plans-Reliefs in Paris, France, displays detailed scale models of major European towns and cities from the seventeenth and eighteenth centuries. The collection was started in 1668 by King Louis XIV so that French military leaders could determine the best way to attack or defend them.

PEN PALS ▶ Two pen pals who had been writing to each other since 1955 met for the first time in 2023. Patsy Gregory traveled nearly 4,000 miles (6,400 km) from Lancashire, England, to meet Carol-Ann Krause in Conway, South Carolina, to whom she began writing when both were 12 years old.

HANDS FREE
Cyclist Robert Murray of Calgary, Canada, rode 81 miles (130 km) in 5 hours 37 minutes without using his hands. He was able to keep going by using his hands to massage his aching legs during the ride.

CAGED CORPSES ▶ Instead of burying or cremating the deceased, the Bali Aga people of Trunyan, Indonesia, leave the corpses in forests to decay in the open air. The bodies are enclosed in triangular bamboo cages to protect them from scavenging vultures, and after the flesh has decomposed, the skeletons are placed on a rock platform for visitors to see.

PRICEY PIECE ▶ A gold LEGO piece donated to a Goodwill store in DuBois, Pennsylvania, was initially listed for $14.95. But the 14-karat gold mask from 2001 turned out to be one of only 30 ever produced, and it eventually sold at auction in 2024 for $18,000.

BLUE PEARL

Nestled in the Moroccan mountains, Chefchaouen is an entire city painted blue! Known as "the Blue Pearl," the city is coated in the color from top to bottom. Almost all of its walls, doors, and even streets are a shade of blue. No one is sure why, though. Some think the color helps keep mosquitoes away. Others believe it represents the sky or the Mediterranean Sea. Whatever the reason, the city has looked *blue*-tiful for more than 500 years!

SUSPENDED SUPPER ▶ Picnickers in Brazil can eat and drink while seated at a table suspended 295 feet (90 m) in the air, hanging over the raging Cascata da Sepultura waterfall. Customers are strapped into harnesses before sitting at the wooden picnic table, which is attached to a zipline on the edge of the fall. Once they are safely secured, the table is rolled out along the zipline to the center of the fall.

HISTORIC TICKETS ▶ Two rare tickets from Ford's Theatre, Washington, D.C., dated April 14, 1865—the night that President Abraham Lincoln was assassinated there—sold at auction in 2023 for $262,500. The front-row dress circle balcony seats originally cost 75 cents.

MOVIE MARATHON
In the span of one year, from July 2022 to June 2023, Zachariah Swope of Pennsylvania watched 777 movies in theaters, averaging more than two movies a day. He watched *Puss in Boots: The Last Wish* 47 times.

CAR COOKIES ▶ On July 18, 2023, it was so hot that staff of the National Weather Service in Texas were able to bake chocolate chip cookies on a car dashboard. The outdoor temperature was 105°F (40°C) but inside the car it was a stifling 190°F (88°C), meaning it took just 4.5 hours for the cookies to bake.

SUPER SHOT ▶ As part of the warm-up before his team's game against the Los Angeles Clippers at the Chase Center, San Francisco, on February 14, 2024, Golden State Warriors basketball star Steph Curry landed a sensational 120-foot (36.5-m), one-handed shot from the tunnel into the basket at the other end of the court.

Ripley's Believe It or Not!

Mini Makeover

Theria Sofa from Jakarta, Indonesia, turns old Polly Pocket toys into mini movie scenes!

Theria began collecting the small dollhouses in 1992. She started painting them in 2021 to give them new life. Since then, Theria has modified more than 1,000 Polly Pocket toys! She turns them into iconic places from movies, TV, and real life. With a steady hand, she carefully paints the inside of each one. She even turns the tiny dolls into matching characters! Collectors love her designs, which can sell for hundreds of dollars!

Before

After: The Wizard of Oz

Before

After: Lilo and Stitch

Coraline

The Nightmare Before Christmas

Artist Theria Sofa with some of her Polly Pocket scenes.

Emperor Bokassa of the Central African Republic had pearl-studded shoes made that cost $85,000! **CHAD** ▶ More than 100 languages are spoken in Chad,

POP DUSTING

In east China's Jiangsu Province, rice farmers use balloons to help their crops! How? They tie a long, thin pipe to giant hydrogen balloons. These lift the pipe into the air. As workers move the floating contraption, chemicals spray from the pipe onto the crops. This helps control pests and diseases without damaging the plants, saving both time and hard work.

SWALLOWED BRUSH ▸ When a piece of turkey caught in her throat and caused her to choke, a woman from Galdakao, Spain, grabbed a toothbrush to try to dislodge it. But she pushed too far and accidentally swallowed the 8-inch-long (20-cm) toothbrush. She was rushed to a hospital and spent over three hours with the toothbrush stuck in her esophagus before doctors successfully removed it.

LOOKALIKE WEDDING ▸ Ed Sheeran superfan Amanda Baron married the singer's doppelgänger Ty Jones in Manchester, England—and the ceremony was attended by lookalikes for Jack Sparrow (from *Pirates of the Caribbean*), former soccer player David Beckham, celebrity chef Gordon Ramsay, and Prince Harry. The couple even had Ed Sheeran song lyrics etched into the wedding cake.

FEARSOME FISH ▸ The whitemargin stargazer fish, which lives in shallow waters in the Indo-Pacific region, can deliver both venom and an electric shock. Buried in the sand with only its eyes and mouth visible, it has venomous spines that can kill a human who treads on it. It also has electric organs located in a pouch behind its eyes, which can discharge a powerful 50-volt shock.

THE RIPLEY'S COLLECTION

DUELING KNIGHTS

Abby Peterson of Webster, Kentucky, carves wooden sculptures with a chainsaw! With it, he is able to achieve a surprising amount of detail. He uses a variety of power tools to complete his works—including a blow torch for adding color!

CATALOG NO. 176044

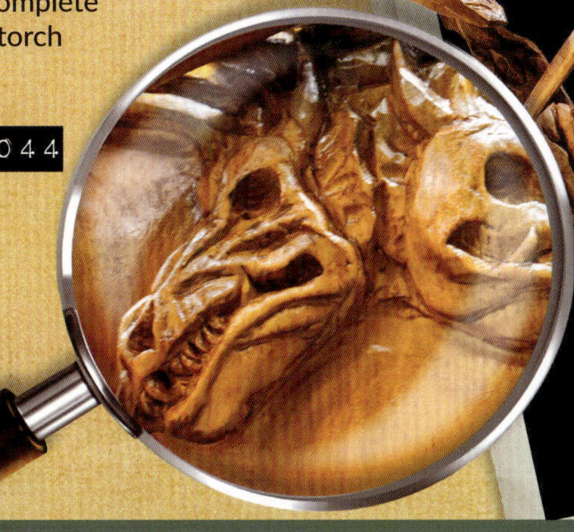

Carved with a chainsaw!

resulting in its nickname of "the Babel Tower of the modern world." **CHILE ▸** Rain falls on Chile's

SEEK THE STRANGE

SIDE EFFECT

GRACEFUL FLIPS IN THE AIR!

BANDALOOP is a dance group with a twist—they perform on the sides of buildings and cliffs! The vertical stage adds an extra level of danger and awe to the art form. Hanging from ropes and strapped into climbing gear, the dancers pull off moves that can't be done on the ground. They tiptoe across windows, take huge leaps through the air, and perform graceful flips—all done next to other dancers and in time with music. BANDALOOP was formed in 1991 by Amelia Rudolph. Since then, the California group has danced on a mountain in China, a cathedral in London, a skyscraper in New York, and more.

Atacama Desert—the driest place on earth—every two to seven years, resulting in a unique superbloom of colored flowers! **CHINA** ▶ Due to water

THEY'RE FLYING HIGH, DEFYING GRAVITY!

DANCING ON THE SIDE OF A CLIFF!

extraction and urban expansion, researchers have discovered that nearly half of China's major cities

SEEK THE STRANGE

MUDDY MAYHEM

Every year, folks at the Dirty Pig Festival welcome spring by splashing around in a giant mud puddle!

This quirky, centuries-old tradition takes place in Hergisdorf, Germany. Villagers and visitors are split into two groups. The "Dirty Pigs" represent the winter season. They roll around in a mud puddle and try to splash others with sludge! The other group acts as spring. They often dress in white and wear colorful hats. They use ropes or sticks to force the Dirty Pigs away from the mud and into a pond. Spring wins over winter when all of the Dirty Pigs are squeaky clean!

are sinking. **COLOMBIA** ▶ There is a traveling library in Colombia known as the Biblioburro that distributes books from the backs of donkeys!

SMALL SLEEP ▸ To renew his energy levels, eccentric Spanish artist Salvador Dalí used to take a short power nap during the day. He did this by falling asleep with a key in his right hand, beneath which he placed an upside-down plate. When he lapsed into a deep sleep, his hand released the key, which fell onto the plate and woke him.

LENGTHY READ ▸ A book club hosted by Gerry Fialka, a movie maker from California, spent 28 years reading *Finnegans Wake*, a notoriously complex 628-page novel by Irish author James Joyce. Monthly meetings to discuss the book page by page started in 1995, and they reached the final page in 2023. Joyce himself took 17 years to write it.

TREASURED TONGUE ▸ KISS front man Gene Simmons had his iconic tongue insured for $1 million in the 1970s.

EARLY ERROR ▸ In the movie *Robin Hood: Prince of Thieves*, which was set in 1194, Morgan Freeman's character produces a telescope, even though telescopes were not invented until 1608.

WILLIAM'S WILL ▸ All that William Shakespeare left to his wife, Anne Hathaway, in his will was his "second-best bed with the furniture."

Sinkholes can form when rainwater collects in the limestone beneath the soil, which then breaks away.

FALLEN FIELD

A giant sinkhole suddenly swallowed the middle of a soccer field! In June 2024, a soccer field at Gordon Moore Park in Alton, Illinois, collapsed into a sinkhole and left a huge crater behind. The sinkhole was around 100 feet (30 m) wide and up to 50 feet (15 m) deep. That's wider than two semitrailers parked back to back! A limestone mine deep underground collapsed and caused the sinkhole. Thankfully, no one was hurt.

COOL COAST

Sand, sea, and snow can be found in the same spot at a beach in Japan! The Tottori Sand Dunes are a unique natural wonder on the country's west coast. These dunes look like a desert, but they're right next to the sea! Some of the dunes reach more than 160 feet (49 m) tall. Snow can cover the sandy hills during winter, creating a striking contrast between the white snow, gold sand, and blue sea.

SEA, SAND, AND SNOW ALL TOGETHER!

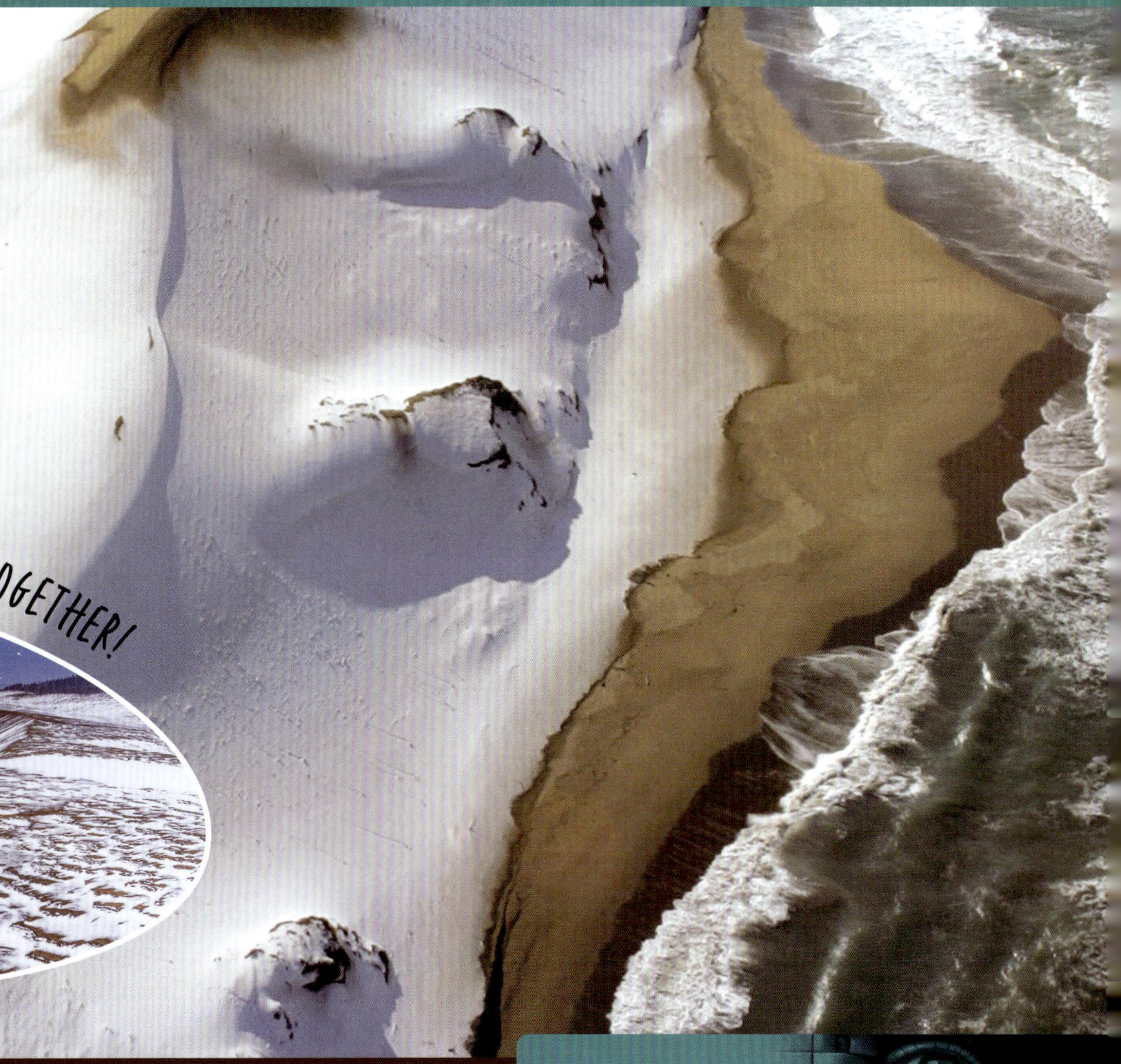

COMOROS ▸ The Comoros is known as the "Perfume Isles" because of its fragrant plant life,

SEEK THE STRANGE

THE RIPLEY'S COLLECTION

INAUGURAL ART

Look closely at this portrait of President John F. Kennedy. It is actually the text of his famous inaugural speech! New Jersey artist Daniel Duffy wrote each word by hand.

CATALOG NO. 171123

The speech includes the famous quote, "Ask not what your country can do for you—ask what you can do for your country."

OSWALD COAT

This U.S. Marine Corps-issued raincoat was once owned by Lee Harvey Oswald—the man who assassinated President John F. Kennedy. He wore it during his time in the military, from 1956 to 1959.

CATALOG NO. 173908

Kennedy set out on what was planned as a two-day, five-city tour of Texas.

```
FOR YOUR INFORMATION AND IMMEDIATE USE
                                                November 20, 1963
                                    Office of the White House Press Secretary
------------------------------------------------------------------
                          THE WHITE HOUSE
                       SCHEDULE OF THE PRESIDENT
                         TEXAS, NOV. 21-22, 1963
              WEDNESDAY, NOVEMBER 20, 1963
                      9:00 p.m. deadline on baggage. Baggage can be
                      left at the White House Transportation Office
                      any time in the afternoon.
              THURSDAY, NOVEMBER 21, 1963
    8:30 a.m.         Press check in at the White House
    9:00 a.m.         Press buses leave Northwest Gate of the White House
   10:00 a.m.         Press plane departs Andrews AFB
   10:45 a.m.         PRESIDENT DEPARTS WHITE HOUSE BY HELICOPTER
                      FOR ANDREWS AFB
   11:00 a.m.         Pool: Smith, Cormier, Costello, Mathias
                      PRESIDENT DEPARTS ANDREWS AFB
   12:30 p.m.         Press plane arrives San Antonio International Airport
    1:30 p.m.         PRESIDENT ARRIVES SAN ANTONIO INTERNATIONAL
                      AIRPORT
    1:40 p.m.         PRESIDENT DEPARTS SAN ANTONIO INTERNATIONAL
                      AIRPORT BY CAR
    2:25 p.m.         PRESIDENT ARRIVES AERO-SPACE MEDICAL HEALTH
                      CENTER, BROOKS AFB
    2:30 p.m.         Dedication program begins
    3:05 p.m.         PRESIDENT DEPARTS AERO-SPACE MEDICAL HEALTH
    3:00 p.m.         CENTER BY CAR FOR KELLY AFB
    3:30 p.m.         PRESIDENT ARRIVES KELLY AFB
                      PRESIDENT DEPARTS KELLY AFB
                      Pool: Merriman Smith, UPI; Frank Cormier, AP;
                      Felton West, Houston Post; Robert MacNeil, NBC
    4:15 p.m.                                         Bob Clark
    4:25 p.m.         PRESIDENT ARRIVES HOUSTON INTERNATIONAL AIRPORT
    5:00 p.m.         PRESIDENT DEPARTS AIRPORT BY CAR
                      PRESIDENT ARRIVES RICE HOTEL
    6pm               Laym toale - Thomas Speech
                                                8 cst
                                                7 cst
    8:35 p.m.         DEPART RICE HOTEL BY CAR
                      Pool: Merriman Smith, UPI; Frank Cormier, AP; William
                      MacKay, Houston Chronicle; Sid Davis, Westinghouse.
                                      MORE
```

FINAL SCHEDULE

An official schedule for President Kennedy's time in Texas for November 21–22, 1963. The document has notes in red pencil and lists key events, including the ill-fated Dallas motorcade where the president was assassinated.

CATALOG NO. 175068

BACK BRACE

President Kennedy wore this brace and others like it to help alleviate his major back pain. In fact, he was wearing a tightly bound lumbar brace the day he was assassinated by Lee Harvey Oswald.

CATALOG NO. 174656

SEEK THE STRANGE

RIPLEY'S Believe It or Not!®

HEATING THE PLASTIC TURNS IT INTO GAS!

FUTURE FUEL

A car fueled by... plastic? Dutch designer Gijs Schalkx took a car that originally ran on diesel and changed it to run on oil created by plastic! To do it, he installed a "de-refinery" on the top of an old Volvo, where he loads household plastics. The rooftop container heats the plastics until they evaporate into gas. The gas then turns into oil, which fuels the car! Unfortunately, the system isn't very efficient. It takes nearly one hour to make just 3 gallons (11 liters) of oil to run the car.

ROTTEN RAIN ▶ A flight from Amsterdam in the Netherlands to Detroit, Michigan, was turned around an hour into the journey after more than a dozen maggots rained down on a passenger. The maggots came from a rotten fish that was being stored in another passenger's bag in the plane's overhead compartments.

REUSED POLES ▶ The hurdles used in track races at the 1900 Paris Olympic Games were made of fallen telephone poles. The 30-foot-long (9-m) poles were laid across the entire width of the track.

SOCCER CIRCUS

There have been more managers of English Football League club Watford since 2015 than there have been Dalai Lamas (Tibetan spiritual leaders) since 1391.

SIMILAR STRANGERS ▶ Two previously unacquainted men named Mark Garland found themselves sitting next to each other on a flight from London, England, to Bangkok, Thailand. Not only did they have the same name, but they also looked alike, lived only 15 miles (24 km) apart, and shared mutual friends and hobbies.

DUBLIN DUCK ▶ A rubber duck, which was one of 150,000 released into the River Liffey in Dublin, Ireland, in 2006, was found 18 years later more than 400 miles (640 km) away on a beach on the Scottish island of Stronsay.

BEEP BALL

If you think it's impossible to play sports without using your eyes, think again! In beep baseball, players with little or no vision are blindfolded and rely on their hearing. The pitcher, one of the sport's few sighted players, throws a beeping ball to the batter. When the ball is hit, a 4-foot-tall (1.2-m) base starts buzzing loudly. The batter runs toward the sound. The goal is to reach the base before the other team picks up the beeping ball. The players don't hold back, often tackling the base and diving for the ball. Adaptive sports like beep baseball allow people of all abilities to take part!

which includes ylang-ylang flowers. **CONGO** ▶ More than 10,000 species of plants and animals live in Congo's rainforests! **COSTA RICA** ▶ Scattered throughout

YULE G.O.A.T.

One of Sweden's biggest Christmas traditions are the Julbocken—giant straw goats the size of buildings!

The most famous of these festive statues, also called Yule goats, is in Gävle. It's over 40 feet (12 m) tall and built every year. But there's a twist! It has become an unofficial tradition for pranksters to try to damage or burn it down. Attempts to protect the goat, such as fences, guards, and security cameras, seem to have no effect. Since it was first built in 1966, the Gävle goat has been destroyed more than 35 times! Still, the town keeps rebuilding it each year.

What is your favorite holiday tradition?
Share your thoughts...

DESTROYED AND REBUILT MORE THAN 35 TIMES!

PRANK PROTECTION!

the jungles of the Diquís Delta in Costa Rica are hand-carved, perfectly round stone balls that are

SEEK THE STRANGE

TransFURmation

Buster, a dog from Oklahoma, completely changed color from black to white!

The transformation is due to a condition called vitiligo. It causes skin and hair to lose color. At first, the white fur appeared in small patches on Buster's face. Less than three years later, his whole coat was completely white! Although dramatic, the change did not hurt the pet in any way. Buster's owner, Matt Smith, says he is a happy dog who loves everyone he meets and enjoys playing with his big brother, Rowdy!

FISHY FIND

Dr. Ben Beska of Newcastle, England, found a goldfish in his grass! Upon a closer look, he realized the fish was still alive! Thinking fast, Ben placed the fish in an old freezer drawer filled with water. He then quickly went out and bought a fish tank and supplies to keep it as a pet. He named the fish Alice. No one is sure how it ended up in his garden, but it is likely a bird dropped it. Alice has since passed away, but Ben has gotten a larger tank and more pet fish!

DIRTY WORK ▶ Dung beetles are worth at least $380 million per year to the U.S. cattle industry because of the work they do to break down manure and churn soil.

KILLER CAMEL ▶ The first camel in Australia shot its owner! Named Harry, the camel was taken on an 1846 expedition across South Australia by English explorer John Horrocks. As Harry leaned to one side, his pack caught on the trigger of Horrocks's loaded shotgun and shot him in the face. Horrocks later died of his injuries.

BIRTHDAY PRESENT ▶ In 1891, Scottish novelist Robert Louis Stevenson, author of *Treasure Island*, legally gave his November 13 birthday to a friend's 12-year-old daughter, Annie Ide, because the girl was unhappy that her birthday fell on Christmas Day.

PEAK PERFORMANCE ▶ Norwegian mountaineer Kristin Harila and her Nepalese guide, Tenjen Sherpa, climbed to the summits of the world's 14 highest mountains—all over 26,000 feet (8,000 m)—in just 92 days in 2023.

FUNNY FELINE

Meet Fedya, the cross-eyed cat who went viral! Fedya lives in Rostov-on-Don, Russia, with his owner, Natalya. She found the kitten in her garden in 2020. At first, she was worried he wouldn't survive. He was very weak and had trouble moving his legs. Natalya nursed Fedya back to health. Now, Fedya is doing great and is internet famous! At first, Natalya was nervous to post pictures of Fedya online. But everyone loved him, and Natalya saw how happy he made people. Today, he has more than 400,000 fans on Instagram!

Côte d'Ivoire! **CROATIA** ▶ There is an organ on the coast of Croatia that continuously plays music

FAST FASHION

Tasmanian jeweler Emma Bugg made a brooch out of a Big Mac burger, and after five years, it still looked the same!

When Emma learned that fast food takes a long time to decompose, she wasn't sure if she believed it. So, she bought a burger to see for herself. A year later, the burger had hardly changed. The only difference was browned lettuce! Emma decided to turn it into a brooch for the world to see. Since then, she's made a new burger brooch every five years. She wants to see if the burgers always stay the same. And it's not only burgers getting special treatment. She's also made a french fries necklace and chicken nugget earrings!

SHARED STORY — SHARE YOUR STORY at RIPLEYS.COM/SHARE

RAMEN RAINBOW

Check out the candy-colored cuisine that Tokyo's Kipposhi restaurant shared with Ripley's! Their picture-perfect ramen is loved by both locals and tourists. The soups come in all different colors, including orange, blue, and green. Even though they might look like the color of candy, the soups are savory! The orange soup has a ginger flavor. The green soup is flavored with grapes. And the blue soup tastes like blueberries—just kidding... it's just souped-up chicken!

and is powered by waves. **CUBA** ▶ Yoandri Hernandez Garrido of Baracoa, Cuba, is known as "Twenty-Four" because he has 12 fingers and 12 toes!

MORE THAN FIVE YEARS OLD!

ROBOT CHAMP ▶ Japan's University of Tokyo developed a robot that can win every game of Rock Paper Scissors. It analyzes its opponent's hand movements milliseconds before they play. The movements reveal which move they are going to play, allowing the robot to pick the winning move every time.

INCA INGENUITY ▶ The Incas built their vast empire, which ruled much of South America from 1438 to 1533, without using either the wheel or horses for transportation.

CHESS CHANCES ▶ There are more than 318 billion different possible positions after each player has made the first four moves in a game of chess.

THE Ripley's COLLECTION

TOUGH TUMBLER

Danielle Lettering's Stanley water cup survived a fire that destroyed her car—there was even ice still inside the cup!

CATALOG NO. 175832

CYPRUS ▶ One of the earliest known examples of people keeping cats as pets is a 9,500-year-old

SEEK THE STRANGE

RIPLEY'S *Believe It or Not!®*

HOOP DREAMS

30 FEET (9 M) IN THE AIR!

SPINNING AND SWAYING!

French performer Julot Cousins takes hula hooping to incredible new heights!

Julot puts on an amazing show with hula hoops and a swaying pole. He climbs the 30-foot-tall (9-m) pole and performs at the top. While on the moving pole, Julot makes hula hoops spin around his body as if he was on solid ground. His act is full of creative stunts. Julot can even perform a handstand on the pole! Before performing his incredible stunts, Julot was a clown, which explains his ability to entertain while performing dangerous feats!

grave in Cyprus where a human and kitten were buried next to each other. **CZECH REPUBLIC ▶** A population of deer in the Czech Republic won't cross the

LIMB TO LIMB

Greek artist Spyridon Dassiotis turned charred trees into haunting wooden figures in a sculpture garden known as the Park of Souls. In 2007, a huge fire burned 38,000 acres of land on Mount Parnitha in Greece. Only scorched earth and a few tree trunks were left behind. Spyridon brought new "life" to the area by carving sculptures of people out of 20 burnt tree trunks!

CAT WOMAN ▸ Italian Chiara Dell'Abate has had over 20 body modifications to make herself look like a cat. She has pointed ears, forehead implants, permanent feline eyeliner, and clawlike fingernails. She had her first modification at age 11, when she had her ears stretched and received the first of more than 70 body piercings. She plans to have her teeth and eyes reshaped like a cat's and hopes to eventually acquire an implant to which she can attach a tail.

RODENT TRIP ▸ British woman Lisa Murray-Lang spent more than $4,000 and traveled 7,000 miles (11,200 km) to scatter some of the ashes of her dead hamster Spud on a beach in Hawaii. Wearing the remainder of his ashes in a vial on a necklace, she then took him on a 1,500-mile (2,400-km) trip around Europe. She says his love of travel began when she made him miniature models of famous global locations and he enjoyed playing in them.

SHORT SHUTTLE ▸ Train enthusiast Neil Hughes completed an 18-hour round trip from his home in Troon, Scotland, just to spend six minutes riding on Britain's shortest branch line. He traveled a total of 1,127 miles (1,813 km), taking two flights and two trains, to ride on the 0.8-mile (1.3-km) Stourbridge Shuttle in England's West Midlands. The short stretch of track links Stourbridge Junction station to the town center, and the journey takes only three minutes each way.

ROBO RUMBLE

At RoboCup, super-smart machines play soccer with a high-tech twist! Robot soccer is played by teams of five or seven. They zoom, pass, and score goals with amazing accuracy! The robots are programmed with custom software. They use AI and machine-learning to understand their surroundings and make real-time decisions during the game. In 2023, Ireland's team, RoboÉireann, scored 67 points in nine matches and took home the cup!

SEEK THE STRANGE

MYTHS AND MONSTERS

No matter where you go in the world, there are stories of monsters. In Japan, there is a group of mythical creatures called *yokai*. Tales of these beings go back centuries, sending chills up the spines of all who hear them. There are hundreds of yokai. Here are just a few.

FUTAKUCHI ONNA

Futakuchi onna is a woman with a second mouth on the back of her head, hidden by her hair. This mouth demands food constantly and can cause the woman pain if not fed. The second mouth often speaks in an eerie voice and can even move the woman's hair like tentacles to grab food!

OKIKU

Okiku is one of most well-known *yurei*, or ghost yokai, in Japanese folklore. She was a maid, and her master owned a set of 10 beautiful plates. Okiku was tricked and accused of breaking one of them. One of her master's samurais threw her into a well and she died. Her ghost haunts the well, where she can be heard counting the plates and crying. After she reaches nine, she lets out a blood-chilling scream!

NURE ONNA

Nure onna is a snakelike yokai with the head of a woman. It lives near water and uses magic to make itself look like a woman holding a baby. When someone tries to help her, the "baby" becomes very heavy and traps the person. Nure onna then uses its true form to attack and drinks the blood of the victim!

KAPPA

Kappa are turtle-like water creatures. Their dish-shaped heads are filled with water, which gives them power. Kappa can be dangerous and are known for their pranks, but they are also very polite. If you bow to a kappa, it will return the gesture. Bowing makes them spill the water from their head and lose their strength!

KAMIKIRI

Kamikiri are small, sneaky yokai that cut off people's hair! These quick, silent creatures have sharp, scissor-like claws and long beaks. They often target brides before their weddings, causing distress and shame. This yokai was especially scary during a time when long hair was a symbol of status and wealth.

YATSUKAHAGI

Yatsukahagi are yokai that began as regular spiders but grew massive after living a long time. Cunning and powerful, they often create illusions to lure humans into their traps. Their victims may not even realize they are caught in the yokai's web. In some stories, it takes a samurai's sword to break the magic!

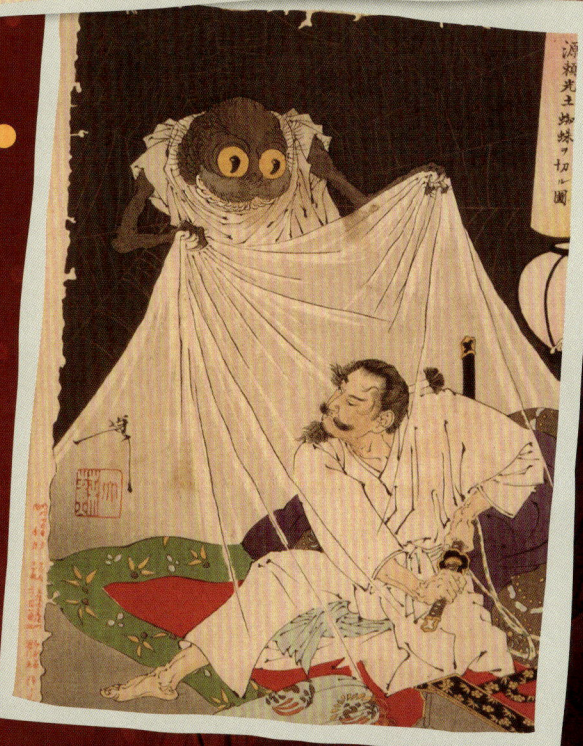

KUROBŌZU

Kurobōzu are dark, shadowy figures dressed in robes. These yokai are said to sneak into homes at night and steal people's breath as they sleep. Their victims are left gasping and terrified. Adding to the fright and disgust, Kurobōzu will also lick sleeping people with their tongues that smell like rotting flesh!

THE RIPLEY'S COLLECTION

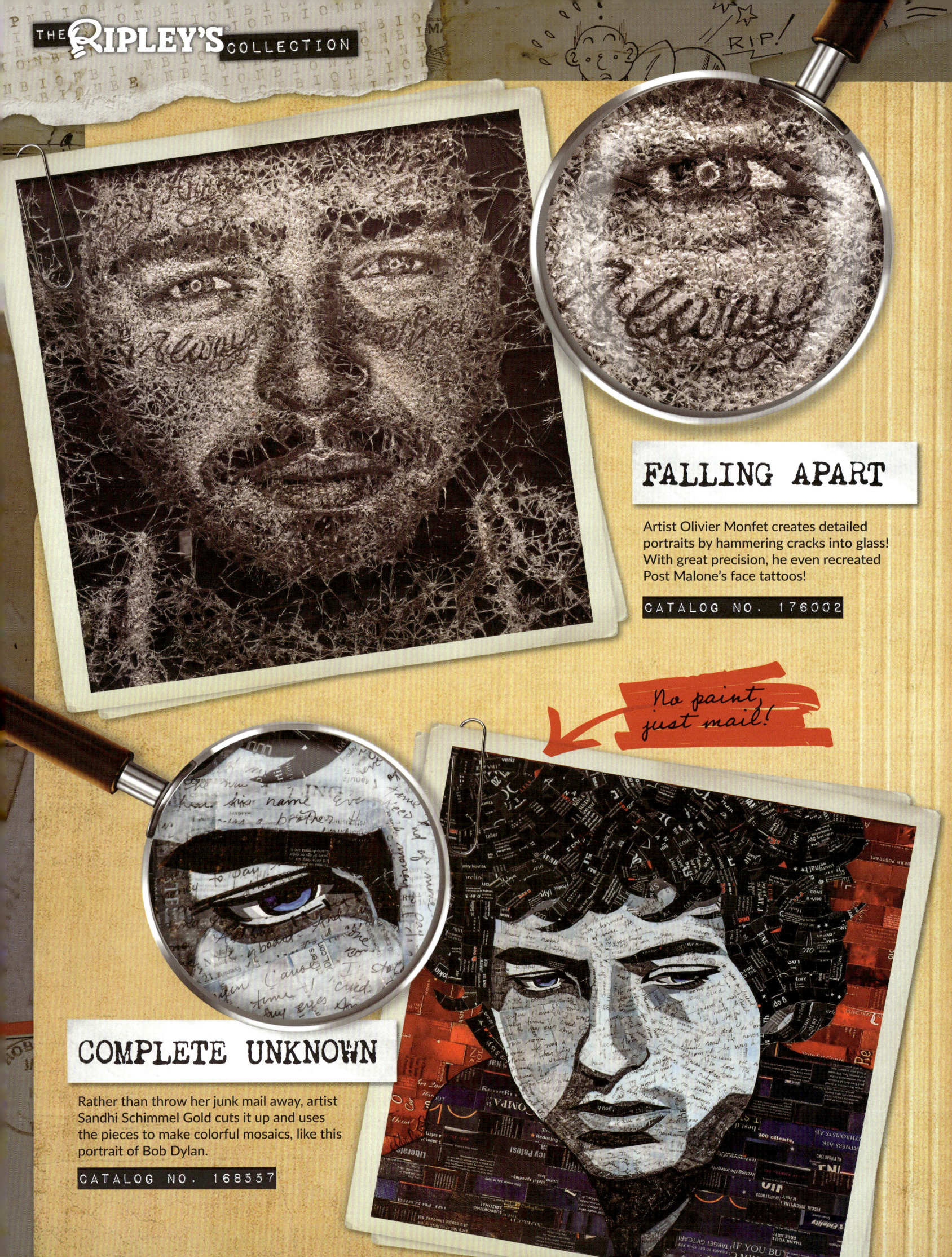

FALLING APART

Artist Olivier Monfet creates detailed portraits by hammering cracks into glass! With great precision, he even recreated Post Malone's face tattoos!

CATALOG NO. 176002

No paint, just mail!

COMPLETE UNKNOWN

Rather than throw her junk mail away, artist Sandhi Schimmel Gold cuts it up and uses the pieces to make colorful mosaics, like this portrait of Bob Dylan.

CATALOG NO. 168557

RARE WIRES

Artist Fekadu Mekasha made this photo-like portrait of Selena Gomez by precisely trimming and stacking layers of wire mesh.

CATALOG NO. 172326

BAD DOG

Using dog fur trimmings from his local groomer, artist Mateo Blanco created this unique portrait of Michael Jackson.

CATALOG NO. 171036

SEEK THE STRANGE

RIPLEY'S *Believe It or Not!*®

WALL'S END

The Great Wall of China totals more than 13,000 miles (21,000 km) and ends at the Bohai Sea!

The Great Wall is actually made up of many walls that stretch across China. The end is located at Laolongtou, where the wall meets the sea. This section of the wall was built in 1579 during the Ming dynasty. It is 2.5 miles (4 km) long and stretches more than 75 feet (23 m) into the water! Emperors of China would visit this part of the wall to honor their ancestors and write poems, some of which are still embedded in the wall today.

Laolongtou means "old dragon head." Do you think it looks like a dragon drinking water from the sea?

The longest piece of the wall is more than 5,500 miles (8,850 km) long!

was left unharmed. **DENMARK** ▶ There are more than twice as many pigs in Denmark as there are people. **DJIBOUTI** ▶ Located in the center of Djibouti,

OFF THE WALL

 After reaching the top of the **Mutianyu Great Wall** section, visitors can **ride sleds back down** on a speed slide!

 In 2005, a **Starbucks** opened at the **Great Wall of China**.

 The **mortar** used in building the Great Wall was made with **sticky rice**.

The Great Wall of China was built over the course of more than **2,000 years**.

 **Fires and smoke signals** were used to send **messages between towers** along the Great Wall.

 It is a **myth** that the Great Wall can be seen from the **Moon**.

Up to **400,000 workers** died while building the Great Wall, and many of the bodies were **buried within its walls**.

 Around **10 million people** visit the Great Wall each year.

CANDY CRAB

This colorful crustacean is known as the candy crab! Covered in pointy spines along its body, the small crab only grows up to 0.8 inches (2 cm) long! It is often found on different types of soft coral. It hides by mimicking the colors of the coral polyps it lives in. It even attaches the polyps to its shell for extra camouflage! The crab can be white, pink, yellow, or red, depending on the color of the coral.

SIMPLE SKI ▸ You can ski to the top of Estonia's 20 highest mountains in a single day. It is a journey of 15 miles (25 km), with the tallest peak, Suur Munamägi, being a modest 1,043 feet (318 m) high.

COLOSSAL CHURCH ▸ The Redeemed Christian Church of God building in Lagos, Nigeria, can hold one million people. The hangar-like structure is 1,640 feet (500 m) wide and over 3,280 feet (1,000 m) long.

COSTLY CHEESE ▸ A single 4.8-pound (2.2-kg) wheel of pungent Cabrales blue cheese sold for $32,408 at auction in 2023. The cheese is matured for up to eight months in the mountain caves of Asturias in northern Spain.

LITTLE LIBRARY ▸ Although it measures only 130 square feet (12 sq m), the Cardigan Library on Canada's Prince Edward Island houses about 1,800 books.

CURIOUS CEMETERY Sad Hill Cemetery, located in a remote region of northern Spain, has over 5,000 grave markers but no bodies. Stretching 984 feet (300 m) in diameter, the cemetery was built for the movie *The Good, the Bad and the Ugly*, starring Clint Eastwood. It became neglected after filming finished, but it has recently been restored and is now a tourist attraction.

NO COMBAT ▸ The European Balkan country of Montenegro was technically at war with Japan for over 100 years, even though the two nations never engaged in combat. In 1905, Montenegro declared war in support of Russia during the Russo-Japanese War, but did not have a navy to fight Japan. When Russia and Japan declared peace later that year, Montenegro was not mentioned in the treaty and so remained at war until 2006 when it finally declared peace with Japan.

UNSINKABLE SURVIVOR ▸ Arthur John Priest, a coal stoker from England, survived the sinking of four ships—*Titanic* (1912), *Alcantara* (1916), *Britannic* (1916), and *Donegal* (1917). He also survived two other collisions at sea and became known as "the unsinkable stoker."

CURRENT CURRENCY ▸ More than 54 billion banknotes are currently in circulation in the United States.

Lake Assal is 10 times saltier than the ocean. **DOMINICA** ▸ The island country of Dominica has a

SEEK THE STRANGE

RIPLEY'S Believe It or Not!®

TIE DYE FOR

Austin Mackereth from Lehigh Acres, Florida, makes amazing tie-dye art!

With careful planning, he turns plain cloth into colorful T-shirts and tapestries. Austin measures, folds, twists, and ties the fabric just right. It looks like a lumpy mess, but he knows exactly where to put the dye. When he unties the cloth, his groovy artwork is revealed!

ARTIST TYING AND DYEING HIS COLORFUL CREATION!

frog on its coat of arms. **DOMINICAN REPUBLIC** ▶ *Tyrannasorus rex* is an extinct scarab beetle that lived in the Dominican Republic 20 million years

RAINBOW RIVER

From June through November, the Caño Cristales turns into a liquid rainbow! The "river of five colors" is 62 miles (100 km) long and runs through a national park in Colombia. When conditions are right, the river bed turns bright red, yellow, green, pink, and blue! The cause is *Macarenia clavigera*, a plant that only grows in this river. The plant blooms in beautiful colors when there's just enough water and sunlight. There's nowhere else on Earth like it!

VOLCANO VICTIMS ▶ Some of the 1,000 victims of the eruption of Italy's Mount Vesuvius in AD 79 may have died after the extreme heat caused their blood to boil and their heads to explode. The eruption launched volcanic ash, gas, and rocks for 20 miles (32 km), while rivers of molten lava swallowed up nearby cities such as Pompeii and Herculaneum.

SHEERAN'S SAVINGS ▶ British musician Ed Sheeran made the video for his 2011 hit "The A Team" for under $25. Within two weeks the song had sold 200,000 copies.

REAL VAMPIRES ▶ According to a survey, more than 5,000 people in the United States identify as real vampires.

ROLLING STUNT ▶ Logan Holladay, the stunt driver for Ryan Gosling's character in the 2024 movie *The Fall Guy*, rolled a car eight and a half times for a sequence in the film. A cannon-like device was fitted beneath the car, and when triggered, it propelled the vehicle into a series of rolls.

SINISTER SALMON

An extinct species of salmon that lived in the waters off North America's Pacific coast seven million years ago grew to a length of nearly 9 feet (2.7 m) and weighed up to 400 pounds (181 kg). The spike-toothed salmon got its name from the two large, 2-inch-long (5-cm), teeth that stuck out sideways from its top jaw, like a warthog's tusks.

MINOR MISS ▶ Although he is of Italian descent, Sylvester Stallone missed out on a minor role in the wedding scene in the 1972 movie *The Godfather* because he was told he didn't look Italian enough.

BOTTOM BITE ▶ While playing for Tennessee's Knoxville Smokies baseball team in 1933, Clarence Blethen, who always removed his false teeth during a game, injured himself when the teeth he kept in his back pocket bit him on the butt as he slid into second base.

CANDY CANVAS ▶ At the University of Wisconsin-Parkside, candy company Haribo created a mosaic out of 150,000 gummy bears. The sweet artwork took four hours to complete and covered an area of 353 square feet (33 sq m).

TONG TWISTER ▶ Rebecca Daynes of Brisbane, Australia, used a pair of kitchen tongs to unravel a deadly eastern brown snake from around the neck of her cat Mabel—without getting bitten.

SHARK SENSATION

An extremely rare black-and-white lemon shark was caught off the coast of Florida! Its spotty coloring, known as "piebald," is caused by a genetic condition. The chances of catching a piebald shark are extremely low. There are only a few recorded instances! The surprise catch was reeled in by Florida angler Jack Appleton in May 2024. Jack measured the shark at more than 7 feet (2.1 m) long and promptly released it back into the water.

Disco's NOT DEAD

Denver artist Lauren Young spreads joy by turning anything and everything into disco balls!

Lauren started by making funky pieces at home for herself. She soon realized that *everyone* needs more disco in their lives! She began creating mirror balls for people to buy or rent for their homes or events. They were a hit! She then started turning wackier and wilder items into disco balls. She's made a mirrored E.T., cowboy boots, and a 15-foot-wide (4.5-m) spider! Imagine that hanging in your hallway!

What fad do you wish would make a comeback? Share your thoughts...

Mount Chimborazo in Ecuador is the furthest away from the Earth's center. **EGYPT** ▶ The Great Pyramid of Giza in Egypt is built of more than 2.3 million

HEAD HANDBAG

Costume designer Janina Udiljak, from Sweden, creates accessories with a twist. One of her most shocking pieces is a purse that looks like a severed head! To make it, Janina scanned the shape of her own head. Then, she 3D-printed the head in two parts. She added hinges to hold the pieces together. Finally, Janina painted the head to look realistic—and even added hair. Now, instead of a brain inside her head, there's a cell phone and keys!

GUT BLUSH ▶ When you blush, the inside of your stomach blushes, too. Your stomach lining turns red because your nervous system triggers an increased blood flow throughout your body.

STORE SIGN ▶ A woman spent a whole year living inside a rooftop store sign at a supermarket in Midland, Michigan. There was enough space inside for her to have a coffee machine, a pantry full of food, a computer, a small desk, and even a houseplant.

IMPATIENT INMATE ▶ After serving 22 years in prison, Russian inmate Kamoljon Kalonov chose to escape from a penal colony in Irkutsk on the very day that he was finally going to be released.

THE RIPLEY'S COLLECTION

CRYSTAL HELMET

This replica Stormtrooper helmet is completely covered in Swarovski crystals! For the truly discerning *Star Wars*™ fan.

CATALOG NO. 175956

stone blocks and held the title of the tallest man-made structure for more than 3,800 years!

RIPLEY'S Believe It or Not!®

Wave CAVE

Blue stone and turquoise water meet at the Marble Caves in Chile to create a dreamlike world.

The caves, found on Lake General Carrera, can only be reached by boat. Their smooth, swirling shapes were formed by more than 6,000 years of waves crashing into the marble walls. When nearby glaciers melt, the lake turns bright blue. Light reflects off the water and onto the marble, deepening its natural blue color. It feels like you're stepping into another world, where the walls shimmer and shift with every ripple of the water.

GOLDEN GRASS

The grass isn't always greener on the other side. Sometimes, the grass is gold! "Golden grass," or capim dourado, isn't really grass. It's actually the long stem of a flower that grows in parts of Brazil. The golden color is from the aluminum-rich soil where the plant grows. Golden grass is harvested by locals and used to create different kinds of crafts. People make bowls, plates, baskets, and even jewelry from the plant stems. And it all gleams like gold!

EL SALVADOR ▸ To commemorate a 1658 volcanic eruption, the town of Nejapa, El Salvador, holds a yearly festival where residents hurl flaming cloth

SNEAKY SPIDER

At first glance, this spider looks like a scorpion with its tail curled, but it's all an illusion! The scorpion-tailed spider, found in Australia, uses its strange shape to scare off predators. It's also called the "drag-tail spider" and loves to hang out in plants, waiting for prey. Although it looks fierce, it's harmless to humans—just a master of disguise in the world of eight-legged tricksters!

LOOPY LAW ▶ Between 1947 and 1986, it was illegal to sell a stove in Vancouver, British Columbia, Canada, on a Wednesday.

SUMMIT STRENGTH ▶ At the King of the Mountain race in Victoria, Australia, runners carry a heavy bag of wheat on their shoulders for the 0.6-mile (1-km) climb to the summit of Mount Wycheproof. Men haul a 132-pound (60-kg) bag and women carry 44 pounds (20 kg). At only 138 feet (42 m) high, it has been dubbed the smallest mountain in the world.

SUPERSTITIOUS STAIRS ▶ According to superstition, the steps leading to the main entrance of a house in the Philippines should not total a number that can be divided by three. This rule also applies to staircases inside the home.

LUCKY FIND ▶ While walking on a beach near Tofino, Canada, in February 2024, Marcie Callawaert spotted the wallet she had lost eight months earlier. She had dropped it into the water while boarding a boat in June 2023, and it had washed ashore the following winter.

TERRAIN TRAINING

U.S. astronauts train for space missions by walking on the hardened lava fields of Hawaii's Mauna Loa volcano because the landscape is like the terrain found on the Moon and Mars. The HI-SEAS research station also has a habitation dome located about 8,200 feet (2,500 m) above sea level, which is used to replicate the conditions that astronauts could face during missions.

GENTLE GESTURE ▶ Most houses in Paraguay don't have doorbells. Instead, visitors rapidly clap their hands for a few seconds to announce their arrival, a gesture considered more polite than knocking on a door. As the weather in Paraguay is usually very hot, residents leave their windows open and are therefore easily able to hear the clapping of visitors.

FISHING FEATURE ▶ Installed in 1990, a fly-fishing rod landmark in Steelhead Park, British Columbia, Canada, stands 60 feet (18 m) tall and weighs about 800 pounds (363 kg). Its reel has a diameter of 3 feet (0.9 m).

HOT SPOT ▶ Home to around 10 million people, the County of Los Angeles in California has a bigger population than 40 U.S. states.

REAL REACTION ▶ For the 2005 movie *The Chronicles of Narnia: The Lion, the Witch and the Wardrobe*, young English actress Georgie Henley was carried onto the set blindfolded so that her initial wide-eyed reaction to the snowy world of Narnia that had been recreated in the studio would be genuine.

balls at each other! **EQUATORIAL GUINEA** ▶ No part of Equatorial Guinea touches the equator!

RIPLEY'S Believe It or Not!®

SWAG WAGON

Fred Keller and Judy Foster of Wasilla, Alaska, built a giant wagon that can go 60 mph (97 kmph)! The husband-and-wife duo used a pickup truck as the base for their drivable version of the classic children's toy. They completed the project in 2010 and enjoyed the surprised looks from other drivers for many years together. After Fred passed away, Judy put the wagon up for auction in 2024. It sold for $73,500.

8-FOOT-LONG (2.4-M) HANDLE!

THIS WAGON GOES UP TO 60 MPH (97 KMPH)!

TANK TEA ▶ Since 1945, all British Army tanks have been fitted with a water-heating device, partly so that soldiers can enjoy a morale-boosting cup of tea. The move was instigated after World War II's Battle of Normandy, when a German tank commander wiped out 14 British tanks in 15 minutes while the crews were outside their vehicles on a tea break.

BEER TESTER ▶ English playwright William Shakespeare's father, John, was paid to drink beer. He was the official ale tester of Stratford-upon-Avon in England.

RAPID RAP ▶ Eminem's song "Rap God" features 1,560 words rapped within 6 minutes 4 seconds, which works out to more than four words per second.

SKELETON SANDS ▶ Namibia's Skeleton Coast is named for the multiple whale and seal bones and more than one thousand shipwrecks that are scattered along its beaches. Many sailors have died there after their ships ran aground in the dense fog that often blankets that stretch of the African-Atlantic coast, leading to some sailors calling it "The Gates of Hell."

BOO-TIFUL BLOOMS!

PHANTOM FLOWER

This spooky flower is called the ghost pipe, but it's really more like a vampire! Instead of getting food from the sun, it sucks nutrients out of underground fungi. The ghost pipe's pale white color is from a lack of chlorophyll, the pigment that makes most plants green. Like a ghost, this plant thrives in dark places. It can be found haunting damp forests in North America and Asia, growing up to about 10 inches (25 cm) tall. Keeping it creepy until the end, the ghost pipe turns from white to black when it begins to die!

ERITREA ▶ Gelada monkeys in Eritrea gather in herds of up to 1,200 individuals, grazing on grass like cows! **ESTONIA** ▶ On New Year's Eve in Estonia,

GRANNY RAP IS WHERE IT'S AT!

GRANDRAPPERS

Who says rap is only for the young? These grannies go from zero to 100 real quick!

In Chilgok, South Korea, a group of elderly rappers known as Suni and the Seven Princesses has taken off! The 80-somethings rap about what they know, with most songs describing their farm life. The leader, 81-year-old Park Jeom-sun, says rapping makes her feel young. They began performing at a community center and quickly gained a following. The South Korean women are also known to dress with flare! Inspired by the success of Suni and the Seven Princesses, other senior rap groups have formed to help fight loneliness.

people traditionally eat up to 12 meals, believing that eating many meals will give them the

Ripley's Believe It or Not!

Ripley's Exclusive

Hair Today, HERE TOMORROW

Zen Hansen of Rigby, Idaho, braids strands of hair into wearable works of art!

Zen is working hard to bring back the historic practice of hairwork and table braiding. Using the same kinds of tools as artists hundreds of years ago, she weaves hair into rings, bracelets, lockets, and more. She took up the craft in 2019, only to find that the last how-to book on the subject was published in 1867! Now, Zen is a hairwork researcher and an expert table braider. She has even developed modern tools and written a book to make the art easier for others to learn!

Ripley's caught up with Zen to find out more about her hairwork and the endangered art form. Check out what she had to say!

Q: *How is working with human hair different from other fibers like cotton or wool?*

A: Hair is thicker and stiffer, and doesn't naturally grab onto itself like other fibers might. This makes hair better suited to braiding rather than spinning, which is common with fibers like wool. Beyond the technical differences, working with hair is a deeply personal experience for me. I know the origin of every strand, whether directly from myself or clients, which adds a layer of intimacy and meaning to each piece you don't get with other fibers.

Q: *What are some unexpected things you've crafted out of hair?*

A: My favorite off-the-wall creation has to be the fly-fishing line I made from my hair. My friend even tied some flies using my hair, and I was thrilled to actually catch fish with the whole setup! Throughout history, hair has been used to make tools such as ropes and nets. Seeing how versatile and functional hair can be in different contexts is incredible.

Q: *What inspires and excites you when it comes to your art?*

A: I love diving into research, and antique hairwork pieces often spark fresh ideas. Humans have always been so creative.

Q: *Which of your hairwork pieces is the most meaningful to you and why?*

A: While the rings I've made with my children's hair are very dear to me, the most meaningful piece features a double-layer snake braid with my brown hair woven inside and my dad's gray hair on top, mimicking a shedding snakeskin. He grew his hair out just so I could work with it.

> " Working with hair is a deeply personal experience for me.

strength of that many people in the coming year! **ESWATINI** ▶ Witches on broomsticks are not legally permitted to fly above an altitude of 500 feet (150 m)

Braiding tables and weights help keep hair organized, so hairworkers can arrange the strands in precise patterns.

Zen combined two different braids to create this piece made from her and her father's hair.

THE RIPLEY'S COLLECTION

HUMAN HAIR JEWELRY

This antique chain and brooch are made with real human hair. In the Victorian era, it was common to wear jewelry made with the hair of deceased loved ones.

CATALOG NO. 4962

in the country of Eswatini. **ETHIOPIA** ▶ A year in Ethiopia lasts 13 months—12 months of 30 days

SEEK THE STRANGE

RIPLEY'S Believe It or Not!®

DRINK UP

The gerenuk can go its entire life without ever taking a sip of water! The lanky antelope lives in east Africa. It gets all of the water it needs by eating plants! It likes to stay in dry areas, where there is less competition for food. To eat, the gerenuk will stretch out its long neck and even stand on its hind legs to reach leaves more than 6 feet (1.8 m) off the ground!

WONDER WORMS ▶ Scientists revived two tiny worms that had been frozen in a dormant state for 46,000 years. The worms, which are thought to have been around at the same time as woolly mammoths and saber-toothed tigers during the Ice Age, had been found 131 feet (40 m) deep in Siberian permafrost, before being thawed out and brought back to life in 2023.

HIDDEN OWL ▶ A baby owl spent four days perched undetected on the lower branches of a newly purchased Christmas tree in the living room of Michelle White's home in Kentucky. Although the family has three dogs, no one noticed anything unusual until someone they hired to clean their carpets saw the owl move slightly.

PAMPERED PETS ▶ In South Korea in 2023, more strollers were sold for dogs and cats than for babies. Overall, 57 percent of strollers sold were for animals, while only 43 percent were for human infants.

FINAL FEAST

A female orca found dead off the Commander Islands in the Bering Sea had six whole sea otters in her stomach and a seventh lodged in her throat. Sea otters are not usually part of an orca's diet, and the last one may have been too big for her to swallow, resulting in her death.

CRIMINAL KOALA ▶ Over several months, a trespassing koala ate thousands of plants, worth $3,800, from Humphrey Herington's nursery in New South Wales, Australia. The mystery of the missing eucalyptus seedlings was finally solved when the koala was caught on the premises, having eaten so much that he was unable to return to his tree.

HEDGEHOG HAT ▶ Finding what she thought was an abandoned baby hedgehog at the side of a road in Cheshire, England, an animal lover took it home to care for it. Worried that it hadn't moved, eaten, or pooped overnight, she took it to an animal hospital where she was informed that it was not a shy baby hedgehog, but the gray pom-pom from a wool hat!

FLEA FROG ▶ Found only on two hillsides in Bahia, southern Brazil, the rare Brazilian flea toad, which, despite its name, is really a frog, measures just 0.3 inches (7.6 mm) long, making it smaller than a human fingernail.

The name "gerenuk" comes from a Somali word meaning "giraffe-necked."

and one month of five days (or six days during a leap year). **FIJI** ▶ After losing its declaration of independence, Fiji had to ask the UK for a photocopy of

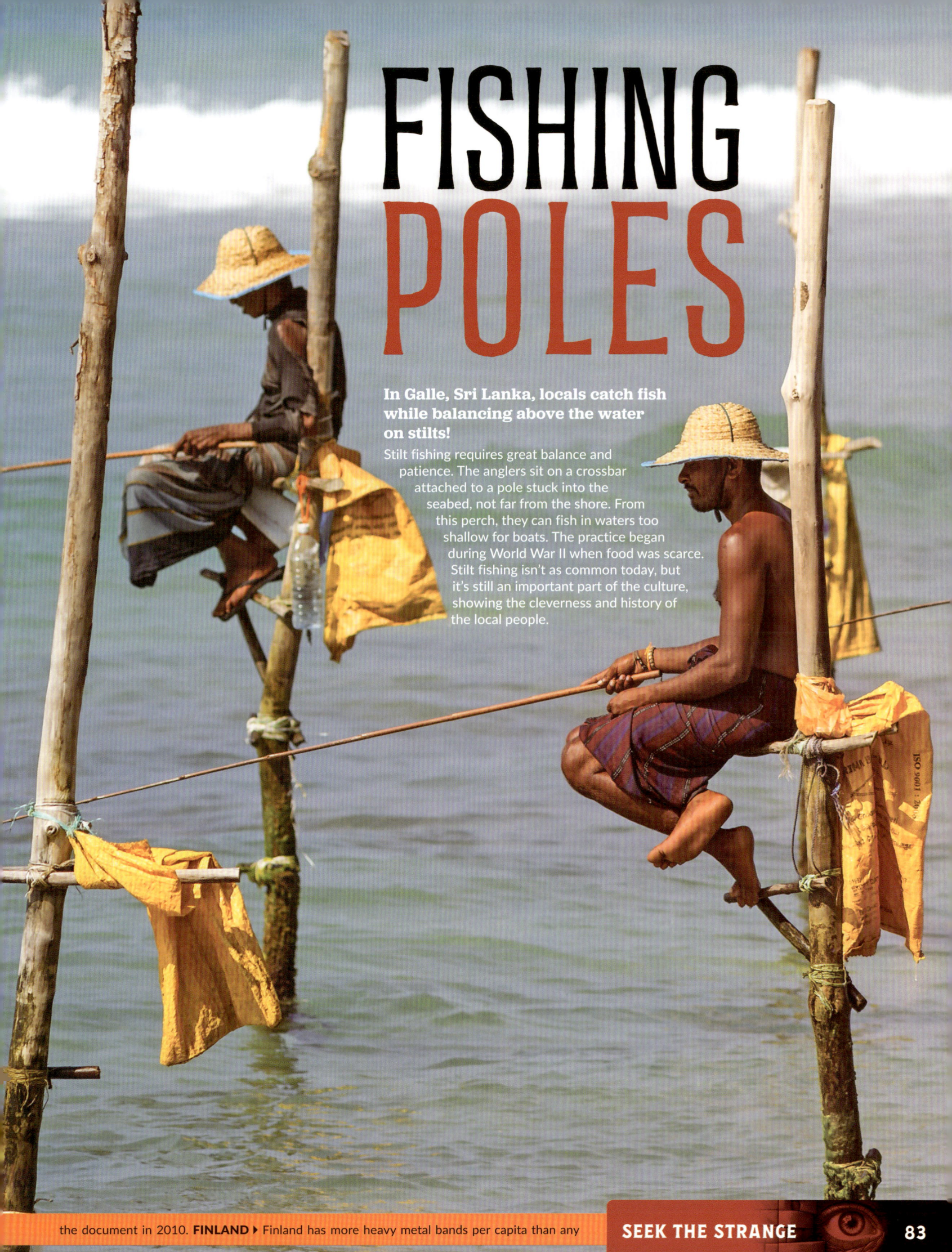

FISHING POLES

In Galle, Sri Lanka, locals catch fish while balancing above the water on stilts!

Stilt fishing requires great balance and patience. The anglers sit on a crossbar attached to a pole stuck into the seabed, not far from the shore. From this perch, they can fish in waters too shallow for boats. The practice began during World War II when food was scarce. Stilt fishing isn't as common today, but it's still an important part of the culture, showing the cleverness and history of the local people.

SEEK THE STRANGE

SIDESHOW SCIENCE

Burnaby Q. Orbax, Neil E. Dee, and Sweet Pepper Klopek use science in their stunt show to perform tricks that push the limits of the human body!

These performers from Ontario, Canada, snap mousetraps on their tongues, hang buckets from their eyes, and walk on broken glass. They use science to stay safe and educate their audience. By understanding how force and pressure work, they can perform painful-looking stunts without getting hurt. They make people cringe, laugh, and learn. It's part-science, part-sideshow, and all-around amazing!

FRANCE ▶ The minimum age to be president of France is just 18 years old! **GABON** ▶ The Abanda Caves in Gabon are home to crocodiles

ROYAL RUN ▶ On January 14, 2024, for the first time in 294 years, not one European country had a female monarch. The stretch began on February 26, 1730, and ended with the abdication of Queen Margrethe II of Denmark.

HEADBANGING HOBBY ▶ At the Heavy Metal Knitting World Championship in Finland, headbanging competitors dance and knit in time to heavy metal music. They are judged on their artistic impression, attitude, originality, knitting presentation, and how well their performance matches the music.

SIZZLING SIDEWALKS ▶ When the Walt Disney Concert Hall opened in Los Angeles, California, in 2003, its steel walls reflected so much light that temperatures on nearby sidewalks reached 140°F (60°C).

COFFIN CONUNDRUM ▶ At an escape room in Barcelona, Spain, participants are given 30 minutes to free themselves from a locked coffin. Players use speakers to communicate with a partner in a neighboring casket and solve a series of puzzles to secure their release.

AMISS ALERT ▶ In December 2023, a great white shark alert was mistakenly sent to Fortrose, Scotland, instead of Fortrose, New Zealand. No great white sharks have ever been seen off the coast of Scotland.

WHEELIN' AROUND

Every April, the village of Pinner in Harrow, England, hosts a wheelbarrow race! It's part of their St. George's Day celebrations. Nineteen teams of two race through the streets. The team members take turns pushing each other in a wheelbarrow. They must stop at refreshment stations along the way and drink half a pint of beer to win!

HANDY MAN

Dave Duran, a.k.a. Handy Handerson, of Chicago, Illinois, is the world's first—and probably only—full-size professional handboarder! What is handboarding, you ask? It's skateboarding with your hands! Most handboarders use smaller boards made for the sport. But Dave performs his tricks on a full-size skateboard. Sometimes he skateboards and handboards at the same time! He took up the sport after breaking his ankle in the seventh grade. The ankle healed, but Dave never stopped handboarding!

that are orange due to bat droppings. **GAMBIA** ▶ Citizens in Gambia cast their votes in elections

SEEK THE STRANGE

THE RIPLEY'S COLLECTION

Magic lanterns were used for both education and entertainment—like this silly slide of a man being attacked by a giant flea!

MAGIC LANTERN

Magic lanterns were projectors that were popular from the late-eighteenth to early-twentieth century. The device used lenses and a light source to project images from slides onto a large surface. Magic lantern shows and slides could be very creative, and some film effects can be traced back to this technology!

CATALOG NO. 175773

SCRUBBED SCRUBBER

In 1875, Peter Lieber of Indianapolis, Indiana, sought to improve early washing machines. He patented this model, which introduced features like rotating brushes for more effective scrubbing. His design never took off, but luckily, washing machines continued to improve.

CATALOG NO. 173761

MECHANICAL CALCULATOR

For most of the 1900s—before electronic calculators became popular in the '70s—many people used devices like this to help with math. Called "slide adders," they could add and subtract by simply moving the numbered slides—no batteries required!

CATALOG NO. 15722

SEEK THE STRANGE

RIPLEY'S Believe It or Not!®

PIERCING *Patterns*

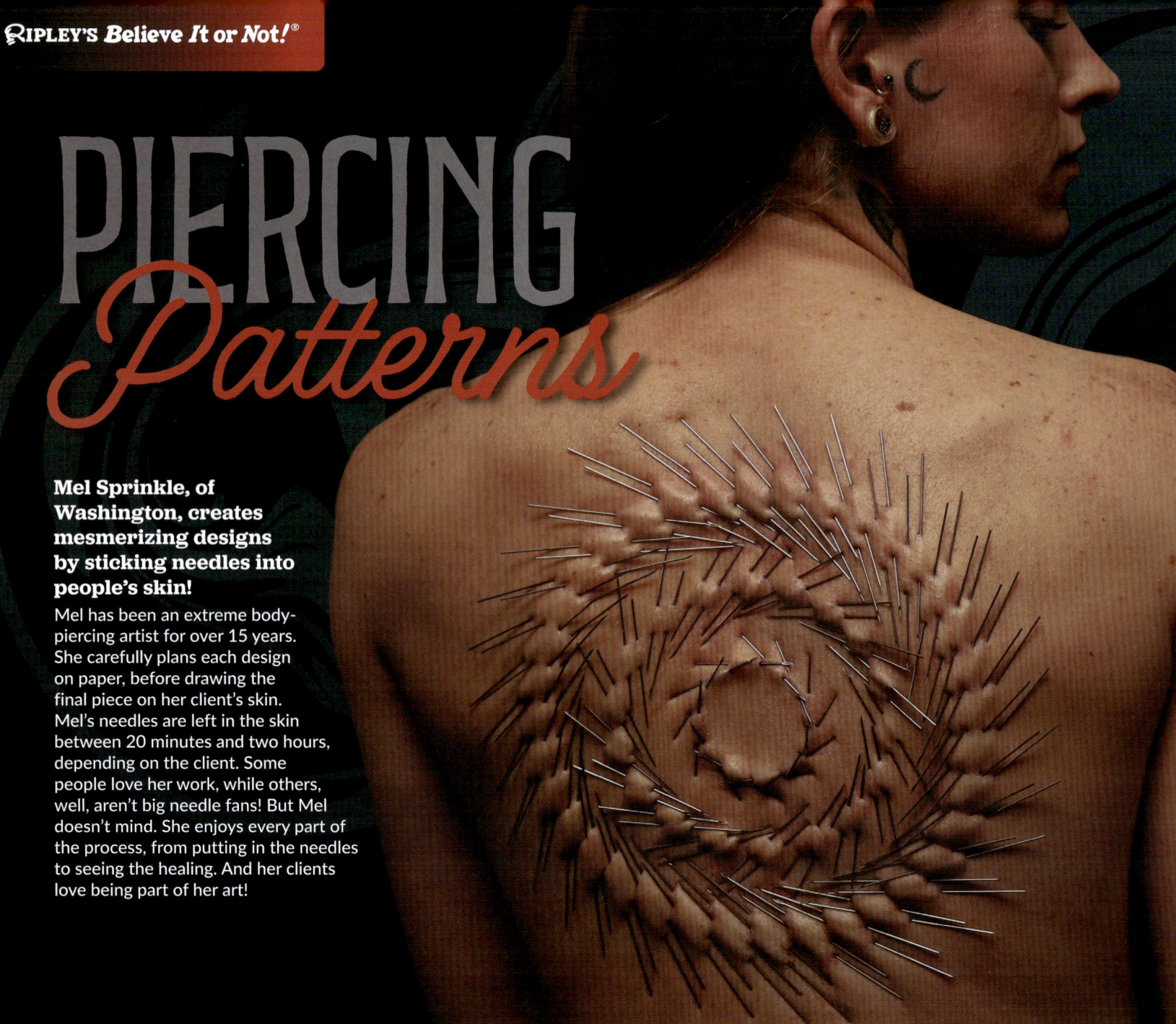

Mel Sprinkle, of Washington, creates mesmerizing designs by sticking needles into people's skin!

Mel has been an extreme body-piercing artist for over 15 years. She carefully plans each design on paper, before drawing the final piece on her client's skin. Mel's needles are left in the skin between 20 minutes and two hours, depending on the client. Some people love her work, while others, well, aren't big needle fans! But Mel doesn't mind. She enjoys every part of the process, from putting in the needles to seeing the healing. And her clients love being part of her art!

SOCKET STRENGTH ▶ Andrew Stanton, from Las Vegas, Nevada, pulled a Cadillac car with his eye sockets. By attaching a hook to each eye socket, he pulled the car with a driver in the front seat. The car weighed 5,319 pounds (2,413 kg) and moved a distance of 33 feet (10 m)! He can also lift 129 pounds (59 kg) with his eye sockets, while simultaneously swallowing a sword.

DÉJÀ VU ▶ In May 2021, Rob Klune became the first person to hit a hole-in-one at the par-3, 226-yard third hole at Pikewood National Golf Club in West Virginia. Two years later, in May 2023, he returned to the course—and once again, he hit a hole-in-one on the third hole.

PLANK POSITION ▶ DonnaJean Wilde, a 58-year-old grandmother from Alberta, Canada, held the abdominal plank position for an incredible four and a half hours.

BALL BANG
In the 1890s, Princeton mathematics instructor Charles Hinton devised a baseball pitching machine—a cannon that fired the ball at the batter. But the "baseball gun," as it was known, was soon scrapped by the college team because the batters didn't appreciate being shot at!

POOL PACE ▶ Adam Lopez ran about 1 mile (1.6 km) through water at a swimming pool in Norwich, England. He completed more than 60 laps in 35 minutes and 24 seconds.

FAST FINGERS ▶ Fourteen-year-old Charlie Eggins, from Brisbane, Australia, solved a Rubik's Cube in 12.1 seconds while blindfolded.

BACKWARD CLIMBER ▶ In February 2024, Ben Stewart, from England, climbed up and down Tanzania's 19,340-foot-high (5,895-m) Mount Kilimanjaro, the highest mountain in Africa—while walking backward. It took him eight days. He trained for the challenge by using a special device that strengthened his neck because of the need to look over his shoulder for long periods. He has also walked backward up the highest mountains in the UK, including Scotland's 4,413-foot-high (1,345-m) Ben Nevis.

by dropping a glass marble into a container that bears the name of their preferred candidate. **GEORGIA** ▶ The country of Georgia celebrates New Year's Day

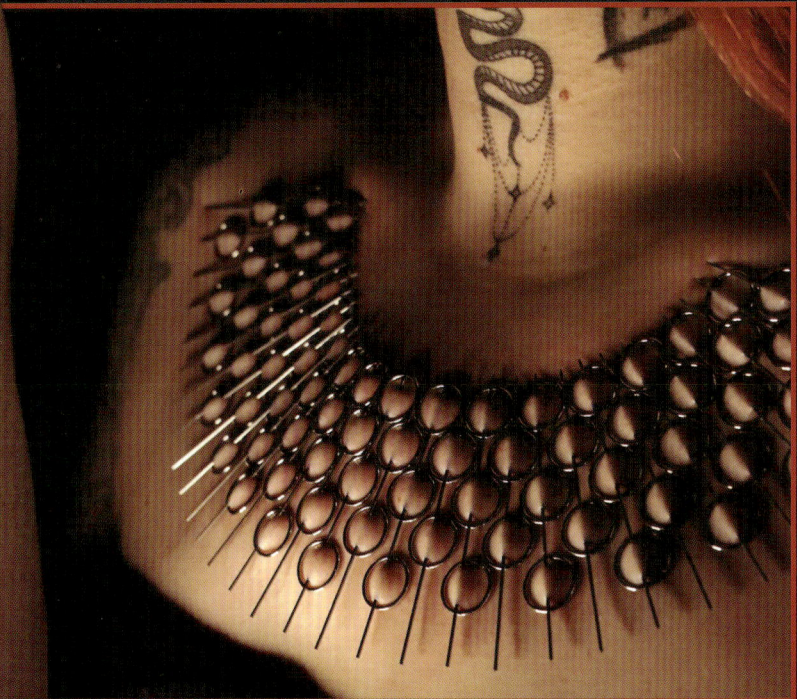

HUNGRY CATERPILLAR

ACTUAL SIZE!

The hickory horned devil caterpillar looks scary and can be really big—up to 5 inches (13 cm) long! But don't fret, it's harmless. The caterpillar is the baby form of the regal moth. Before wrapping itself in a cocoon, it eats a huge meal. This is the last food the insect will ever have, because when it becomes a moth, it doesn't eat at all!

When it becomes a moth, it stops eating.

twice—on January 1, then again on January 14, which is known as "Old New Year" according to

SEEK THE STRANGE

RIPLEY'S Believe It or Not!

HISTORIC HEE-HAW

The town of Oatman, Arizona, has more donkeys than people! In the 1920s, Oatman was a booming gold mining town. The miners used small donkeys, or burros, to carry heavy loads. When the mines shut down, the donkeys were set free! Thousands of burros today are direct descendants of the gold mine burros. More than a dozen wander into town every day. In 2020, a donkey named Walter was named the town's honorary mayor!

TREASURE TROVE ▶ While renovating the kitchen of their farmhouse in Dorset, England, Robert and Betty Fooks uncovered $75,000 worth of ancient coins beneath the floor. The hoard of more than 1,000 coins dated back to when the house was built in the mid-seventeenth century.

MACABRE MEMENTO ▶ When her husband Derek died, Tina Loudfoot kept part of his bowel preserved in a jar of formaldehyde as a reminder of their happy marriage. Derek had previously undergone surgery to remove his colon and had asked the hospital if he could keep the bowel. He proudly displayed it in his living room and even took it to the pub, until the landlady said he was scaring away customers.

WICKED WAITERS ▶ More than 100 Chicago waiters were arrested in 1918 for poisoning customers that they considered to be bad tippers. Victims had their food or drinks laced with a powder that caused vomiting, headaches, dizziness, and depression.

TREE TRAVEL ▶ Two 65-foot-long (20-m) rope bridges have been built in England's Forest of Dean to help hazel dormice travel safely between treetops. Dormice are vulnerable to predators on the ground, only going down to hibernate.

SLOTH SUCTION ▶ Sloths suck termites and other insects from their nests like a vacuum cleaner. They are even able to seal their nostrils to improve suction and stop the insects from crawling up their nose.

FUNGI FROG

In 2023, scientists in Karnataka, India, found something very strange: a frog with a tiny mushroom growing from its side! The frog seemed healthy and moved normally, so they didn't touch it. This bizarre find confused experts worldwide. No one had ever seen a mushroom grow on a frog before! The mushroom is believed to be a type that usually grows on dead wood, but no one knows how it ended up on a living frog. It's a big mystery!

the dates of the Julian calendar. **GERMANY** ▶ The town of Nördlingen, Germany, was built inside a 15-million-year-old meteor crater and is embedded with

SO HIGH UP!

CANOE BELIEVE IT?

At the Pontcysyllte Aqueduct in northern Wales, you can canoe 126 feet (38 m) above the ground!

Also called the "stream in the sky," it's the longest and highest aqueduct in the UK! An aqueduct is like a bridge that helps move water. Completed in 1805, the Pontcysyllte Aqueduct took over a decade to design and build. Surrounded by scenic views, people can travel across the aqueduct in a boat or canoe. There's even a pathway to walk or bike across the top!

72,000 tons of tiny diamonds. **GHANA** ▶ Craftsmen in Ghana create custom "fantasy coffins" in

RIPLEY'S Believe It or Not!®

ROLL MODELS

Bryan Sisk, a.k.a. The Maki Master, creates realistic portraits out of sushi ingredients!

His canvas is a layer of rice on top of dried seaweed, or *nori*. To get started, he draws an outline in squid ink. He fills the shape in with slices of fish like tuna and salmon. Sometimes Bryan uses octopus or vegetables and will use different sauces for the shading and small details. When he is done, he rolls the artwork up and slices it into bite-size pieces!

Robert Downey Jr.

Miley Cyrus

Bob Marley

Jiro Ono

Kim Kardashian

PORTRAITS ARE ROLLED, SLICED, AND SERVED!

the shape of foods, animals, vehicles, and other objects to represent the customer's life! **GREECE** ▶ At midnight on New Year's Eve, Greek households

SUITCASE SUSHI

Imagine getting off a flight and going to pick up your bag. But next to the suitcases rolling around, you see trays of giant sushi! This is what happens at Oita Airport in Japan. It turned baggage claim into a moving menu! It is like a giant version of the conveyor belts seen at some sushi restaurants. The display encourages visitors to try the local food.

UNCLAIMED SUSHI?

LANGUAGE LEARNING ▶ RM, singer of Korean pop band BTS, learned English partly by binge-watching all 10 seasons of *Friends* on DVD.

POOP PLACES ▶ "Places I've Pooped" is a smartphone app that shows on a map all the places you have pooped. You can even follow your friends and see where they have pooped.

SHOUT-OFF ▶ The annual Tennessee Williams Festival in New Orleans, Louisiana, features a Stanley and Stella Shouting Contest where competitors yell "Stellaaa!" or "Stanleyyy!" to mimic the characters from Williams's play *A Streetcar Named Desire*.

BEATLES BASS ▶ In 2024, Sir Paul McCartney was reunited with the bass guitar he had played on early Beatles hits. The bass guitar was stolen from their van in 1972. The Hofner bass, which McCartney played more than 250 times at Liverpool's Cavern Club, was found gathering dust in the attic of a home in Sussex. It is valued at around $12.5 million.

CREATIVE CHALK ▶ Preeti Gundapwar spent three days creating a 2,438-square-foot (226-sq-m) chalk drawing of the northern lights on the sidewalk outside her home.

SCHOOL SPELLING ▶ A road sign painted in 2023 outside Mountview Middle School in Holden, Massachusetts, was misspelled as "SHCOOL."

SECRET SHOW

In the hope of achieving his artistic breakthrough, an employee of the Pinakothek der Moderne art museum in Munich, Germany, secretly drilled holes in the gallery wall and put his own painting on display among those of Pablo Picasso, Paul Klee, and Andy Warhol.

LONG LENGTH ▶ A total of 100 people gathered on a beach near Pembrey, Wales, to take part in a tug-of-war contest with a rope that stretched for a length of 1,696 feet (517 m).

DELICIOUSLY DIRTY ▶ Abe-chan, a restaurant in Tokyo, Japan, serves pork skewers that taste very rich because they are dipped in a sauce jar that has not been cleaned for 60 years.

FAVORITE FILM ▶ Professional magician Darren McQuade has collected more than 2,000 items of *Ghostbusters* memorabilia and even appeared as a background actor in the latest *Ghostbusters* movie. His rarest items include a *Ghostbusters 2* Christmas cracker box and don't forget the *Ghostbusters* stunt kite!

BITE BLOCK

Created by UK artist Laurence of WhatHoWhy on social media, this real sushi roll is completely encased in museum-quality acrylic, keeping the item inside preserved for years to come!

CATALOG NO. 175399

Rolling through time!

enjoy vasilopita, a cake with a coin baked inside that is said to bring good luck to whoever finds it!

SEEK THE STRANGE

RIPLEY'S Believe It or Not!®

TALL ORDER

Humans have been building larger-than-life statues for thousands of years. They often honor deities, historical figures, or even ideas. There are always new monuments being built. Some aim to reach higher than all others. Here are five of the tallest statues in the world—you can't miss them!

LAYKYUN SEKKYA

Laykyun Sekkya in Myanmar includes two figures, one standing and one reclining. Both depict the founder of Buddhism, Siddhartha Gautama. The standing statue is 380 feet (116 m) tall! The monument took 12 years to build, starting in 1996 and opening in 2008. For locals, the statue is a sacred place to pray.

If you could build a giant statue of someone, who would you pick?

Share your thoughts...

THE STATUE OF BELIEF

At 369 feet (112 m) tall, the Statue of Belief in India is the world's tallest statue of the Hindu god Shiva. Also known as the Vishwas Swaroopam, the monument can be seen from over 12 miles (19 km) away! Unlike many other statues, the figure is shown seated. The bold color from its copper coating also helps it stand out.

VISIBLE FROM 12 MILES (19 KM) AWAY!

GRENADA ▶ The Molinere Underwater Sculpture Park located off the west coast of Grenada is the first public art exhibit of its kind in the world.

THE STATUE OF UNITY

The Statue of Unity in India is the tallest statue in the world at 597 feet (182 m). That's nearly four times taller than the Statue of Liberty! It honors Sardar Vallabhbhai Patel, an important Indian leader. The statue is made from thousands of tons of bronze, steel, and concrete. There is a viewing area in the chest where visitors can look out over the river from more than 440 feet (134 m) high!

THOSE ARE BIG SHOES TO FILL!

SPRING TEMPLE BUDDHA

The Spring Temple Buddha in China is 420 feet (128 m) tall, making it the second tallest statue in the world. The figure stands on a 66-foot-tall (20-m) pedestal that's shaped like a lotus flower. The lotus doubles as a monastery. Visitors willing to climb hundreds of stairs (or pay for a lift) can touch the statue's toes, which are as tall as an adult human!

USHIKU DAIBUTSU

The Ushiku Daibutsu in Japan is a bronze Buddha that stands 394 feet (120 m) tall. Its base and lotus-shaped platform add an extra 67 feet (20 m) to that height! Completed in 1993, it was the world's tallest statue for about 15 years. Included inside the giant figure is a room filled with around 3,400 small Buddha statues!

THOUSANDS OF STATUES INSIDE THE STATUE!

GUATEMALA ▶ Day of the Dead celebrations in Guatemala include colorful displays of giant

SEEK THE STRANGE

RIPLEY'S Believe It or Not!®

BIG BLANKET

More than 4,000 people gathered in Paris, France, for a giant picnic on an enormous blanket! Held on May 26, 2024, the event took place on the city's famous avenue, the Champs-Élysées. The massive red-and-white checkered cloth stretched over 708 feet (216 m) long! Hungry Parisians enjoyed free meals from local restaurants and views of the iconic Arc de Triomphe.

LONGEST PICNIC EVER?

LOAFING AROUND

Every Easter, the town of San Biagio Platani, Italy, is covered with bread sculptures! The tasteful designs are made to look like the inside of a church. Pasta, grains, and even fruit are also used for decor! Called the Arches of Bread festival, the tradition dates back to the seventeenth century. Today, the festival is a friendly contest between locals. People come from all over to see the savory structures!

paper kites that take months to make and can measure up to 60 feet (18.3 m) across! **GUINEA** ▶ The Centre d'Art Acrobatique Keita Fodeba in Conakry, Guinea,

PASTRY WAR ▶ A three-month-long conflict between Mexico and France was known as the Pastry War. It started in 1838 partly because Mexico refused France's demand to pay Monsieur Remontel, a French pastry cook living in Mexico. He claimed that Mexican army officers had damaged his shop in Tacubaya and asked for 60,000 pesos in compensation.

MUMMIFIED MONKEYS ▶ Thanks to an airport sniffer dog, four mummified monkeys were discovered in the luggage of a passenger arriving at Boston's Logan International Airport on a flight from the Democratic Republic of the Congo in early 2024.

SUPER SELLOUT
From June 12, 1995, to April 4, 2001, every seat at Jacobs Field was sold out for 455 consecutive Cleveland Indians baseball games. During that period, a total of 19,324,248 tickets were sold.

FOUNTAIN FOLLY ▶ A man in Switzerland was hospitalized after trying to hug Geneva's Jet d'Eau fountain, which spouts water over 460 feet (140 m) into the air at speeds of 124 mph (200 kmph). He was launched skyward by the force of the fountain and landed on hard concrete.

POWERFUL PUTT ▶ With a single putt, Jay Stocki of Illinois sent a golf ball across a hilly golf course and into a hole 401.2 feet (122.3 m) away! The record-breaking putt took place on September 26, 2023, at Blackwolf Run in Kohler, Wisconsin.

FRANKLY FABULOUS
A 65-foot-long (20-m) hot dog drizzled in mustard stole the show in the city that never sleeps!

Hot Dog in the City was a sculpture designed by artists Jen Catron and Paul Outlaw. In April 2024, it was installed in the middle of Times Square in New York. Every day at noon, the giant hot dog would tilt upward on hydraulics and shoot rainbow confetti into the sky! The sculpture was part of an exhibit and other hot dog–themed events, like the Condiment Wars wrestling match, the Hottest Dog Show, and a hot dog eating contest.

THE RIPLEY'S COLLECTION

Not exactly pocket change!

KATANGA CROSS

This copper cross was once used as money in Central Africa. Called a "Katanga cross," it is named after a region that is now part of the Democratic Republic of the Congo. The cross measures about 8 inches (20 cm) wide and weighs over 2 pounds (1 kg)!

CATALOG NO. 169166

FIELD MASS KIT

This cross-shaped container was likely used during wartime and possibly on the battlefield. It contains things like a candle and anointing oil, which a Catholic priest would use to perform religious rituals such as the Last Rites for the dying.

CATALOG NO. 174043

VAMPIRE DEFENSE

This large cabinet dates back to around 1900 and includes everything you'd need to defeat a vampire: wooden stakes, a mallet, a cleaver, a hammer, daggers, crucifixes, holy water, garlic, and a Bible. Vampire-killing kits became popular following the publication of Bram Stoker's *Dracula* in 1897.

CATALOG NO. 174075

Vampire-killing stakes!

SEEK THE STRANGE
99

Tons of asparagus were once taken by train to markets to be sold at auction.

CHEERS FOR SPEARS

The British Asparagus Festival is a yearly celebration of asparagus! It begins on April 23, Saint George's Day, and lasts two months. The star of the show, besides the actual veggie, is Gus the Asparagus Man! He is often joined by the Aspara-Fairy, Saint George, and Jemima Packington, the Asparamancer, who claims to use asparagus to tell the future. The festival is held in the Vale of Evesham. The area has grown asparagus for a very long time and is famous for it to this day!

BALLAD BATTLES ▶ For a period of several months, drivers in Porirua, New Zealand, used siren-type speakers to blast out Celine Dion ballads across the city during the night. Teams competing in the siren battles attached loudspeakers to their cars and bicycles to find out who could play the songs the loudest and the clearest.

DOG ABUNDANCE ▶ There are more than 1,800 hot dog stands in Chicago, Illinois.

STILL OPEN ▶ Sanquhar Post Office in Dumfries and Galloway, Scotland, has been in continuous operation for over 300 years. Since it first opened in 1712, there have been only 17 postmasters.

COUNTLESS CUSTOMERS ▶ Coppelia Park, an ice cream parlor in Havana, Cuba, has enough tables to seat 600 customers at a time. In one day it serves 4,200 gallons (16,000 liters) of ice cream to more than 30,000 people.

TREACHEROUS CROSSING ▶ To get to school in Villa Leidy, Colombia, some students must walk carefully across a makeshift bridge that spans the alligator-filled Gaira River. The bridge consists of a single narrow pipe with a length of rope for pedestrians to hold on to.

BULKY BERG ▶ An iceberg that broke free from Antarctica in 2023 weighed nearly one trillion tons. It was 920 feet (280 m) thick and covered an area of 1,500 square miles (3,885 sq km)—more than three times the size of New York City.

DECLARED DEAD ▶ Manoel Marciano da Silva, from Brazil's Tocantins region, spent 28 years of his life legally dead. His ex-wife and two witnesses had declared him dead in 1995, but he only found out about it in 2012 when he was stopped from voting in a local election because he was listed as deceased. It subsequently took him two years to prove to a court that he was still alive so he could collect his pension. His death certificate was finally annulled in 2023.

RARE TIDE The tide on the Qiantang River in eastern China sometimes flows in spiraling waves that resemble fish scales on the water surface—a rare phenomenon known as a "fish scale tide." It is believed to be caused by rotating currents, which result in the waves colliding at oblique angles to create a scale pattern. It only lasts for about 10 minutes before fading.

SKY HIGH

The Giant Kite Festival in Sagamihara, Japan, is home to some of the largest kites in the world!

Known as the Oodako matsuri, the festival started in the 1800s. The kites are built out of bamboo and handmade paper. The kite-flying has signified many things, from celebrating new babies to praying for healthy crops. Over the years, the kites have grown larger and larger. It can take up to 100 people to get these giant flyers in the air and keep them there. In 2024, the largest kite was 47.6 feet (14.5 m) wide and weighed more than 2,094 pounds (950 kg). Now that's a big kite!

MORE THAN 47 FEET (14.3 M) WIDE!

IT TAKES AN ARMY TO BUILD A KITE!

SEEK THE STRANGE

RIPLEY'S *Believe It or Not!*®

PET GALA

Fashion designer Anthony Rubio creates clothing for dogs based on celebrity looks from the Met Gala!

The Met Gala is the must-watch event of the year for fashion-loving humans. But what about our style-savvy furry friends? In May 2024, more than a dozen chic canines walked the red carpet of the Pet Gala in Anthony's copycat creations. The event took place at the AKC Museum of the Dog in New York City. It helped raise money for the museum, which put the outfits on display for a month after the Pet Gala.

The lovable Livie slayed as Gigi Hadid!

LOVING THAT LIP COLOR ON YOU!

GLAM GILLS

A very special fish lives in the waters of the Galápagos Islands. It has legs like a frog, bright-red lips, and a little lure that dangles from its head. The red-lipped batfish is unlike any other fish in the ocean. Even though it can swim, you're more likely to see it walking on the seafloor using its finlike legs. People who have seen it up close agree: the red-lipped batfish is one of a kind!

is the second-oldest independent nation in the Western Hemisphere, having gained its independence from France in 1804. **HONDURAS** ▶ Every year,

Ted Gram the poodle said, "Bad Bunny? More like Bad Puppy!"

Miley-Jo paw-*fectly* nailed her Cardi B look!

NATURAL CURLS

There's a toucan in South America that looks like it has curly hair! The curl-crested aracari is a large, colorful bird that lives in the rainforest. While it may look like this toucan went to the salon for a perm, its 'do is totally natural. The shiny black curls on its head are really feathers! Toucans already stand out from other birds thanks to their large beaks. But the curl-crested aracari manages to stand out even more thanks to its unique style!

fish appear to fall from the sky in Yoro, Honduras, during heavy rainstorms, an event locals call

RIPLEY'S Believe It or Not!®

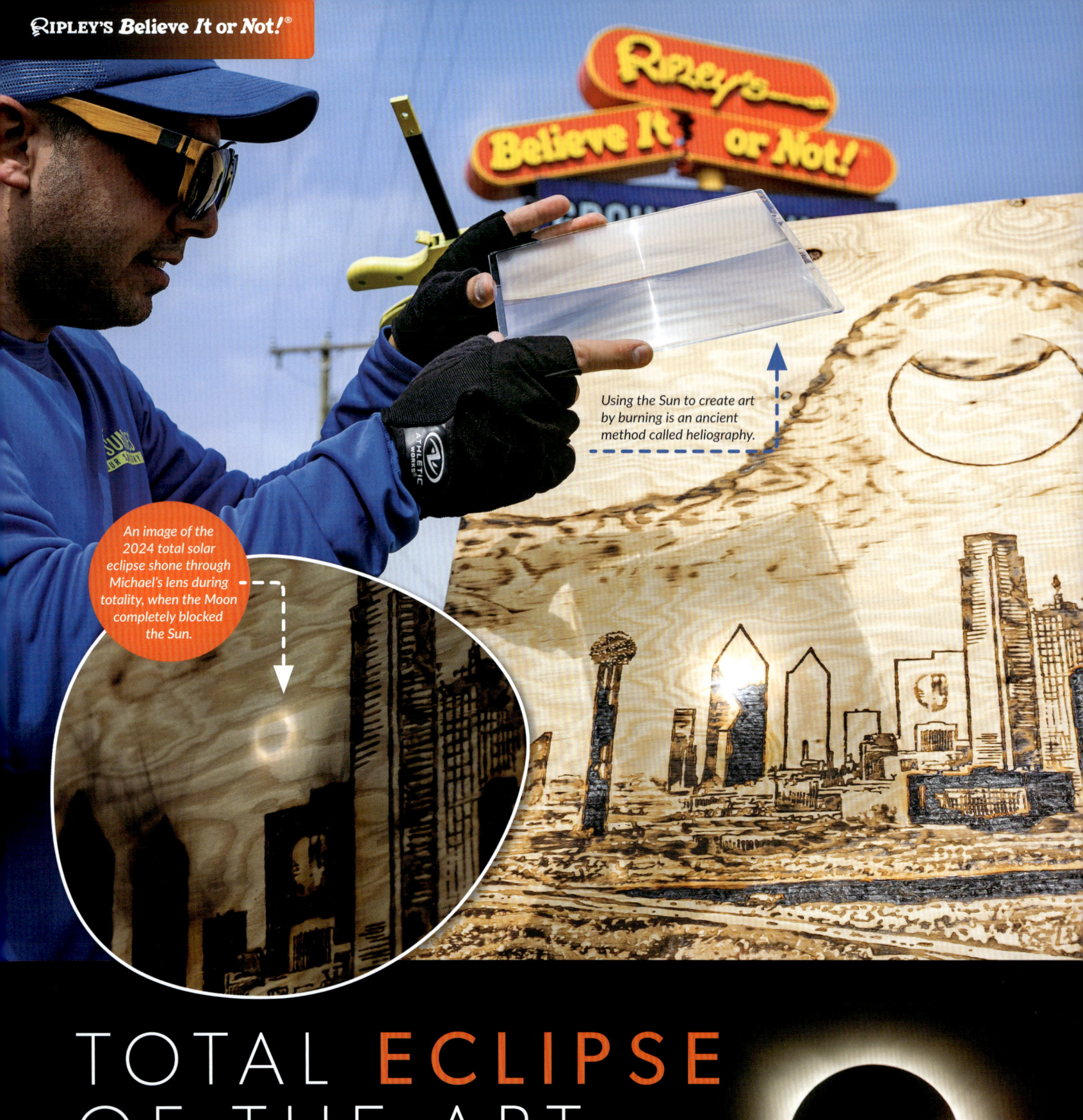

Using the Sun to create art by burning is an ancient method called heliography.

An image of the 2024 total solar eclipse shone through Michael's lens during totality, when the Moon completely blocked the Sun.

TOTAL ECLIPSE OF THE ART

Artist Michael Papadakis used the power of the Sun to turn the 2024 total solar eclipse into a work of art!

Also known as Sunscribes, Michael uses mirrors and lenses to focus the Sun's powerful rays onto a wooden canvas. The wood is burned by the heat, which Michael uses like a paintbrush. He went to Ripley's Believe It or Not! in Grand Prairie, Texas, to create a piece of art during the total solar eclipse on April 8, 2024. He was able to create burns until the moment of totality when the Moon completely blocked the Sun. During that time, Michael used his lens to shine an image of the eclipse onto the canvas!

Lluvia de Peces. **HUNGARY** ▶ When driven over at the right speed, Road 67 in Hungary plays the song "Road 67" by the Hungarian band Republic.

TOTALLY AWESOME

There are four kinds of solar eclipse: **total, annular, partial, and hybrid.** They occur when the Sun, Moon, and Earth align.

A total solar eclipse happens when the Moon **completely blocks the Sun**, casting a dark shadow onto Earth.

A total solar eclipse occurs somewhere on Earth **every 18 months or so**. The next one will be on **August 12, 2026**.

An average of **375 years** pass before a total solar eclipse is visible again from the same spot on Earth.

The only place on Earth to view a total solar eclipse is from **within the Moon's shadow**.

The short period of time when the Sun is completely blocked by the Moon is called **totality**. It can last from **a few seconds up to about 7.5 minutes**.

During **totality**, the **temperature drops**, **some animals go silent**, and the sky looks like a **sunset** in every direction.

The **white light** of the Sun's outer atmosphere, or **corona**, is only visible to the **naked eye during totality**.

QUICK CUBER ▶ Daryl Tan Hong An of Singapore can solve a Rubik's Cube underwater in 9.3 seconds. He has also solved a Rubik's Cube in 13 seconds with his left hand while juggling two balls in his right hand.

OLDER NEW ▶ British musician Gary Numan is two weeks older than Academy Award–winning actor Gary Oldman. Both were born in March 1958.

LOTTERY LUCK ▶ Wayne Murray from New York City won $10 million lottery prizes in both 2022 and 2023. He purchased the winning tickets from the same convenience store.

PASTOR'S PATENT

The bulletproof vest was invented by a priest. Polish-born Casimir Zeglen, who was a priest at a Catholic church in Chicago, Illinois, applied for a U.S. patent for the device in 1896.

INCONVENIENT STORE ▶ A tiny convenience store in China's Shiniuzhai National Geological Park is perched on the side of a vertical cliff 393 feet (120 m) above ground. There is only room for one worker inside the hut, which sells water, cakes, and sodas to climbers. The store can only be accessed by a network of fixed iron handrails and cables, and restocking takes place via a rope that pulls supplies up from the foot of the cliff.

STATION LOVE ▶ Train company employee Rehana Khawaja loves London's Marylebone Station so much that she changed her middle name to Marylebone.

THE RIPLEY'S COLLECTION

ECLIPSE ART

On April 8, 2024, cities across North America witnessed a total solar eclipse. Ripley's teamed up with artist Michael Papadakis, a.k.a. Sunscribes, to capture the rare event as a unique work of art. The finished piece features the skyline of Dallas, Texas, burned onto a wooden canvas.

CATALOG NO. 175888

The power of the Sun!

ICELAND ▶ Phone books are arranged alphabetically by first name in Iceland. INDIA ▶ A heat

SEEK THE STRANGE

WINGS & THINGS

Artist Luci Jockel turns bee parts into delicate works of art, like this veil made from more than 20,000 bee wings!

Where does Luci find so many bee wings? From beekeepers! They give Luci bees that have died from natural causes like harsh weather, harmful parasites, and even hungry bears! Each honeybee has two sets of wings, but Luci also uses other parts, like the thorax, in her work. She dries the insects before gently removing the parts she needs. With a steady hand, she rearranges them into something new. Luci uses her art to highlight the fragile link between humans and nature.

21,600 BEE WINGS!

What do you do to feel connected to nature?
Share your thoughts...

ROMAN REMAINS ▶ A chicken's egg that was discovered recently in a watery pit at an old Roman dig site in Buckinghamshire, England, has remained unbroken for 1,700 years. Scientists even found that the egg still contained its liquid. The "Aylesbury Egg," as it is known, has stayed intact for so long because the clay in the heavy, waterlogged soil formed a protective barrier that kept the air from decomposing it.

GRUESOME GUEST ▶ A neurosurgeon who was investigating the mysterious symptoms of a 64-year-old Englishwoman at a hospital in Canberra, Australia, removed a 3.1-inch-long (8-cm) parasitic roundworm larva from the patient's brain. She had been experiencing forgetfulness, abdominal pain, and night sweats. The worm's eggs are often shed in the droppings of carpet pythons, which are common in Australia.

KING'S COINS ▶ Since the reign of King Charles II in the late seventeenth century, the tradition has been for British monarchs to be depicted on coins facing in the opposite direction to their predecessor. The one exception was Edward VIII, who came to the throne in 1936. He should have been shown facing right, but insisted on left because he preferred his profile from that side. Ultimately, he only reigned for 325 days before abdicating, which meant that there was no time for any coins to be issued in his name.

SNAIL MAIL ▶ A postcard sent from Sydney, Australia, in August 1981 was finally delivered to its destination—an address in Kent, England—42 years later in December 2023.

BUG FLIPS

There's a tiny arthropod that can complete 368 full backflips per second—spinning away just like Sonic the Hedgehog! The globular springtail is about the size of a flea. The bug relies on its quick jumps and flips to get away from predators. They can jump and flip more than 2 inches (5 cm) high in the air. That's over 60 times their height! Don't blink if you see them, or they might disappear!

FLIPPING OUT!

BAT-FAN

Brad Ladner is a comic book fan with more than 8,200 items of Batman memorabilia. Among his rarest pieces are a Batman cigarette box and a costume continuity binder from the set of the 1989 *Batman* movie.

WARNING WINGS ▶ The postman butterfly from Central and South America develops its own poison by eating toxic plants. As caterpillars, they eat passionflower vines and retain the plant's toxic chemicals for the rest of their lives. The vivid red patterns on the butterfly's wings warn predators that it is poisonous.

CROAKING COLLECTION ▶ Helen Claypool of Kirksville, Missouri, was known as the "Frog Lady" due to her collection of more than 15,000 frog items, including clocks, phones, earrings, and lawn ornaments. She began collecting them at age six and documented each one, with an accompanying photo, in 47 logbooks.

CUTTING HEDGE

Gardeners at Powis Castle in Wales have to use cherry pickers to trim the 46-foot-tall (14-m) shrubs! The gardens have over 3 acres of hedges, including 14 massive yew tumps, or shrubs. Keeping them looking great is a big job. It takes up to 12 weeks to trim them each year. Today, powered shears make the job easier, but trimming still takes time. In the past, 10 men spent four months trimming the hedges by hand using shears and ladders!

are considered sacred and may not touch the ground for the first 105 days after being born.

RIPLEY'S Believe It or Not!®

Crafty CARS

Houston, Texas, is home to the biggest and oldest art car celebration in the world!

Hundreds of cars, bikes, and other wheeled wonders decked out in crazy colors and fun designs cruise together in a parade. Crafty artists transform their vehicles into moving masterpieces. Some even use tape, paper, blankets, and candy to jazz up their rides. Others are turned into sculptures that look like giant animals, fruits, or even shoes! The Houston Art Car Parade started back in 1988, and now more than 300,000 spectators attend every year.

IRAN ▶ In 2007, Iran captured 14 squirrels on suspicion of espionage! **IRAQ** ▶ The world's earliest writing system emerged in what is modern-day Iraq more

than 5,000 years ago. **IRELAND** ▶ If one of your grandparents was born in Ireland, you can claim

SEEK THE STRANGE

THE RIPLEY'S COLLECTION

MATCH TO THE FUTURE

Folk artist Pat Acton recreated the setting of the 1985 film *Back to the Future* out of matchsticks! The massive model shows the town square of Hill Valley, California, as it appeared when Marty McFly traveled back in time to 1955. Pat spent just over two years building the diorama and even added interactive features!

CATALOG NO. 175460

723,000 matchsticks!

1.21 GIGAWATTS

With the push of a button, the time-traveling DeLorean speeds down the street. Lights flash and thunder rolls—mimicking the scene in which Marty McFly returns to the year 1985!

MATCH TO THE FUTURE PART II

HIGH SCHOOL

> "If you put your mind to it, you can accomplish anything."
> Marty McFly

MANURE TRUCK

Incredible detail!

CLOCK TOWER

"Roads? Where we're going, we don't need roads."
Dr. Emmett Brown

GAS STATION

SEEK THE STRANGE

MATCH TO THE FUTURE
PART III

LOU'S CAFE

CONTROL STATION

Lights and music!

TOWN STREET

> "Wait a minute, Doc. Are you telling me that you built a time machine... out of a DeLorean?"
> Marty McFly

HILL VALLEY SIGN

SEEK THE STRANGE

EN POINTE

In April 2024, more than 350 ballet dancers stayed en pointe, or on their toes, at the same time for a full minute! They tiptoed in one spot and did not drop or touch each other the entire time. The feat took place in New York City, but the dancers were from around the world. Some people joined the challenge at the last minute. One dancer even squeezed into shoes three sizes too small so they could take part!

STAY ON YOUR TOES, PLEASE!

WORLD TOUR ▶ Setting off in June 2023, Douglas Concha of Honolulu, Hawaii, cycled around the world in nine months, riding 18,000 miles (29,000 km) across six continents and 23 countries. During his adventure, he suffered food poisoning twice and had three accidents, including one that put him in the hospital for 10 days.

CROWING CONTEST ▶ The annual Kentucky State Fair stages a rooster crowing contest to determine which bird can crow the most times in 15 minutes. The contest apparently started as a way of settling a dispute between two feuding farmers.

STREET STUNT ▶ In 2023, Brooklyn-based bicycle stunt rider Leh-Boy Gabriel Davis rode through the streets of New York City with a couch balanced vertically on his head! He also rides while balancing basketballs, garbage cans, and flat-screen TVs on his head.

BALLOON BEAST ▶ As part of the 2024 Chinese New Year celebrations, balloon artists Sze Tai Pang and Kun Lung Ho led more than 60 volunteers to construct a dragon sculpture at a shopping mall in Hong Kong. The sculpture measured 137 feet (42 m) long and was made from about 38,000 balloons.

COAST PEDAL ▶ Canadian quadriplegic Kevin Mills handcycled all the way across Canada from coast to coast, traveling a distance of over 5,220 miles (8,400 km). He set off on May 24, 2023, from Cape Spear Lighthouse in Newfoundland and, pedaling with his arms and shoulders on his customized bike, finished four months later on September 30 in Victoria, British Columbia. On the way, he overcame hurricane-force winds, bumpy gravel roads, and steep climbs through the Rocky Mountains.

STATIONARY SKETCHES Artist Garry Trinh, from Sydney, Australia, goes into stationery stores carrying a piece of paper and uses every sample marker or pen to create an abstract artwork. He spends up to two hours on his in-store doodles without ever buying a single pen. In 2023, his creations went on display at a local gallery.

SAME SCHOOL ▶ In 2023, 76-year-old Paul Durietz marked 53 years teaching social studies at Woodland Middle School in Gurnee, Illinois. He started teaching there on September 1, 1970.

Irish citizenship no matter where you live or were born. **ISRAEL** ▶ Albert Einstein was offered the presidency of Israel in 1952, but he turned it down.

TEQ *Yeah!*

What two activities would you combine into a new sport, and what would you call it?
Share your thoughts...

SPECIALLY CURVED TABLE WITH A DIVIDER

Kick it up a notch (literally) with teqball—a sport that mixes soccer and table tennis!

Instead of kicking a ball into a net, teqball players use their feet, head, or chest to pass and hit a soccer ball over a specially curved table with a divider down the middle. You can't use your arms or hands, though! Players and teams can only touch the ball three times before sending the ball back to their opponent. The goal is to try to score 12 points and win a set. The team with the best of three sets wins!

ITALY ▶ Giant mirrors reflect light onto Italy's Alpine village of Viganella, which is located in a

SEEK THE STRANGE

RIPLEY'S Believe It or Not!

REVOLUTIONARY
Riding

At Mexican rodeos, teams of women perform thrilling dances on horseback while riding sidesaddle in heavy dresses!

The event started in Mexico in the 1950s. The women, called *escaramuzas*, compete in teams of eight. They are judged based on their skill and precision. They ride their horses with both legs on one side and wear dresses with ruffled layers. Each dress weighs 15 pounds (6.8 kg)! The women fighters of the Mexican Revolution inspired their outfits. They would ride horses in circles to create dust and confuse their enemies!

When riding sidesaddle, both legs must stay on one side of the horse!

valley and receives no direct sunlight between November and February. **JAMAICA** ▶ Chocolate milk was invented in Jamaica. **JAPAN** ▶ Thanks to a marketing

CASH CATCH ▶ While fishing for walleye on the Lake of the Woods in Minnesota, 14-year-old Connor Halsa reeled in a wallet stuffed with $2,000 in cash. The wallet, which was retrieved from 20-foot-deep (6-m) water, had been lost there a year earlier by Iowa farmer Jim Denney. He was tracked down by a business card inside the wallet and the money was returned to him.

PAIRED PAINS ▶ When Daisy Devane, from Bedfordshire, England, suffered a cardiac arrest, Jeremy Williams, an emergency responder who was treating her, also collapsed in her living room from a major heart attack. While he was timing the chest compressions that were being administered for CPR, he suddenly began to feel pains in his own chest. Both were rushed to a hospital and eventually recovered.

OVER ORDERED ▶ Dan Dafydd, a shopkeeper on the Orkney island of Sanday, which is located off the north coast of Scotland, accidentally ordered 80 cases of Easter eggs instead of just 80 Easter eggs. He was sent 720 chocolate eggs for an island with a population of only about 500 people.

CRASH COURSE ▶ On only his second day in the job, an instructor-in-training at the Community Driving School in Lakewood, Colorado, crashed a vehicle through the school's front window—right beneath a sign that says "Learn To Drive." He had been attempting to park.

SUPER ZUCCHINI ▶ Henry D'Angela, of Thorold, Canada, grew an 8.4-foot-long (2.6-m) zucchini in his garden.

GLADIATOR GALS
Women in ancient Rome didn't just watch gladiator battles—they fought in them, too! The female fighters wore less armor than men and no helmets. Why? That way, everyone could see they were women. Some even fought by torchlight to add extra drama! These battles were not common, though. Male gladiators were well-documented in ancient Rome, but only a few writings and artworks of these female fighters have ever been found.

POWER NAP
Ready, set, nap! Hundreds of people took part in a sleeping contest in Seoul, South Korea. Participants wore pajamas and tried to sleep for 90 minutes. They had to snooze through distractions like tickling, whispering, and insect buzzing sounds. The winner was the person whose heart rate changed the most, showing they had the best sleep. South Korea has one of the lowest sleep quality scores in the world. The event was held to remind people that rest is really important for staying healthy in a busy world.

SNOOZE OR LOSE!

campaign that started in the 1970s, eating Kentucky Fried Chicken on Christmas has become a

SEEK THE STRANGE

RIPLEY'S Believe It or Not!®

Love BUG

Bugkiss is a real product made for kissing insects and other creepy crawlies!

The device was created by the artist and inventor known as Legboot. For the prototype, he attached a tiny pair of doll lips to a pacifier with a metal spring. He even made attachments for kissing extra-small bugs! Like much of Legboot's art, Bugkiss was meant to be a joke. But when videos of him using it to kiss real bugs went viral, people really wanted to buy their own Bugkiss! So he turned it into a real product, and now anyone can "smooch without smoosh!"

> " People just want to feel what it's like to enter the bug world.

Ripley's reached out to Legboot to learn more about Bugkiss. See what he had to say!

Q: How do you feel about the response to Bugkiss, both positive and negative?
A: I wasn't expecting it to become so popular so quickly. I also wasn't prepared for how many people seem to want to use it unironically. I designed the product as a novelty gag gift or joke product and never intended it to be put to actual use. I will admit that using it—even as a joke—has made me a little bit more compassionate and thoughtful toward bugs and small critters than I was before.

Q: Why do you think so many people were drawn to the idea of kissing bugs?
A: I guess people just want to feel what it's like to enter the bug world and connect with a creature that would otherwise be inaccessible.

Q: You've kissed many creatures using Bugkiss, including a worm that reportedly "kissed back." What was that like?
A: I won't pretend to understand worm psychology, but that was the impression I got from a human point of view. More likely the worm was blindly casting about to find some soil.

Q: Do you have any tips for first-time Bugkiss users?
A: The most important thing to keep in mind is to never approach insects that could cause you harm, or to which you may cause harm while interacting. Other than that, it's pretty simple: just hold the device in your mouth and slowly bring the small lip attachment into contact with the bug.

time-honored tradition in Japan. **JORDAN ▶** More than 85 percent of the ancient city of Petra in Jordan is still underground and unexplored.

IS THE WORM KISSING BACK?

Legboot also made a book so Bugkiss users can keep track of the bugs they smooch!

FOR KISSING EXTRA-TINY BUGS!

TWIG TRAP ▶ During the bird mating season, some crocodiles and alligators balance twigs on their snouts to lure nest-building water birds to their deaths.

CLIFF COLONY ▶ Every year, around 74,000 adult burrowing parrots gather to nest on the 8 miles (12 km) of cliffs at Balneario El Cóndor in Argentina. More than 70 percent of the species' total worldwide population nests there.

ALIEN LIFE ▶ Scientists have estimated that there are at least 36 intelligent alien civilizations living in our galaxy.

THE Ripley's COLLECTION

MOO SHOES

Created by Jim Wells of Ontario, Canada, these boots help protect cows from hoof infections. Plus, they're super stylish!

CATALOG NO. 14210

KAZAKHSTAN ▶ Lake Chagan, a.k.a. Atomic Lake, in Kazakhstan was created by a nuclear

SEEK THE STRANGE

CATCH a Breeze

Sometimes beaches get covered in thousands of living blue blobs!

The jelly-like creatures are known as by-the-wind sailors. They can grow up to 4 inches (10 cm) long and live on the surface of the ocean. By-the-wind sailors rely on the ocean current, the wind, and the small sails atop their bodies to travel. This mode of transportation does not always work in their favor. Sometimes they end up stranded on sand in the thousands, surprising and delighting beachgoers with their bright blue color.

LITTLE LIVING SAILBOATS!

explosion in 1965 and is still radioactive. **KENYA** ▶ In June 2016, a monkey tripped a transformer at a hydropower plant in Kenya and caused a nationwide

BEAR-Y UNIQUE

Meet Qizai: one of the world's only brown-and-white pandas! He's one of just seven brown-and-white pandas ever known. The first recorded brown panda was discovered in 1985. Qizai was found in 2009 in China's Qinling mountain range, where all of the other brown pandas were also discovered. Qizai stands out because of a mutation in his DNA, which turned his fur brown instead of black!

CROC ESCAPE ▶ Australian cattle farmer Colin Deveraux survived an attack by a deadly, 10.5-foot-long (3.2-m) saltwater crocodile. He was in a swamp in the Northern Territory when the croc grabbed the man's right foot and dragged him into the water. During the struggle, he managed to bite the croc on the eyelid, which forced it to let go. As he made his escape, the crocodile briefly chased him before giving up.

DONUT RAID ▶ A mother black bear and her cub raided a Krispy Kreme donut van after the driver left the doors open while delivering to a military base convenience store in Anchorage, Alaska. The bears devoured 26 packs of donuts before they were chased away.

SMELLY SEARCH ▶ Cecil, a seven-year-old goldendoodle dog, chewed up $4,000 in cash that his owners had left in an envelope on the kitchen counter of their home in Pennsylvania. They managed to reassemble most of the shredded bills and retrieved others in a smelly search through the dog's poop and vomit, until only $450 was missing.

SUPER SENSOR ▶ Sharks can track their prey just by listening for its heartbeat. Sharks have special receptors to detect the faint traces of bioelectricity that are given off by each heartbeat. They can even find fish hidden beneath the sand on the ocean floor!

PUP TRUCK

Poochies Pupsicles is an ice cream truck in London, England, that's just for dogs! The pink-and-white van is run by Emmie Stevens. She takes it to places like dog parks and special events. On the menu are homemade ice cream and popsicles. They come in dog-friendly flavors like mango, banana, and peanut butter. The canine customers can even get sprinkles on top!

YUM YUM!

electrical blackout. **KIRIBATI** ▶ The Pacific island nation of Kiribati is the only country in the world

RIPLEY'S Believe It or Not!®

WASTE NOT!

The Elephant PooPooPaper Park in Thailand uses elephant dung to make paper! Visitors to the outdoor museum learn the 2,000-year-old history of paper and can even watch poo paper get made in front of their very eyes! The best part about poo paper? It helps save the elephants' natural habitat! By using fibers from elephant poop, fewer trees need to be cut down for paper. And before you ask—the pages are clean, safe to use, and don't smell!

How to Make Poo Paper!

1 Gather and clean your elephant poop!

2 Boil and mix with other plant fibers.

3 Thinly spread the pulp across a screen.

4 Let it dry in the sun—et voilà!

THE END RESULT: POO PAPER!

GOLD GALORE ▸ Every day, Mount Erebus in Antarctica spews tiny gold crystals worth $6,000. The 12,448-foot-high (3,794-m) active volcano emits 2.8 oz (80 g) of gold a day and its gold dust has been detected more than 600 miles (965 km) away.

RAT REFRESHMENT ▸ A market stall in San Luis Potosi, Mexico, has been selling rat broth for over 50 years. Each bowl costs $5.80 and contains a whole field rat. The stall is currently run by José Remedios Hernández, who inherited the business from his mother.

PLENTIFUL PARKING ▸ There are an estimated two billion parking spots in the United States—more than six spaces for every registered car.

LASTING LIGHT ▸ Okunoin cemetery in Japan is home to 10,000 lanterns, many of which have been constantly alight for 900 years. The lanterns were donated by worshippers. At 1.2 miles (2 km) long, Okunoin is Japan's largest cemetery with over 200,000 tombstones.

LEAFY GREENS
Former Chinese Communist leader Mao Zedong (1893–1976) never brushed his teeth. Instead he rinsed his mouth daily with tea and also chewed leaves. But these turned his teeth green and he ended up losing all of his upper teeth in the last years of his life.

SUMMIT SOCCER ▸ The crater of the inactive 8,900-foot-high (2,713-m) Teoca volcano near Mexico City is home to a soccer pitch where 10 amateur teams play on weekends. The pitch, which is about 70 years old, is reached by a single road to the summit.

POPULAR PLACE ▸ Home to around 10 million people, the County of Los Angeles in California has a bigger population than 40 U.S. states.

TOILET TREAT ▸ Gordos, a restaurant in Holon, Israel, serves chocolate ice cream in a real toilet bowl.

POOP BEETLE ▸ When scientist James Tweed first spotted what turned out to be a new species of longhorn beetle in Queensland, Australia, he mistook it for bird poop. The beetle is about 0.4 inches (1 cm) long and its body is covered in fluffy white hairs.

LOOKING SHARP

Every year, a Minnesota neighborhood celebrates the sharpening of a 20-foot-tall (6-m) pencil!

The giant pencil was once a 180-year-old oak tree on homeowner John Higgins's yard. A storm blew down most of the tree in 2017. Instead of chopping the rest down, John asked an artist to turn it into a No. 2 pencil! In 2022, sculptor Curtis Ingvoldstad carved new life into the wood. It was named the "Loti pencil" after the Minneapolis neighborhood where it is located. Every summer, the community hosts a sharpening party. The sculpture is shaved down 1 foot (0.3 m) and given a fresh point!

from Kyrgyzstan with around 500,000 lines in its longest form! **LAOS** ▶ Fishermen in Laos use

SEEK THE STRANGE

THE RIPLEY'S COLLECTION

AUTO-GRAPHED

This 1965 Chevrolet Corvette has been signed by some of the biggest names in rock music history! Many of the signatures were added when a Texas radio station owned the car, which was later given away in a contest. More and more rock stars signed it over the years, and now there are more than 60 autographs covering the car!

CATALOG NO. 175881

Guns N' Roses

AC/DC

STRAWBERRY SQUID

Strawberry squids are covered in tiny lights and have lopsided eyes!

The seedlike dots on its body are called photophores. They help the squid send messages and disguise itself in the deep, dark sea where it lives. That's also where its unusual eyes come in handy! One eye is much larger than the other. The squid keeps its large eye pointed toward the surface to help it see the shape of prey against the little bit of sunlight from above. The smaller eye is used for spotting other creatures that glow in the darkness below!

Don't give me that side-eye!

SLIMY YET SATISFYING

This skinny snake slurps up slimy slugs and snails for supper! Small, docile, and nonvenomous, the blunthead slug snake is as harmless as its tiny head, big eyes, and cartoonish smile make it appear—to humans, at least. But it is a deadly hunter of snails and slugs in Southeast Asia forests. The snake has extra teeth on one side of its jaw, which it can move separately from the rest of its mouth. This helps it saw through the "door" of a snail's shell and pull the slimy snack right out!

LOYAL COMPANION ▶ When 71-year-old Rich Moore died of hypothermia while hiking on the 12,500-foot-high (3,810-m) Blackhead Peak in Colorado, his loyal Jack Russell terrier Finney stayed by him for more than two months until her master's body was discovered. She survived by eating small animals like mice.

FLAG FOUNDER ▶ Alaska's flag was designed by 14-year-old Benny Benson, who won a territory-wide contest in 1927 that received about 700 entries. His prize was a $1,000 educational scholarship and a watch. His design became the state flag when Alaska was admitted to the Union in 1959.

STARING SWAN ▶ A female swan visited Telford Park School in Shropshire, England, every day for more than a year—just to stare at her own reflection in a school window.

PAWS ABOARD!

FIRST-CLASS CANINES

Instead of being cramped in bags or stuck in cargo, dogs on BARK Air are treated like first-class passengers! Dogs often have a tough time traveling. BARK Air was created to make flying fun and stress-free for our furry friends. The planes are prepped with soothing smells, music, and colors. Once they have boarded, dogs can also get calming treats, noise-canceling earmuffs, and jackets to help them stay comfortable.

(312 m) above sea level, once had a tower built on its peak in an attempt to make it taller than

SEEK THE STRANGE

Fancy FRIDGES

The hottest, uh, coldest new trend in kitchen design? Decorating the inside of your fridge!

Called "fridgescaping," the fad is about styling the inside of your fridge to make it look pretty. Lynzi Judish of New York joined the trend in 2024. She surrounds her food with things like fresh flowers, picture frames, antiques, and even lights! She is often inspired by TV shows and movies, seasons, and holidays. Fridgescaping has some online critics, but Lynzi loves her hobby. Her designs have earned her many fans who enjoy seeing what she comes up with.

A Beetlejuice *fridgescape*!

A fridge fit for a hobbit!

TREASURED TOY ▶ A very rare rocket-firing Boba Fett action figure from *Star Wars*™ sold at auction in 2024 for $525,000. The 1970's toy, which is less than 4 inches (10 cm) tall, is believed to be one of only two still in existence. It was never sold to the public because the projectile was a choking hazard for children.

SMALL SPOON ▶ Indian microartist Shashikant Prajapati carved a wooden spoon that measures only 0.06 inches (1.6 mm) long. He used a craft knife and a surgical tool to carve the tiny utensil from a single piece of wood.

STAGE NAME ▶ U.S. rapper Megan Thee Stallion (born Megan Jovon Ruth Pete) took her stage name from her tall stature.

TECHY TODDLER ▶ Victor De Leon III, a.k.a. "Lil Poison," became a professional gamer at age six. He started video gaming when he was just two, began competing when he was four, and signed with Major League Gaming two years later.

DOUBLE DUPE

Etienne Constable of Seaside, California, received a letter from local authorities instructing him to erect a 6-foot-high (1.8-m) fence to conceal the boat he had parked on his driveway. Constable did so—but hired his neighbor, a mural artist, to paint a photorealistic image of the boat and driveway on the side of the fence that faces the road.

ESCAPE ERROR ▶ Twenty inmates of a prison in Maracaibo, Venezuela, successfully tunneled out of their cells—but when they emerged beyond the outside wall, the would-be escapees were met by a group of police officers on a training exercise.

CANDY PROTEST ▶ After the price of a chocolate candy bar increased from 5 cents to 8 cents on April 29, 1947, 200 Canadian youngsters marched to and protested at the capitol building in Victoria, British Columbia, effectively shutting down the provincial government for a day.

INSIDE OUT ▶ UK baby Dorothy Montgomery was born with many of her internal organs—kidneys, liver, bowels, ovaries, and intestines—on the outside of her body. She had an extreme form of gastroschisis, a very rare condition where a hole in the abdominal wall allows some organs to poke out of the stomach. After being swathed in plastic wrap to keep her insides moist, she was transferred to a hospital in Southampton where surgeons were able to push her organs back inside.

Bridgerton? More like Fridgerton!

Lynzi's enchanted forest fridgescape.

STITCH SWITCH

Colorado artist Michelle Herringer turns knitwork into porcelain! First, she knits patterns into different shapes, like small bowls and pouches. Depending on the size, shape, and pattern, it can take her anywhere from one day to several weeks to knit a piece! Michelle then uses different objects to help the knitting hold its shape while she dips it in liquid porcelain. The piece dries for several days and is then fired in a kiln. The end result is a hard sculpture that looks as soft and delicate as yarn!

prepared a serving of hummus weighing over 23,042 pounds (10,542 kg). **LESOTHO** ▶ Lesotho is

SEEK THE STRANGE

Ripley's Believe It or Not!

The name "Godzilla" comes from the combined Japanese words for "gorilla" and "whale."

KING of the ZIPLINES

At Nijigen no Mori Park in Japan, you can zipline straight into Godzilla's mouth!

Even though it is just the top half of the monster's body, the sculpture is still a massive 75 feet (23 m) tall and 180 feet (55 m) long—half the size of a football field! It's thought to be the only "life-size" Godzilla in the world. Known as "King of the Monsters," Godzilla has been many sizes over the years. The creature started at 164 feet (50 m) in 1954 but is more than twice that height in later movies!

landlocked yet shares a border with just one other country, South Africa! **LIBERIA** ▶ In 2009, a state of emergency was declared in Liberia due to a giant

SWINGING BY

In Berlin, Germany, people can swing above the rooftops and see the city at a whole new level—literally! The Berlin High Swing is Europe's highest swing. Riders can soar 394 feet (120 m) above the streets from the Park Inn Hotel. Passengers are strapped in with a safety belt and can see incredible views of the city. Would you try it?

PACIFIC VOYAGE ▶ Tom Robinson, from Australia, rowed 7,500 miles (12,000 km) across the Pacific Ocean in a homemade wooden boat, spending a total of 265 days at sea. He set off from Peru in July 2022, bound for Australia. He stopped off at various islands along the way. But in October 2023 a huge wave caused his boat to capsize off Vanuatu. He clung on to the upturned hull for 14 hours before being rescued by a passing cruise ship.

DRONE DROP ▶ Cameron Heinig caught a tennis ball dropped by a drone flying 470 feet (143 m) above ground in Almond, New York. He and his friend Julian, the drone pilot, had spent two summers preparing for the feat, during which he sometimes used a baseball glove to help him catch the falling ball. In the end, he caught the ball with his bare hands and was relieved that it did not prove too painful.

NO ARMY ▶ Costa Rica has no army. It banned the military in 1948 following a civil war, and its abolition was formally drafted into the country's constitution the following year.

PRICEY PROP ▶ A wooden door panel that was used as a prop for the 1997 movie *Titanic* sold at auction in 2024 for $718,750. The film's central characters Jack and Rose (played by Leonardo DiCaprio and Kate Winslet) desperately cling to the door as it floats in the icy waters of the North Atlantic.

MARINE MAGIC

Combining her love for scuba diving and magic, 13-year-old Avery Emerson Fisher performed 38 magic tricks in three minutes while underwater in a tank at the Aquarium of the Bay in San Francisco.

SPEEDY STOPS ▶ After months of careful planning and studying maps, University of California Berkeley students Winnie Zhuang, Paul Liu, Ameen DaCosta, and Jacob Champlin traveled to all 50 Bay Area Rapid Transit (BART) stations in only 5 hours and 47 minutes.

CHERISHED CHOC ▶ Ainslie Peters has an unusual family heirloom—a 50-year-old Cadbury Creme Egg. It was bought as a gift for her grandmother Jean in 1973 by her future husband on their first date. Instead of opening it, Jean displayed it in a cabinet as a reminder of their encounter.

MONSTER MATCH

Artist Mike Bell transformed a simple matchbook into a 3D portrait of Godzilla surrounded by skyscrapers!

CATALOG NO. 169275

swarm of caterpillars. **LIBYA** ▶ Within the caldera of Libya's extinct Waw an Namus volcano lies

RIPLEY'S Believe It or Not!®

SUPER
SMALL

Pygmy animals are smaller versions of the larger species. They often look and act in a similar way, too. And what pygmies lack in size, they more than make up for in stealth! They can hide in the smallest nooks and chase prey into places out of reach from bigger animals, all while looking absolutely adorable!

TEENY HIPPO

The pygmy hippo weighs just 600 pounds (270 kg)—10 times less than the mighty common hippo. A male common hippo can tip the scales at a whopping 7,000 pounds (3,175 kg). Amazingly, the pygmy hippo still manages to munch 145 pounds (65 kg) of plants a day!

Moo Deng, a baby pygmy hippo at Khao Kheow Open Zoo in Thailand, stole hearts all over the world in 2024 with her funny faces.

RODENT RUNT

Is it a mouse or a teeny kangaroo? The pygmy jerboa looks a bit like both and is the smallest rodent in the world! Although its body measures a teeny 2 inches (5 cm) long, the pygmy jerboa's tail can add another 10 inches (25 cm)!

Pygmy jerboas eat desert plants and even dig up the roots if the leaves are gone!

ITTY BITTY FROGGY

Pygmy frogs are incredibly small—they can sit on a human fingertip! The yellow-striped dwarf frog is one of the smallest in the world. It measures an easy-to-miss 0.5 inches (1.3 cm) long. The dwarf frog lives in Cuba, hidden among the leaves on forest floors.

an oasis! **LIECHTENSTEIN** ▶ The tiny country of Liechtenstein could fit inside the city of Orlando, Florida, with room to spare. **LITHUANIA** ▶ The popular

Pygmy seahorses live on coral in the waters near Australia, Indonesia, and Japan.

ACTUAL SIZE!

SHRUNKEN SEAHORSE

The first pygmy seahorse was discovered in 1969 by George Bargibant, a marine biologist. There are now seven known species of pygmy seahorse. They only grow up to 1 inch (2.5 cm) long, compared to the largest seahorse, which is 14 inches (35 cm) long!

PETITE PRIMATE

The slow loris loves hanging around in trees! The pygmy primate can safely grab onto weaker branches because it weighs just 14 ounces (400 g). But grabbing onto a pygmy slow loris isn't safe or recommended—the tiny animal has a venomous bite! Glands near its elbows secrete a toxin. The slow loris then licks the toxin, which coats its teeth!

WORLD'S ONLY VENOMOUS PRIMATE!

MICRO OWL

You need to keep your eyes peeled to spot a pygmy owl! The ferruginous pygmy owl has a wingspan of just 9 inches (23 cm)—that's from one wing tip to the other. This is teeny when put against the largest owl's wingspan—80 inches (200 cm) for the Blakiston fish owl.

Mushroom Festival held yearly in Varėna, Lithuania, includes a mushroom picking tournament.

SEEK THE STRANGE

RIPLEY'S Believe It or Not!®

BLANKET STATEMENT

Jeff Holloway of Oklahoma creates art using his bedspread! Every morning, Jeff makes a new picture in the fabric of his blanket. Depending on the image, he uses different tools to help move the fabric. He's used things like brushes, popsicle sticks, and even cardboard to help make his art. Jeff has drawn images of horses, flowers, cars, and landscapes! It goes to show that art can be made anywhere!

DRIVING SAUCER

A flying saucer took to the streets instead of the sky to reach the Roswell UFO Festival! Alien enthusiast Steve Anderson built the UFO using a 1991 Geo Metro. He and a friend spent eight months turning the old car into a street-legal UFO. The dashboard was covered in alien-themed buttons, and the horn made laser sounds! In June 2024, Steve drove from Indiana to New Mexico in the UFO car. Along the way, he was pulled over by police four times!

LUXEMBOURG ▶ In 2020, Luxembourg became the first country in the world to offer completely free public transportation for both residents and visitors.

BIRD Besties

Dave Brooker, who lives in Maidstone of Kent, England, has a special friendship with his pet turkey!

Trouble Version Two, a.k.a. T2, goes everywhere with Dave, from the store to the dentist! People are often surprised when they see T2 in Dave's car or in public. T2 even hangs out with Dave at the pub, where she likes to eat cheese and onion chips. Their bond is so strong that Dave has even stopped eating turkey at Christmas. Dave and T2 are best friends and even sleep in the same room!

If you could have any animal as a pet, what would it be?

Share your thoughts…

SMUGGLED STASH ▶ A Taiwanese man was arrested in 2023 after trying to smuggle two live otters and a prairie dog, which were hidden in his underwear, onto a plane at Suvarnabhumi International Airport in Bangkok, Thailand.

WEIGHTY WHALE ▶ The extinct colossal whale, which lived about 40 million years ago, is estimated to have weighed as much as 375 tons, making it almost twice the weight of a blue whale, the heaviest animal in the world today.

STICKY SWIM

Asian rhinos are excellent swimmers, but their African relatives are not and can drown in deep water. If they need to cool down, they just wallow in mud.

BLOOD-SUCKING BUG ▶ A newly discovered species of giant-headed vampire wasp from South America, *Capitojoppa amazonica*, stings its victim, sucks its blood, and then eats it from the inside by depositing larvae under its skin.

LUCKY DOG ▶ A woman was shopping at a convenience store in Guangdong, China, when her golden retriever broke free from its leash and ran into a nearby lottery store, where it bit into a scratch-off ticket. She was forced to buy the ticket—and it won her $139.

MADAGASCAR ▶ Darwin's bark spider of Madagascar can build webs up to 82 feet (25 m) wide

SEEK THE STRANGE

Inked EATS

Chef Joseph Kasteleiner, from Berlin, Germany, tattoos food with squid ink!

In 2023, Joseph was gifted a tattoo machine. It was only a matter of time before he combined his passions for art and cooking. He soon wondered if he could tattoo food with squid ink, which is often used to color foods like pasta. It worked perfectly! Today, Joseph inks everything from meat and vegetables to pasta and tortillas. The tattoos turn his dishes into works of art!

Each ingredient reacts differently to the squid ink, so Joseph must experiment to find the perfect combination of tattooing and cooking methods.

with its silk! MALAWI ▶ Lake Malawi, Africa's third largest lake, has an estimated 1,000 different species of fish—more than every lake in North

COLOR COLLECTOR

Hidden deep within the maze of shops in Tehran's Grand Bazaar in Iran lies a treasure trove of colored pencils! Mohammed Rafi's shop—measuring just 30 square feet (3 sq m)—is packed from floor to ceiling with 50,000 pencils of 200 different colors. He has owned his little shop for 35 years. Mohammed only sells single pencils. His customers include children, artists, and tourists. Mohammed can find the right pencil color for anyone!

SOAPY SHIFT ▶ The 200-year-old former Elmwood Hotel in Halifax, Canada, was moved to a new location with the help of two excavators, a tow truck, and 700 bars of soap. The 220-ton, three-story building was pulled 30 feet (9 m) across a steel frame to be closer to the street. The soap was used to help it slide smoothly over the frame.

TALENTED TODDLER ▶ Ghanaian artist Ace-Liam Ankrah had his first exhibition of paintings before he was even 18 months old. He sold nine of his 10 artworks on display at the Museum of Science and Technology in Accra, and even received a prestigious commission from Ghana's First Lady.

MATCHSTICK MOZART ▶ Tomislav Horvat from Croatia used 210,000 matchsticks to create a life-size sculpture of Mozart playing a grand piano. Even the piano strings were made of matchsticks! For the past seven years, Horvat has been building a full-size figure of Michelangelo working on his famous sculpture of David, using 430,000 matchsticks. To prevent these large structures from collapsing, he molds a supporting structure of papier-mâché or wood.

GLITCH GLAM

Fashion brand Loewe made clothes that look straight out of a video game! The collection, called "Pixel," includes items like hoodies, pants, T-shirts, and even a purse. The effect makes the wearer look like their clothes haven't fully "loaded." The illusion is achieved with thick black outlines and blocky colors.

PIXELATED PANTS!

America combined! **MALAYSIA** ▶ Malaysia is the only nation in the world with a rotational

SEEK THE STRANGE

THE RIPLEY'S COLLECTION

URINAL SLIPPERS

It was once common in parts of Japan and China for bathrooms to have heavy ceramic slippers like the ones shown here. They weren't used for walking around. Rather, they showed the best spot to stand when using the urinal!

CATALOG NO. 20759

Easy to clean!

FOOT BATH

Foot-binding was practiced in China until the twentieth century. To begin the foot-binding process, feet were soaked in warm water and herbs to ease the pain. These baths were often beautifully adorned, as foot-binding was mostly practiced by the wealthy.

CATALOG NO. 18240

A thankfully outdated practice!

KINGLY KICKS

King Henry VIII of England's extravagant footwear was influenced by his struggles with gout, which caused severe foot pain. To manage his condition, he favored shoes like these with wider toes.

CATALOG NO. 9434

Worn by a king!

SEEK THE STRANGE   141

HUSSEIN'S BARBER SHOP IS AN ART GALLERY!

CUT and PASTE

Iraqi barber Hussein Faleh uses hair clippings from his clients to create art!

After washing and cutting a client's hair, Hussein collects the trimmings that fall to the floor. He then cleans the hair again before storing it in containers. Not all hair works well for his art, though. It's taken years of trial and error to figure out which hair is best. Hussein has created images of famous people and many animals. He used to make his hair art on the shop floor and then sweep it away. Today, he saves his art and displays it on the walls of his salon.

monarchy, in which nine royal families take turns reigning for five years apiece. **MALDIVES** ▶ In October 2009, the Maldives' President Mohamed Nasheed

DOG'S DINNER ▶ Donato Frattaroli and Magda Mazri from Massachusetts were married at Lake Garda, Italy, in August 2023—despite their golden retriever eating Frattaroli's passport only two weeks before the big day. The groom managed to get an emergency replacement passport so their dream wedding, which had taken 18 months to plan, could go ahead.

VENOMOUS VISITOR ▶ A tennis match between former U.S. Open champion Dominic Thiem and Australia's James McCabe at the Brisbane International tournament in December 2023 was halted by the umpire when a deadly eastern brown snake slithered onto the court.

SHAMROCK SHOCK ▶ A golden retriever puppy was born in Florida with lime-green fur. The rest of the litter were the usual golden color, but Shamrock had a rare pigmentation at birth due to biliverdin, a green bile sometimes found in the womb of a mother dog. The strange color faded after a few weeks.

SLOW ESCAPE ▶ Ty, a 60-pound (27-kg) African sulcata tortoise, escaped from her home in Florida in April 2020. She was eventually found three and a half years later—just 5 miles (8 km) away.

HUMAN HIBERNATION

Karolina Olsson from Sweden seemingly remained in a state of hibernation for 32 years and 42 days. She fell asleep in 1876 at age 14 after complaining of a toothache and did not properly wake up until 1908. She didn't eat during her years in bed—although she was given two glasses of milk each day—and no one heard her speak. Yet when she did finally wake, she was able to remember everything she had learned before falling asleep and went on to live to the age of 88.

SUDDEN SWARM ▶ Five million bees in boxes fell off the back of a truck while traveling in Burlington, Canada, in August 2023. The bees were being transported on a trailer. Drivers were asked to keep their windows up and pedestrians were told to stay away while a dozen beekeepers spent about three hours rounding up the cloud of angry bees. The truck driver was stung more than 100 times but was not seriously injured.

SWIFT STRIKE ▶ Australia's death adder snake can attack, inject venom, and return to its striking position in only 0.15 seconds.

CAVE CAPTURE ▶ Charlie the hunting dog was rescued after being trapped in a cave for three days—with a bear! The dog fell down a narrow shaft into the cave near Knoxville, Tennessee, and was trapped 40 feet (12 m) below ground just yards away from a sleeping 200-pound (91-kg) black bear.

PET PIGEON ▶ Abby Jardine takes her pet pigeon, Pidge, in her bag to restaurants and bars in New York City. She rescued the bird from a street near her apartment when it was just three weeks old and unable to fly. She has even potty-trained Pidge by taking her to the bathroom every half hour and holding her over the toilet.

DOUBLE DOG

Lucy the dog has spots on her ear that look like a tiny version of her own face! The funny markings were first spotted when she was a puppy at a dog shelter in New York. The staff was amazed when they noticed the resemblance. It's like Lucy was born with a cartoon selfie on her ear! The shelter shared Lucy's selfie spots online, and she was adopted soon after!

AN EAR-IE RESEMBLANCE!

Ripley's Believe It or Not!

MORE THAN 4,000 YEARS OLD!

FORGOTTEN FOREST

A storm revealed a 4,500-year-old forest buried under sand and water! In 2014, Storm Hannah washed away tons of sand from the beach in Borth, Wales. In the aftermath, stumps of oak, ash, and birch trees appeared! The stumps date back to the Bronze Age. Scientists believe that the forest flourished before the sea level rose, and it eventually fell over. Now, you can see the stumps at high and low tides.

GIANT PUMPKIN ▶ Travis Gienger, a horticulture teacher from Anoka, Minnesota, grew a massive 2,749-pound (1,247-kg) pumpkin—big enough to fill nearly 700 pumpkin pies.

STICKY SENTENCE ▶ A man was sentenced to 18 months in jail after stealing 200,000 Cadbury Creme Eggs from an industrial complex in Shropshire, England.

STATION STOPS ▶ Over a period of six weeks, Dave Jones, a railway worker from England, visited 2,542 train stations in the UK. He averaged 62 stations a day, jumping out to take a photo of the station sign at each stop.

CARD COLLECTOR ▶ Since the 1990s, Californian Morten Soerensen has collected more than 1,100 key cards from hotels all around the world.

SCI-FI SUPERFAN ▶ Lily Connors, from Swansea, Wales, has more than 10,000 items of memorabilia relating to British TV sci-fi series *Doctor Who*. She started collecting them at age eight and now has about 400 Daleks in various sizes, a full-size robotic dog K9, and a full-size Cyberman. Her dad Tom even built her a TARDIS wardrobe that has been signed by actor Peter Capaldi, who played the twelfth incarnation of the Doctor from 2013 to 2017.

TREE-LIEVE IT OR NOT!

The largest, most dense organism ever is **Pando**—a group of more than **40,000 genetically identical aspen trees** that share a root system in Utah. It covers **106 acres** and weighs nearly **13 million pounds (5.9 million kg)**!

At Tuskegee National Forest in Alabama, forestry student Abubakar Tahiru **hugged 1,123 trees** in just one hour!

The traveler's tree of Madagascar has **bright blue seeds** that are easily seen by **ruffed lemurs**, which help **pollinate the plant** but have limited color vision.

California is home to the world's **tallest, largest, and oldest trees**.

"Old Knobbley," an **800-year-old** oak tree in Essex, England, has its own **website and children's book**.

The Chained Tree of Peshawar in Pakistan has been shackled to the ground since 1898 when a **drunken British officer "arrested" the banyan tree** for running away from him.

The Midway-Frogtown Arborators Band of Minnesota is a group of brass musicians who climb trees and **play concerts from the branches**.

a fourteenth-century king of Mali, is considered one of the richest people to have ever lived—worth an estimated $400 billion! **MALTA** ▶ Many churches in

TREE *Triumph*

A woman lived in a tree for over two years to save it from being cut down!

In 1997, activist Julia "Butterfly" Hill wanted to save a 1,000-year-old tree in California's Redwood Forest from being cut down by loggers. To protest, she climbed the 200-foot-tall (60-m) tree and stayed there for 738 days on an 8-foot-wide (2.4-m) square of plywood. She remained through pouring rain and freezing wind with only a tarp to keep her sheltered. Friends and other protestors delivered food, water, clothing, and batteries. In 1999, she finally won. The lumber company agreed not to cut down the tree or others nearby, and Julia put her feet back on solid ground!

DETERMINED TO SAVE A 1,000-YEAR-OLD TREE

RESPECT YOUR ELDERS

Malta have two clocks that show different times so as to confuse the devil about the time of the

SEEK THE STRANGE

POWER TRIP

In 2023, travel influencer Lexie Limitless set off to become the first person to circumnavigate the world in an electric vehicle!

The trip marked 100 years since explorer Aloha Wanderwell became the first woman to drive around the world. Lexie took on the challenge in an electric Ford Explorer. She began her trip in Nice, France. She traveled through six continents, including Asia, South America, and Africa. In March 2024, Lexie finished her journey! It ended back in Nice. The whole trip took 200 days!

What's the furthest you've traveled from home?

Share your thoughts...

One of Thomas Parker's electric cars built in the late 1800s!

ELECTRIC BEGINNINGS

Did you know that the first electric car dates back to the 1830s? It was built by Scottish inventor Robert Anderson. He was the first person to build a carriage that didn't need horses! But back then, batteries didn't last long and needed to be replaced very frequently—perhaps after only a few minutes of driving. In 1884, English engineer Thomas Parker created a new prototype. He drove his electric car to work every day!

LOST CONTINENT ▸ Scientists recently discovered parts of a lost continent that vanished 155 million years ago. Argoland, which was 3,100 miles (4,990 km) long, broke off from northwestern Australia and vanished. Its remains were found hidden beneath the jungles of Myanmar and Indonesia.

CAR CRASH ▸ Alaskans celebrate the Fourth of July each year with a spectacularly destructive car launch. More than a dozen empty vehicles—including police cruisers, trucks, and buses—are launched in turn over a 300-foot-high (90-m) cliff at Glacier View, before smashing into pieces at the bottom.

LONG HIGHWAY

U.S. Route 20 passes through 12 states and runs 3,365 miles (5,415 km) from Newport, Oregon, to Boston, Massachusetts—nearly half as long as Earth's diameter.

PLANE EXTRAVAGANCE ▸ Russian developer Felix Demin converted a Boeing 737 jet airplane into a luxury two-bedroom villa on the Indonesian island of Bali. The cockpit has been turned into the bathroom, and one of the wings is now an outside terrace overlooking a swimming pool.

TORNADO TOSS ▸ When a deadly tornado tore through Clarksville, Tennessee, on December 9, 2023, it ripped the roof off Sydney Moore's rented mobile home and swept away her four-month-old son. Incredibly, he was found safe and well, lodged in a fallen tree 30 feet (9 m) away.

THE Ripley's COLLECTION

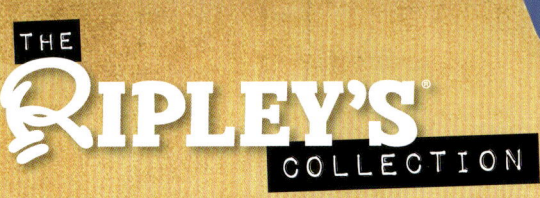

PLANE PIECE

This piece of fabric came from Amelia Earhart's Lockheed Vega 5B. That was the plane that she piloted as the first woman to fly solo across the Atlantic Ocean! Her historic flight took place in 1932. The feat broke gender barriers and made Amelia a household name. Sadly, Amelia and her navigator Fred Noonan disappeared over the Pacific Ocean in 1937 during an attempt to fly around the world. Their fates remain a mystery to this day.

CATALOG NO. 175814

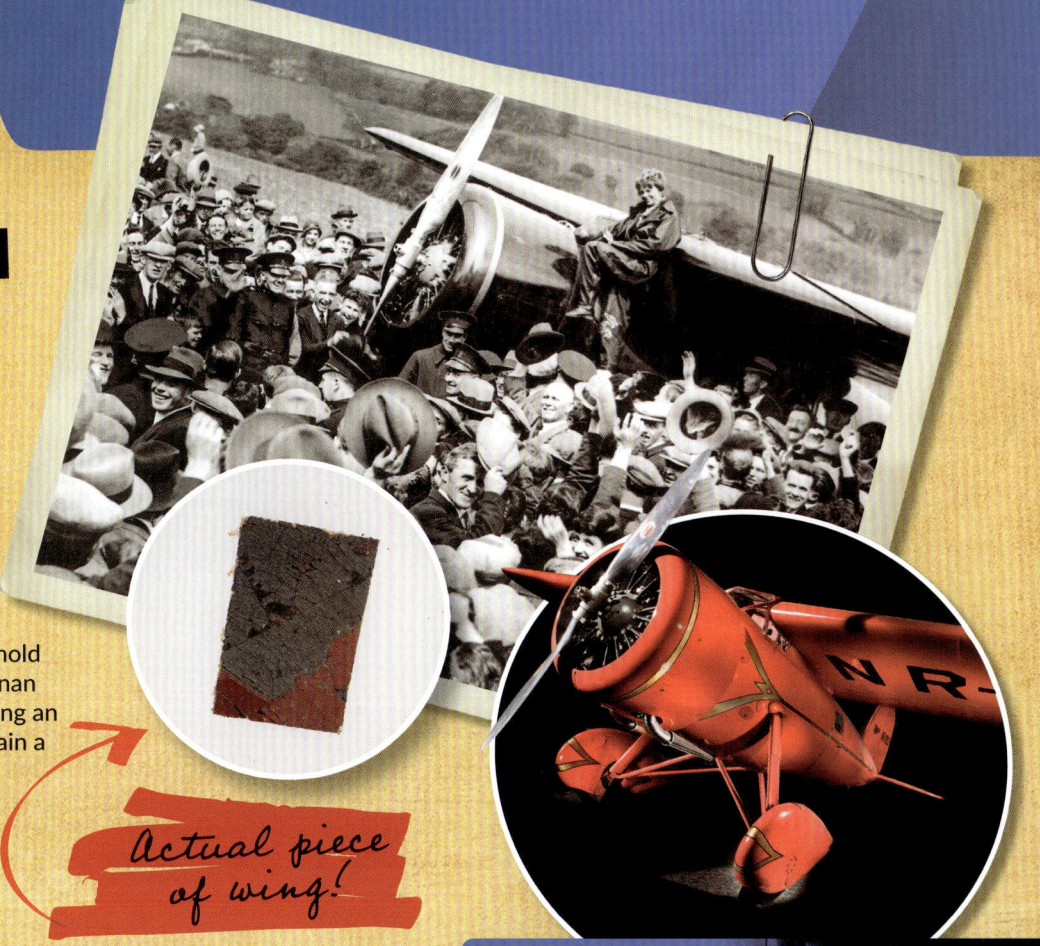

Actual piece of wing!

transporting iron ore from inland Mauritania to the coast can reach more than 1 mile (1.6 km)

SEEK THE STRANGE

RIPLEY'S Believe It or Not!®

WAKE UP!

PULLED BY A DRONE!

In November 2023, extreme athlete Brian Grubb combined wakeskating and BASE jumping in a jaw-dropping stunt that had never been done before!

Pulled by a drone, Brian wakeskated across a pool on the roof of the Address Beach Resort in Dubai. It launched him off a ramp and into the air—more than 965 feet (294 m) above the ground! Brian let go of the rope for a BASE jump 77 stories down to a beach. This incredible stunt, which Brian named WakeBASE, was a dream he'd had for seven years. Brian not only had to learn about BASE jumping, but he also had to create a drone strong enough to pull himself!

in length. **MAURITIUS** ▶ Silt deposits off the island of Mauritius create an illusion that looks like an undersea waterfall. **MEXICO** ▶ If you clap your hands in

front of the Mayan Kukulcan pyramid in Chichén Itzá, Mexico, the echo sounds like a chirping bird.

SEEK THE STRANGE 149

RAINBOW CONNECTION

Rainbow swamps look like something out of a fairy tale but are totally real! The seemingly magical colors only show up in the right conditions. The water has to be completely still for a long time. This lets oils from dying plants float and form a thin film on the surface. When the sun hits the oils just right, the wetlands transform into a dazzling dreamland!

COSTLY CHOCOLATE ▶ A single bar of To'ak dark chocolate costs $450. It is made with rare cacao harvested from only 14 farms in Ecuador's Piedra de Plata valley and aged in barrels of whisky, bourbon, sherry, or tequila.

KEEP MOVING ▶ It is illegal to stop walking on some pedestrian bridges in Las Vegas, Nevada. Anyone who stops can be fined $1,000 or face six months in jail.

BREAD BATTLE ▶ Italian ciabatta bread was invented as recently as 1982. It was created by Arnaldo Cavallari, a baker near Venice, to rival the popular French baguette.

ROYAL CEMETERY ▶ According to a 500-year-old document, there are 48 Scottish, eight Norwegian, and four Irish kings buried at Reilig Odhrain, a small cemetery on the Scottish island of Iona.

GREAT GENES ▶ Cornflakes and their corn genome possess 12,000 more genes than humans.

WITCH BOTTLES ▶ Since 2017, at least eight "witch bottles" have mysteriously washed ashore on Gulf of Mexico beaches in Texas. The bottles, which contain things such as iron nails, rusty pins, herbs, hair, and urine, are traditionally designed to deter evil spirits.

HOLE SALE

The Costco in Mérida, Mexico, has a sinkhole in its parking lot! The sinkhole, or cenote, was found during the store's construction in 2015. It extends far beneath the surface and likely formed thousands of years ago. Instead of filling in the natural sinkhole, the builders preserved it! They added a garden and fenced the cenote in. Visitors can look into the clear fresh water from a viewing platform.

MICRONESIA ▶ The megapode bird of Micronesia buries its eggs in volcanic ash to keep them warm. **MOLDOVA** ▶ The wine cellars at Milestii Mici in

CLAWS OUT!

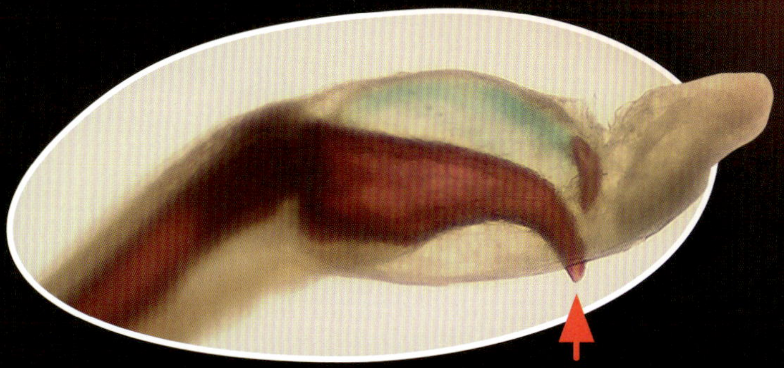

BONE CLAW!

The wolverine frog will break its own bones when threatened, unleashing sharp claws!
The talons sit under the skin of the toes on the hind legs. In the face of danger, the frog snaps its toe bones in half, and the claws poke through the skin—much like the X-Men superhero, Wolverine! Also known as a horror frog, it grows up to 5 inches (13 cm) long and lives in Cameroon. There, hunters of the frog use spears to avoid getting scratched!

The male of the species has another unusual feature: hair! Actually thin strands of skin, the "hair" is thought to help the frog absorb more oxygen.

Moldova are so large you can navigate them by car! **MONACO** ▶ About one-third of Monaco's

SEEK THE STRANGE

THE RIPLEY'S COLLECTION

RECORD RECORDER

On May 6, 1954, Sir Roger Bannister of England became the first person recorded to run 1 mile (1.6 km) in under 4 minutes. This stopwatch was used by Guinness World Records founder Norris McWhirter to time the legendary feat.

CATALOG NO. 175353

Upside-down and backward handwriting

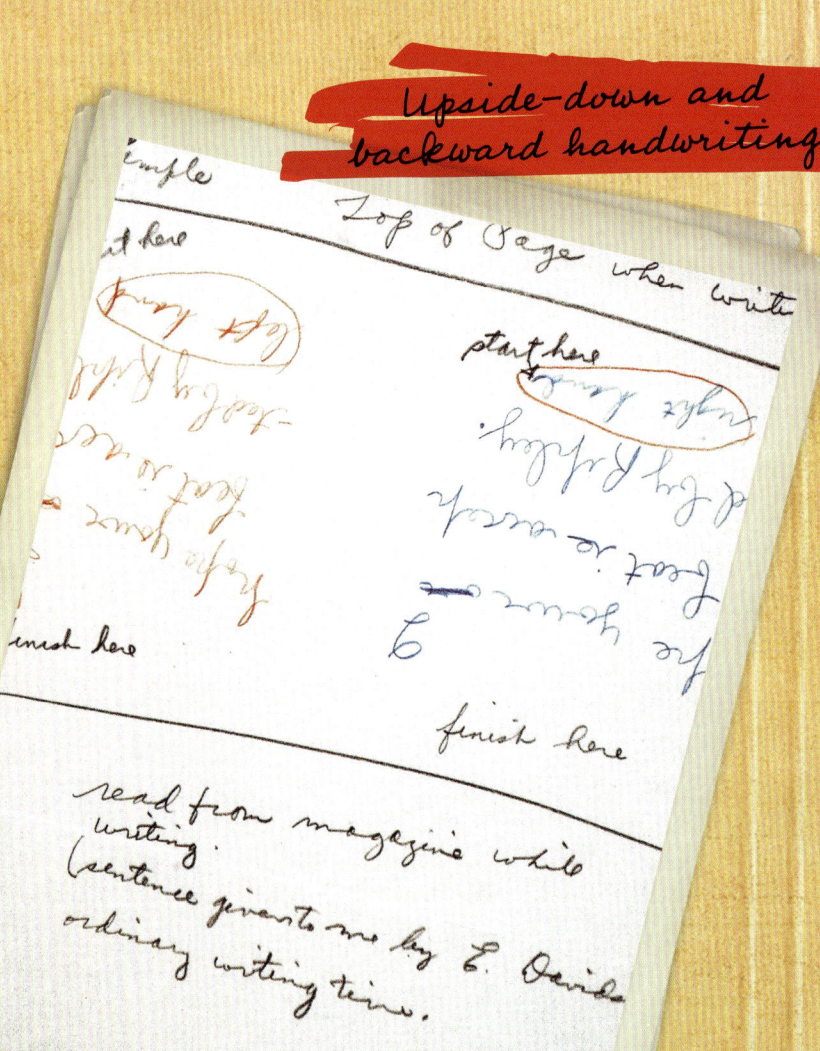

WILD WRITING

In 1942, Lillian Lee from New Orleans wrote to Robert Ripley to tell him about her amazing ability: she could write upside down and backward with both hands at the same time. She could even do it all while reciting poetry!

CATALOG NO. 13547

TINY BIKE

Built and ridden by Charlie Charles of Las Vegas, Nevada, this bike weighs less than 1 pound (0.45 kg), and is a whopping 6 inches (15 cm) long and 4.5 inches (11.5 cm) wide.

CATALOG NO. 11027

Actual size!

Charlie rode the bike through a Las Vegas shopping mall on an episode of the Ripley's Believe It or Not! television show in the early 1980s.

SEEK THE STRANGE

RIPLEY'S Believe It or Not!®

TWINNING

There are only three known sets of twin elephants in the world!

In 2024, a set of rare twin elephants was born at Thailand's Ayutthaya Elephant Palace and Royal Kraal. The baby boy and girl were a big surprise. The staff expected the mother to have just one baby! Only one percent of elephant births result in twins. Male-female twins are even rarer! Elephants are sacred to the people of Thailand and are a national symbol. Monks even visited to bless the elephants!

TREE-MENDOUS!

Adak "National Forest" in Alaska is home to just 33 trees! During World War II, a general planted Christmas trees on Adak Island to help remind soldiers of home. But it is a tough place for plants to grow. It's cold and windy. Most of the trees died, but about 30 survived. Today, this tiny group of trees is unofficially called "America's smallest national forest."

citizens are millionaires. **MONGOLIA** ▶ The Golden Eagle Festival in Bayan-Ölgii, Mongolia, honors the Kazakh tradition of training the birds as

ELEPHANT TWINS ARE VERY RARE!

BRAND-NEW BUG ▶ A new species of moth discovered in 2021 by enthusiast Barbara Mulligan in Walpole Park, England, turned out to be an almost identical match for an unnamed species found 9,000 miles (14,500 km) away in Walpole, Western Australia, 135 years earlier, in 1886.

BURIED BONES ▶ While fishing with her father on the shores of the Oka River in western Russia, eight-year-old Maryam Mirsaitova found 100,000-year-old woolly mammoth bones. The bones had been exposed by a recent landslide.

SEAL SMELL ▶ A polar bear can smell a seal that's under 3 feet (0.9 m) of ice. The bear's sense of smell is 100 times better than a human's.

SUCCESSFUL SURGERY ▶ Ariel, an abandoned spaniel puppy from Pembrokeshire, Wales, was born with six legs. She underwent surgery to remove her extra limbs and was soon adopted by a new family.

UV VOLES ▶ Kestrels hovering in the sky detect voles on the ground by tracking their urine trails, which reflect ultraviolet light. Unlike humans, kestrels can see ultraviolet light.

BAFFLED BIRDS ▶ Two dumpster-diving vultures ate some food that had fermented so much that it made them too drunk to fly. The pair were unable to stand and kept passing out. But after animal rescuers gave them fluids, plenty of rest, and a good breakfast, the birds were well enough to be released back into the wild.

BOILING BLUES

You can cook eggs in a bubbling, bright-blue hot spring called Umi-Jigoku, or "Sea Hell!" This steamy spring in Beppu, Japan, is famous for its light blue color caused by iron sulfate. The water gets so hot it reaches nearly 212°F (100°C)—perfect for boiling eggs right in the pool! While it's too hot for even a quick dip, visitors love watching the water bubble and steam while enjoying a snack cooked in nature's kitchen. It's a fun and tasty way to enjoy one of Japan's hottest spots!

hunting companions. **MONTENEGRO** ▶ The village of Brezna, Montenegro, holds an annual

SEEK THE STRANGE 155

RIPLEY'S Believe It or Not!®

MANHOLE MARVELS

In Japan, some manhole covers are also works of art!

The manhole covers are made of cast iron, and many are very colorful. Almost every city in the country has its own unique design! Some are about Japan's history and stories. Others show things the local area is proud of, like Mount Fuji. Some of the covers even feature famous cartoons! Each cover is hand-painted, and they last about 15 to 30 years. Because they are so popular, the unique artworks are sometimes sold when they get old and must be replaced! Fans of the covers are called "manholers."

What would you put on a manhole cover design for your hometown? Share your thoughts...

contest to see who can stay lying down the longest. **MOROCCO** ▶ Inaugurated in the year AD 859, the al-Qarawiyyin Library in Fez, Morocco, is the oldest

HOME IN ONE

These big bulbs may look like giant golf balls, but they are actually homes! In the Dutch town of Den Bosch, there's a community of 50 round homes that look oddly like golf balls. They're only 18 feet (5.5 m) wide, and each one has 11 windows. The building material is very light, making it simple to disassemble the homes and transport them to another place. They were built in the 1980s as an experimental design for small, easy-to-build houses. The style never quite caught on, but the original homes are still lived in today!

GETAWAY GONE-AWAY ▶ While three masked robbers were raiding a check-cashing business in Commerce City, Colorado, another thief was stealing their getaway vehicle, leaving them stranded. The gang tried to flee on foot but two of them were quickly arrested.

STAGGERING SHOT ▶ A shot by Northern Ireland golfer Rory McIlroy at a 2023 golf tournament in Dubai, United Arab Emirates, landed in a spectator's lap as she lay on the grass near the green. The ball was lodged between her legs but when she stood up, he was allowed to play a drop ball from the spot where she had been lying.

LOUSY LEECH ▶ When a 53-year-old Vietnamese man developed trouble speaking and began spitting blood, doctors in Hanoi discovered that he had a 2.4-inch-long (6-cm) leech sucking the blood from his throat.

PERFECT POWER

When he was first created, Superman's superpower was his ability to jump over tall buildings in a single bound. But when artists began animating the character, they found that it was too complicated to draw him bending his knees to jump, so they made him fly instead.

BIRD BANDIT ▶ A man robbed a customer at knifepoint at a McDonald's restaurant in Fairfax County, Virginia, while accompanied by three parrots. The suspect had two parrots perched on the brim of his black cowboy hat and a third parrot sitting on his shoulder.

LONG-LOST LIPSTICK ▶ Scientists discovered a nearly 4,000-year-old lipstick in Iran. The makeup vial contained a waxy reddish substance composed of various minerals, including hematite, manganite, and braunite.

COLORFUL CLOUDS

A pilot's glory is a rainbow that can only be seen from above the clouds! This round rainbow forms thanks to tiny water droplets in the clouds that bend and spread sunlight in a special way. When sunlight gets close to a water droplet, it creates electromagnetic waves. The waves then bounce around inside the droplet. When the waves escape, they create rays of light. The result is a beautiful, round rainbow that looks like it follows the plane! But there's a catch: This awesome sight can only be seen when you're right between the light source and the water droplets.

SEEK THE STRANGE

Flowery FASHION

Artist Beth Williams creates clothing with living plants!

Beth makes dresses, tops, and masks using biodegradable fibers and plants. She matches materials like felt and yarn with the right seeds, which are then cared for to help them grow. It can take months for the plants to turn into clothing pieces. Beth tries to keep the living clothing alive for as long as possible. When the plants die, they are composted.

THIS STYLE REALLY GROWS ON YOU!

Beth Williams

POOZEUM

George Frandsen

THE STINKER

FECES FOSSILS

The Poozeum in Arizona is a museum all about dinosaur poop! Founded by George Frandsen, the Poozeum is home to more than 8,000 coprolites, or fossilized pieces of poop, including dino droppings! There are coprolites of all sizes, shapes, and colors. One coprolite looks like a rainbow on the inside! The rainbow colors are most likely from thin layers of minerals that formed inside the poop. When light strikes it just right, the rainbow colors appear!

RAINBOW POOP FOSSIL!

DARWIN DOODLES ▶ The young children of nineteenth-century English naturalist Charles Darwin doodled on the backs of pages of the draft manuscript for his groundbreaking scientific work *On the Origin of Species*. Their drawings included colorful imaginary birds and soldiers riding vegetables into battle.

GOLDEN DRINK ▶ After Roman general Marcus Licinius Crassus, the richest man in Rome, was killed in battle in 53 BC, it is rumored that the leaders of the opposing Parthian army poured molten gold down his throat as a symbol of his thirst for wealth.

ZERO VOTES ▶ In 2024, Félix-Antoine Hamel became the first person in Canadian history to receive zero votes in a contested federal election. He was running in the Toronto-St. Paul's by-election but could not even vote for himself because he is not a Toronto resident. He described himself as the true unity candidate because everyone decided not to vote for him.

TWIN LIVES ▶ Identical twin sisters Stephanie Buckman and Sammie Nowakowski live next door to each other and work together in Jacksonville, Florida. They met their husbands on the same day in 2014, got pregnant at the same time, and even their pet golden retriever dogs are siblings from the same litter.

DETECTOR DISCOVERY ▶ In 1970, Marilyn Birch lost her engagement ring while feeding hay to the cattle on the family farm in Pontardawe, Wales. Fifty-four years later, metal detectorist Keith Phillips found it 8 inches (20 cm) below ground in a field while searching for buried treasures.

THE RIPLEY'S COLLECTION

PETRIFIED PEANUTS

This odd-shaped lump is a petrified cluster of peanut shells! Found in Germany, this bizarre fossil is more than 1,000 years old.

CATALOG NO. 24671

kyawthuite was discovered in the bed of a stream in Myanmar and weighs just 0.01 ounces (0.3 g).

SEEK THE STRANGE

RIPLEY'S Believe It or Not!®

EDIBLE ARENA

Hirofumi Hayashi of Kasukabe, Japan, built a mini Colosseum out of chocolate!

The carpenter also known as CHiPa normally works with wood. But he wanted to test his skills. So he made a copy of the Roman monument out of Meiji brand chocolate! He melted some and used it like glue to stick the tiny pieces together like bricks! The finished model looked good enough to eat. And that is just what CHiPa and his friends did!

COLI-SEE 'EM ALL!

Did you know there are more than 230 coliseums around the world? The Romans built these structures across their empire, including in places that are now France, Spain, and Africa.

Amphitheatre of Durrës: This coliseum in Albania was almost lost to time! It was damaged by an earthquake in the fourth century and then buried in the 1500s. It was rediscovered in the 1960s!

Arènes d'Arles: During the Middle Ages, this coliseum in France was transformed into a city. The walls were used as protection against invaders!

NAMIBIA ▶ The Himba women of northern Namibia cover their hair and skin in a bright red paste made of butterfat and red ocher to protect themselves

SAVE US A PIECE!

HEAD ROMES

Fences outside of the Colosseum in Rome are covered in hundreds of headphones! Audio tours are a common way to learn more about the historic Italian structure. Rather than keep the earbuds, some visitors left them on a nearby fence. More and more people started doing the same. Soon, it was completely covered!

Pula Arena: Located on the coast of Croatia, this arena was once home to gladiators and big cat fights. It's still intact and is used for concerts today!

Amphitheatre of Tarragona: The stands of this amphitheater in Spain were carved directly into the rock. The arena was used for things like gladiator battles, religious ceremonies, and even as a prison!

Amphitheatre of El Jem: Built around AD 238, this amphitheater in Tunisia is one of the largest in the world. It could fit up to 35,000 people inside!

from the Sun. **NAURU** ▶ The country of Nauru has no official capital! **NEPAL** ▶ Nepal is the only

SEEK THE STRANGE

BORN FOR THIS

Maddie Cottle Dock, a.k.a. Maddox Dock, was in the circus before she could walk! Decades later, she's carrying on her family's legacy under the big top!

Just three days after Maddie was born, she joined her performer parents on the road. At three years old, she took to the stage for the first time. At age six, she began learning balance and magic tricks. While training with her older sister, she discovered her passion: roller skating! Now in her early twenties, she performs high-speed skating stunts with her partner Jamil Avanzi. As a fourth-generation circus performer, Maddie is keeping her family's nearly 200-year-old legacy alive.

Ripley's jumped at the chance to ask Maddie about her life in the circus. See what she had to say!

Q: How does it feel to carry on a family legacy that spans nearly 200 years?

A: It's the most amazing feeling in the world, but sometimes it can be overwhelming. I'm very lucky to have a family that comes from a long line of performers. They're always there to support and push me in the right direction.

Q: You've learned many circus skills over the years, from magic tricks to pyramid bike acts. Which was the most challenging to master?

A: Out of all my skills, the most difficult to learn had to be unicycling and juggling. They're something I could never get the hang of from a young age.

Q: The circus life involves constant travel and a relentless schedule. What keeps you motivated?

A: From a young age, I have loved to express myself and have fun. I also enjoy performing for the audience. They come to have fun, laugh, and sometimes cry! I love to see them with happy faces.

Q: What advice would you give to young people who dream of joining the circus?

A: I would say, "Go for it!" Maybe some days aren't easy, but it's always rewarding. My grandfather loved to encourage people to give circus acts a go.

Q: What does the future look like for Maddie Cottle Dock?

A: My partner and I have got a lot of new exciting things coming together. I don't believe in being comfortable. I think you can always be bigger and better. My grandfather used to say, "Nothing extraordinary was done by being ordinary." Even though he's not here with us anymore, it pushes me to try more out-of-the-box things.

> "I don't believe in being comfortable. I think you can always be bigger and better."

THE RIPLEY'S COLLECTION

SCRIMSHAW SCAPULA

This giraffe scapula, or shoulder blade, has been decorated with Africa's "Big Five"—the most popular animals to see on a safari. An art technique called scrimshaw was used to carve and stain the bone.

CATALOG NO. 175845

NEW ZEALAND ▸ New Zealand's Mount Taranaki, or Taranaki Maunga, is legally recognized as a

RIPLEY'S Believe It or Not!®

SIDEWALK AQUARIUM

Some people turned a puddle in Brooklyn, New York, into a fishpond! A leaking fire hydrant created the puddle. Residents added some goldfish. It was dubbed the Bed-Stuy Aquarium. Neighbors took turns feeding the fish each day. People even donated decorations, such as pearls and seashells! But three months later, the fire hydrant was fixed and the hole was filled. Undeterred, residents soon built a new fishpond on the same sidewalk!

PEDALING POODLE ▶ A giant poodle called Xu Laifu can ride a bicycle as well as a three-year-old child. His owner spent a year teaching him how to use his front legs to steer the handlebars and his back legs to pedal. The talented dog also learned to ride a skateboard in just five days.

MEDICAL MARVEL ▶ Rakus, a Sumatran orangutan in Indonesia, was seen treating a large wound on his cheek using a paste made from the akar kuning plant. He chewed both the stem and leaves, repeatedly applying the chewed-up plant to the gash for several minutes. Following his self-treatment, the wound closed up and healed in a month.

CURIOUS CAT ▶ Carrie and Matt Clark's cat made a six-day, 630-mile (1,014-km) journey after accidentally being mailed in an Amazon return box. She had jumped into the package undetected at the family home, and despite going almost a week without food or water, was in good health when she was eventually rescued by an Amazon worker at a depot in California. Luckily, one of the box's seams had come unglued, enabling her to breathe.

DAREDEVIL DUCK ▶ A stowaway duck hitched a ride on Cedar Point's high-speed Millennium Force roller coaster in Ohio. The duck landed on the ride and stayed put even though it reached speeds of 93 mph (150 kmph).

EYE TEETH ▶ A whale shark's eyeballs are covered in tiny teeth called dermal denticles, which protect its eyes from attacks by other shark species.

BUTT BREATHERS

To survive winter while hibernating under water, turtles, salamanders, and frogs breathe through their butts—a process known as cloacal respiration.

CAMPUS CAT ▶ Ahead of students' graduation in 2024, Max the tabby cat was made an honorary "Doctor of Litter-ature" by Vermont State University's Castleton campus in recognition of his friendliness. For more than four years, he has befriended students, posing for selfies and accompanying them on college tours.

SNAKE STUDY ▶ The University of Michigan Museum of Zoology has a collection of about 70,000 dead snakes, mostly preserved in jars of alcohol for scientific study.

SHARED STORY
SHARE YOUR STORY at ripleys.com/share

FISHY FINDS

Andrew Brown from Florida shared his fishy finds with us—red drum fish with heart- and number-shaped spots! No, really! Since 2015, Andrew and his Instagram followers have kept track of the shapes found on the red drum fish they've caught. The shapes include letters, numbers, hearts, and even Mickey Mouse! In just five years, they found all 26 letters of the alphabet and numbers 0–9!

person with human rights. **NICARAGUA** ▶ At Cerro Negro in Nicaragua, thrill-seekers can surf down the side of an active volcano! **NIGER** ▶ Niger has the

KITESURFING CANINE

Champion kitesurfer Zara Hoogenraad rides waves and catches air with her dog, Dice!

Before she started kitesurfing with Zara, Dice would try to follow her owner as she sped across the water. She'd run up and down the beach or even swim out to Zara and try to jump on the board! On a trip to Brazil in 2022, Zara decided to find out if Dice really wanted to kitesurf. She picked the eager dog up, caught some wind, and they zipped across the water together. Dice loved it! Today, the dynamic duo shreds waves all over the world. They even make short jumps into the air together!

What's your pet's special talent? Share your thoughts...

SURF'S UP!

Zara only takes Dice kitesurfing when conditions are safe.

RIPLEY'S Believe It or Not!

BAGGINS CLAIM

Wellington International Airport in New Zealand was transformed into Middle Earth with giant sculptures of characters from *The Hobbit*!

To celebrate the release of *The Hobbit: The Desolation of Smaug* in 2013, special effects creators of the movie designed Hobbit-themed sculptures to hang from the ceiling. Travelers were greeted by a 43-foot (13-m) Gollum chasing several 13-foot-long (4-m) fish. Two eagles hovered over passengers. Each had wingspans of 15 feet (4.5 m) and weighed almost one ton! Gandalf the Grey was mounted to the top of one of the eagles with his legendary staff. Though Gollum is gone, the eagles and one giant dragon remain.

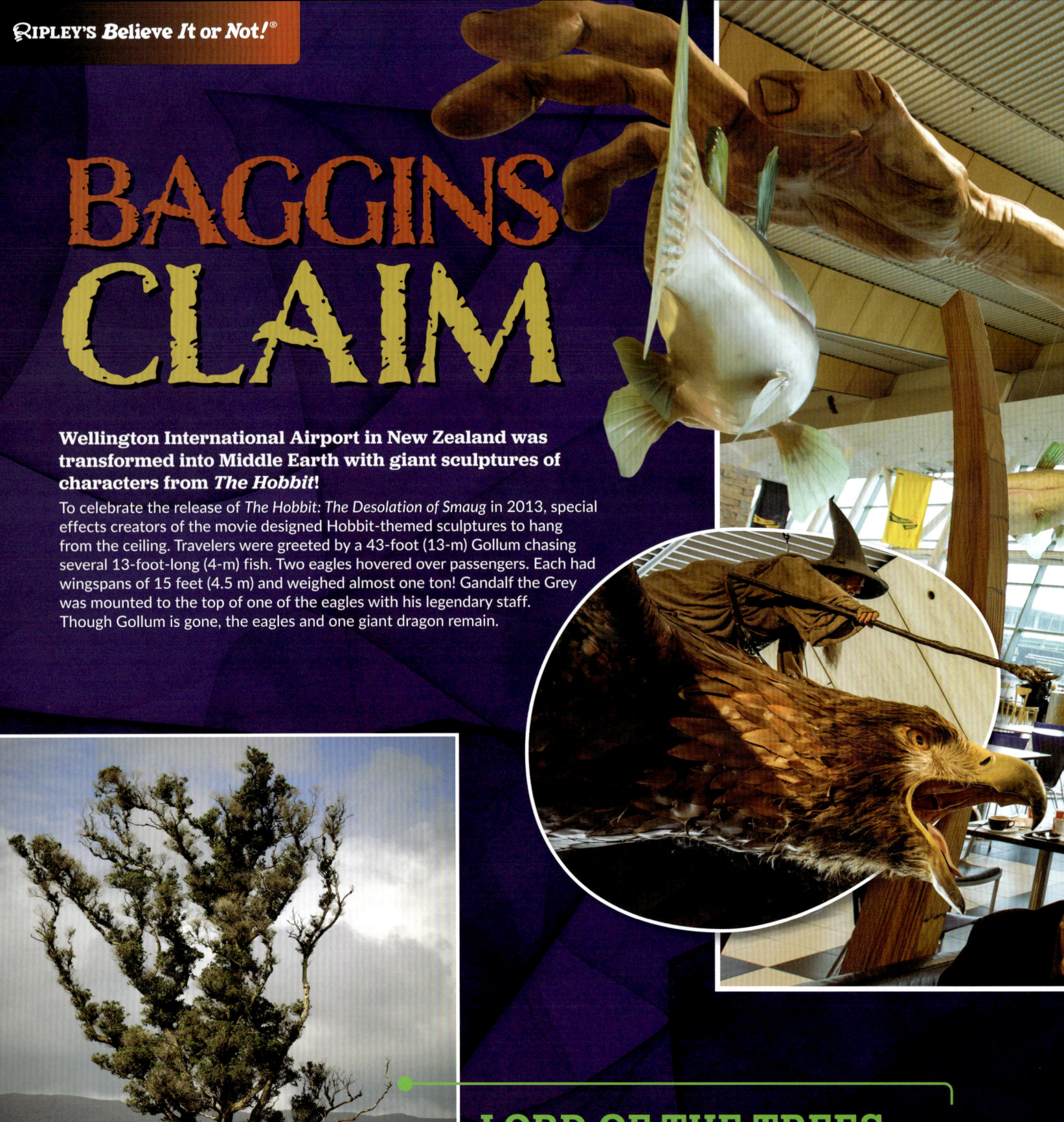

LORD OF THE TREES

This tree looks like it sprouted legs to go on a stroll! Known as "The Walking Tree," the 105-foot-tall (32 m) northern rātā tree won New Zealand's Tree of the Year contest in 2024. Northern rātā trees start their lives by growing on another tree. When its roots reach the ground, it surrounds the host tree. The Tree of the Year contest has been held in New Zealand since 2022. Its goal is to celebrate and bring awareness to the roles trees play in our lives. With 42 percent of the votes, The Walking Tree beat the competition by a landslide! Many voters said it reminded them of Ents from *The Lord of the Rings*.

Ubang, Nigeria, men and women speak separate languages. **NORTH KOREA** ▶ North Korean dictator Kim Jong-un has his own personal, portable toilet

MOVIE MISTAKES ▶ NASA shows the 1998 sci-fi disaster movie *Armageddon* during its management training program. New managers are instructed to spot as many errors in the movie as they can. At least 168 mistakes have been found.

TIRED TYPEWRITER ▶ Over a period of 46 years, U.S. writer Cormac McCarthy wrote five million words—his books and letters—on the same Olivetti typewriter. He bought it in a Tennessee pawnshop in 1963 for $50.

NOVEL NAME ▶ Following the success of the TV show *Game of Thrones*, 560 babies born in the U.S. in 2018 were named Khaleesi (a title given to the wife of a warlord), ranking it among the 1,000 most popular girls' names.

GRAMMY GREATS
Former U.S. president Barack Obama has won more Grammy Awards than Britney Spears. Obama won Best Spoken Word Album in both 2006 and 2008, whereas Britney has just one Grammy Award for her song "Toxic."

FILM CREDIT ▶ When Steven Spielberg returned to college in 2002 to complete a Bachelor of Arts degree that he had started but not finished in 1969, he submitted for course credit *Schindler's List*, the 1993 movie for which he won an Academy Award for Best Director.

MISSING PROPERTY ▶ More than 26,000 phones are lost on the public transport network of London, England, every year.

COSTLY COMIC ▶ A copy of *The Amazing Spider-Man Issue No.1* from March 1963 sold in 2024 for $1.38 million. The comic book features Spider-Man's first encounter with the Fantastic Four and sold for 12 cents when it was first printed.

THE RIPLEY'S COLLECTION

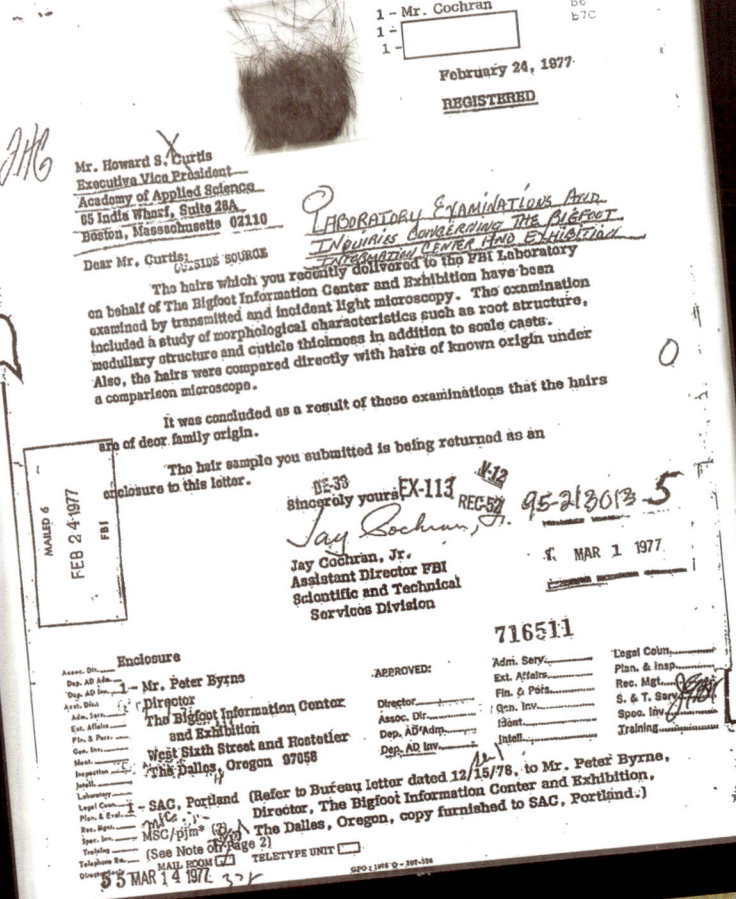

BIGFOOT EVIDENCE

In the 1970s, Oregon Bigfoot hunter Peter Byrne sent hair and tissue samples he believed came from Bigfoot to the FBI. The agency analyzed the samples and sent Peter this letter stating their findings: the hair came from a deer.

CATALOG NO. 175390

Peter continued to believe in Bigfoot until his passing in 2023 at age 97.

This chupacabra sculpture looks similar to a canine with severe mange.

CHUPACABRA FOOTPRINT

The notorious chupacabra is a vampire-like creature said to drain the blood of livestock. This footprint casting was taken after a sighting in rural Miami, Florida, in 1996. It is thought that what people believe to be a monster might actually be a coyote with mange.

CATALOG NO. 22453

WOLPERTINGER TAXIDERMY

The Wolpertinger is a mythical creature born from the works of crafty taxidermists located in Bavaria during the 1800s. They combined parts from wildly different animals, then sold the creations to tourists as "local wildlife." Many myths grew around the Wolpertinger over time—such as its saliva causes thick hair growth wherever it touches your skin!

CATALOG NO. 17270

So cute, it's unreal!

SEEK THE STRANGE

Ripley's Believe It or Not!®

Fly FISHING

Believe it or not, some bats hunt and eat fish!

Known as fishing bats, these creatures use echolocation to detect ripples on the water's surface caused by fish. They swoop down, extend their claws, and snatch the fish right out of the water. The greater bulldog bat of Central and South America is one of the best-known fishing bats. They have long toes and sharp claws that help them catch their slippery prey. These bats are specialized hunters, making them unique among their insect-eating relatives.

WHO NEEDS A FISHING LINE WHEN YOU HAVE SONAR?

2 million years old, North Macedonia's Lake Ohrid is one of Europe's deepest lakes. **NORWAY** ▶ Norway once knighted a penguin! **OMAN** ▶ Mountain Dew

MONEY MAGNET

Reel in hidden treasure! New York couple Barbi Agostini and James Kane were shocked when they found a safe with $100,000 inside while magnet fishing in Queens. They used a strong magnet to pull the safe out of a creek and found it stuffed with hundred-dollar bills! They told the police, but since no one knew who the money belonged to, they were allowed to keep it. Some of the money was wet and damaged. Barbie and James plan to use the money to buy better magnet fishing equipment to find more treasures!

A REEL FIND!

NEW HOME ▶ In 2017, Stephanie Barstow's Bengal cat Duke went missing from his home in England. Seven years later he was found alive and well, living in a factory just 900 feet (274 m) away!

DOG DETECTOR ▶ Gunner, a white kelpie dog adopted by Leading Aircraftman Percy Westcott, saved the Australian city of Darwin from being bombed by Japanese air raids during World War II. The dog's sense of hearing was so acute that he could hear airplanes when they were still many miles away, making him at least 20 minutes and sometimes hours faster than the city's official air raid sirens. He was also able to distinguish between the engine sounds of Allied and Japanese planes and only became agitated when enemy planes were approaching. He was so reliable that his warnings were passed on to the local air base, allowing fighter planes to be scrambled to defend the city.

SPIDER SOMERSAULTS ▶ The flic-flac spider, which lives in Morocco's Erg Chebbi desert, can cartwheel its way out of danger—both forward and backward. When threatened, it leaps off the ground and launches its body into a succession of speedy somersaults to make its escape. It can cartwheel at 6.6 feet (2 m) per second, which is double its walking speed, and can even cartwheel uphill.

MEDITATION MISTAKE ▶ Seeing several people lying on the floor at a café in Lincolnshire, England, a concerned passerby called the police to report a mass killing. Officers rushed to the scene, only to find that the suspected massacre was merely a yoga class in meditation.

TRAP TREE

Every Christmas, the coastal town of Stonington, Maine, stacks hundreds of real lobster traps into the shape of a giant Christmas tree! The tower contains more than 400 lobster traps, 400 buoys, and thousands of multicolored lights. Local artists paint many of the buoys. Every year, the tree gets bigger and better. In 2023, the lobster trap tree was 35 feet (10.6 m) tall, which was 8 feet (2.4 m) taller than the year before!

is the top-selling beverage in Oman. **PAKISTAN** ▶ The Sheedi Mela festival in Pakistan ends with

SEEK THE STRANGE

CroBRO

California dude Steven Borzachillo is giving crochet a twist with his new style: *Brochet!*

Steven doesn't make blankets and scarves. Instead, he crochets weapons! He's made a fluffy ninja star, a soft spear, and even a yarn cannon! To make things extra brutal, he also crochets bloody guts and body parts. For Steven, Brochet isn't about violence. It's his way to make people laugh! He also hopes it shows that crochet is for everyone and inspires others to pick up the hobby.

LOOK OUT!

HE'LL LEAVE YOU IN STITCHES!

FLUFFY GUTS!

MADE IN BRAIDS

Shana Everson, from Syracuse, New York, makes wigs that form pictures out of braids! Her first themed wig was a jack-o'-lantern for Halloween. She has since made wigs for other holidays, sports teams, movies, and more! It takes Shana between three days and a few weeks to make each wig. To start, Shana sketches her design. Then, she braids the color patterns into the hair. She adds final details with paint and yarn to make them picture-perfect!

RED LIGHTS FOR EYES!

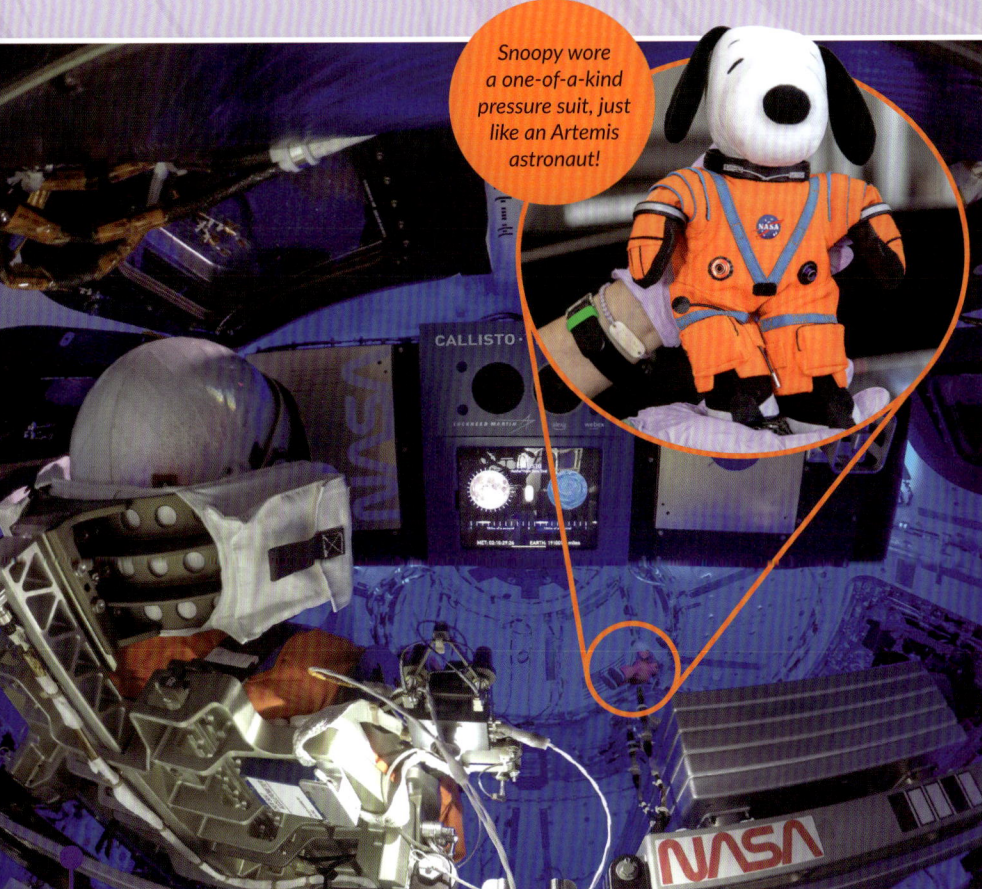

Snoopy wore a one-of-a-kind pressure suit, just like an Artemis astronaut!

ONE SMALL PAW

5-4-3-2-1, it's liftoff for Snoopy! In November 2022, a small Snoopy doll went to space inside the *Orion* spacecraft. There were no astronauts on board. The mission, called Artemis I, was to help prepare for future crewed flights to the Moon. Snoopy was used as a zero-gravity test. When scientists back on Earth watched the video from inside *Orion* and saw Snoopy floating, they knew it had reached the point where everything was weightless! Snoopy spent 25 days in space and traveled beyond the Moon. In total, he covered more than 1.4 million miles (2.25 million km)!

RIPPED FROM HISTORY

"SPIKE" ← Drawn by "SPARKY"

A HUNTING DOG THAT EATS PINS, TACKS, SCREWS AND RAZOR BLADES IS OWNED BY C.F. SCHULZ, St. Paul, Minn.

SNOOPY'S START

As a teenager, cartoonist Charles Schulz sent a drawing of his dog named Spike to *Ripley's Believe It or Not!* He claimed the dog "eats pins, tacks, screws, and razor blades." Ripley featured the artwork and story in the February 22, 1937, cartoon panel. It was Schulz's first professional publication. The cute little dog would later become famous as "Snoopy" in the *Peanuts* comic strip!

Raft RACE

The Lewes to Newhaven Raft Race sees teams racing homemade rafts while being pelted with flour and eggs!

The yearly event is held on the River Ouse in England. Rafts are decorated with different themes each year. Crowds gather on shores and bridges to cheer for their favorite team. But some fans go even further—they throw things like flour and eggs at the rafts they want to lose! The event is a fun way the local community raises money for charity.

GETTING PELTED WITH FLOUR AND EGGS!

CROWDS CHEER AND THROW THINGS!

Palestine is a tree called al-Badawi, thought to be the oldest olive tree in the world at possibly 5,500 years old. **PANAMA** ▶ Panama is the only country

JOY RIDE

Black bears at Woburn Safari Park in England rode on a swan boat! After rain formed a pond in the bears' enclosure, the park staff added the boat. The curious bears sniffed the boat, swatted at it, and even climbed aboard! The playful activity was a hit. Enrichment makes life more enjoyable for the animals and delights visitors and staff.

SUSTAINED SILENCE ▶ For 32 years, Saraswati Devi only allowed herself to speak for an hour a day. She began her vow of silence in 1992 after an important temple in Ayodhya was demolished and only ended it in 2024 when a new temple was built in the city.

FINGER PHOBIA ▶ A man in Quebec, Canada, had two fingers on his left hand amputated even though they were perfectly healthy because, ever since childhood, he had been convinced that they did not belong on his body. The fingers had given him repeated nightmares that they were either rotting or burning, but once they were removed, the nightmares stopped. Doctors said he was suffering from a very rare condition called body integrity identity disorder.

PRESERVED LEMON

A 285-year-old lemon found in the back of an old cabinet drawer sold at auction in Shropshire, England, in 2024 for $1,780. By contrast, the cabinet fetched just $40. The antique lemon was intact but had turned a dark-brown color.

UNUSUAL EVENTS ▶ On April 5, 2024, the New York Yankees baseball team was taking part in pre-game batting practice when a 4.8 magnitude earthquake rocked New York City. Three days later, they played immediately following another natural phenomenon—a solar eclipse.

PARTY PROBLEM ▶ In 2024, right-wing political party Reform UK dropped Tommy Cawkwell as a candidate for York Central because he had been "inactive"—unaware that he had died two months earlier.

LOST BIRTHDAYS ▶ Mary Forsythe of Oklahoma turned 100 on February 29, 2024, but because she was born on Leap Day, it was only her 25th actual birthday.

COOL CRUISE

Artist Ivan Karpitsky from Belarus made a boat out of ice! He carved big blocks of ice into the right shapes to build the boat and added a steering wheel and paddles. Then, he went cruising on a lake. That's right, the boat actually worked! However, the rudder was just for show and did not control the boat's direction. Just like ice cubes in a drink, the boat floated because ice is less dense than water! That's pretty cool—literally!

in the world where you can watch the Sun rise over the Pacific Ocean and set on the Atlantic!

SEEK THE STRANGE

DOOMED DESIGNS

Inventors like to solve problems. They try to come up with the next best thing to make people's lives easier. But not all inventions are clever or successful, and some are just plain silly! Here are some odd creations that never quite caught on.

CAR SCOOP

By the twentieth century, there were more cars on the road. This put pedestrians at risk. So, along came inventors with the "safety scoop" or "pedestrian catcher!" It worked by pulling a lever to release a scoop, so the car would sweep a person off their feet, rather than hitting them. But it only worked if the driver was quick enough—and if the car was slow enough!

WHEELY BRIGHT

Back in the 1960s, Goodyear Tire & Rubber Co. invented something cool: car tires that glowed! These weren't made of basic black rubber. They were made of a special clear material that let light through. The tires could be dyed in any color, like bright green, yellow, blue, and red. Goodyear even added lightbulbs inside to make them glow!

MEWING MACHINE

If you had rodent trouble in Japan in 1963, you didn't have to get a cat! This "Cat Mew" machine was invented to solve the problem. To scare away mice and rats, every six seconds it "mewed" and its eyes lit up.

PAPUA NEW GUINEA ▶ The Anga people of Papua New Guinea mummify their dead by smoking the remains over fire. **PARAGUAY** ▶ Paraguay is the only

DONUT DUNKER

Donuts are delicious but sometimes messy. Glaze can stick to your fingers, and powdered sugar can drop on your clothes. But Russell E. Oakes's donut-dunking device could have been your saving grace. You used it to hold your donut, dunk it in a cup, and put it in your mouth—with no mess!

STROLLER SOUNDS

Listening to the radio was popular in the 1920s. It was easy and cheap entertainment for the whole family to enjoy. And this included the baby! This stroller from 1921 had its own antenna and loudspeaker. It was made to help keep the baby quiet.

EXPERT EARS

It can be hard to hear a movie when people are talking through it. But inventor Russell E. Oakes had a solution: just slip on his custom headphones! The amplifiers over the ears would pick up sound in the direction they faced. You could even flip them around to hear what someone was saying behind your back!

What problem do you have that a new invention could fix?

Share your thoughts...

country with a two-sided flag! **PERU** ▶ The Boiling River, a 4-mile-long (6.4-km) stretch of water

SEEK THE STRANGE

Shed & SHRED

At the World Dog Surfing Championship, dogs catch waves instead of balls!

The event takes place every year on the California coast. Dogs of all breeds and sizes can compete in the competition. Each dog gets 10 minutes to catch as many waves as they can. Points are awarded based on how long the dog can stay on the board, whether they sit, stand, or lay down, and even the size of the wave! More important than the points are the charities the event helps support. That, and how much fun the dogs and their humans have shredding waves together!

DOUBLE SHREDDING FUN!

COWABUNGA, DUDE!

deep in the Amazon rainforest in Mayantuyacu, Peru, regularly reaches 186°F (86°C). **PHILIPPINES** ▶ The national flag of the Philippines is flown upside

The Blue Angels leave smoke trails behind their jets so the pilots can easily see each other!

TIGHT FLIGHT

The Blue Angels use next-level teamwork to perform daring midair stunts at high speeds! These jets are flown by U.S. Navy and Marine pilots. During air shows, the pilots do loops and flips and sometimes fly with as little as 18 inches (46 cm) between each jet! They go up to 700 mph (1,126 kmph) while performing—that's just under the speed of sound! Believe it or not, that's only halfway to the jets' top speed!

PILOT'S POINT OF VIEW!

TREACHEROUS TREK

The Caminito del Rey in Malaga, Spain, was once the most dangerous trail in the world! The path was made in the early 1900s to help transport materials and laborers to a hydroelectric dam. It was built about 330 feet (100 m) high into a cliffside. The narrow footbridge is just 3 feet (1 m) wide and nearly 5 miles (8 km) long. It has no return route. Over the years, the walkway fell apart and became very dangerous to use, but it was completely renovated in 2015.

down with the red stripe on top during times of war. **POLAND** ▸ The Gruba Kaśka pumping

THE RIPLEY'S COLLECTION

LOADED DICE

This dice collection once belonged to a prominent crime family in Chicago during the 1940s. The dice were made for cheating in illegal gambling dens! Some are weighted or misshaped, while others have spots in the wrong places.

CATALOG NO. 175248

WANTED POSTER

John Dillinger is one of the most infamous criminals in U.S. history. Between 1933 and 1934, Dillinger and his gang robbed banks, staged three jailbreaks, and killed multiple people. His crime spree ended on July 22, 1934, when he was shot and killed by the FBI.

CATALOG NO. 8388

PRISON DOOR

Made with iron plates and weighing hundreds of pounds, this door was once part of Manchester Prison in England. Previously known as Strangeways, the prison was built to house the most dangerous of criminals.

CATALOG NO. 16533

Housed the most dangerous criminals

RIPLEY'S Believe It or Not!®

PIT PONY CLUB

Sultan the Pit Pony is a huge earth sculpture in Wales that is best seen from above! Designed by Welsh artist Mick Petts, the figure is 656 feet (200 m) long and up to 50 feet (15 m) tall in some places. Pit ponies were small horses once used in mines to pull carts of coal before machines took over. The sculpture honors the hard work of these ponies and the area's mining history. Sultan was completed in 1999—the same year the last pit pony in the UK retired!

Sultan is made from more than 60,000 tons of coal shale, stone, and dirt!

PIT PONY AT WORK!

DUCK DEVOTEE ▶ Charlotte Lee owns a collection of over 5,600 rubber ducks, which are housed in glass cases and occupy an entire room of her home in Seattle, Washington. She purchased her first seven rubber ducks in 1996 to brighten up a dark bathroom but now has ducks from all over the world, some dating back to the 1930s.

FAST-FOOD FREEBIES ▶ Lee Choon Chiek has spent four decades collecting more than 70,000 McDonald's toys, Happy Meal boxes, and other items of memorabilia associated with the restaurant chain. He displays them, along with four Ronald McDonald statues, in his private museum in Alor Setar, Malaysia. His collection started in 1982 when he attended the opening of Malaysia's first McDonald's, in Kuala Lumpur, where he was given a red-and-yellow metal pencil holder with his chicken burger. Among his exhibits are the world's first Happy Meal box from 1979 and a selection of McDonald's condiment packets from around the world.

BIG BIRD

A pair of finger bones discovered in Poland once belonged to a Neanderthal child who might have been eaten by a giant prehistoric bird! Analysis of the 115,000-year-old bones showed they came from a child around six years old. The porous nature of the bones indicated that they had passed through the digestive system of a large bird.

BOMB DECOR ▶ A 64-pound (29-kg) bomb from the late-nineteenth century sat as a garden ornament outside a house in Wales for 100 years. The house's current owners, Sian and Jeffrey Edwards, always thought it was a "dummy" with no charge and used to bang their trowel on it to remove soil. It turned out to be live and, in 2023, a bomb disposal unit detonated it.

DEVOTED DAD ▶ Mark Owen Evans from Wales has the name of his daughter Lucy tattooed on his body 667 times.

PLANT PLASTIC ▶ In 1941, Henry Ford unveiled a plastic car that he claimed was tougher than steel. Called the Soybean Car, its bodywork was made from a mixture of plant fibers. The vehicle had a tubular steel frame to which 14 plastic panels were attached and weighed only 2,000 pounds (908 kg), making it 1,000 pounds (454 kg) lighter than a steel car. But, largely because of World War II, it never went into production.

station in Warsaw, Poland, uses live mussels to monitor water quality. **PORTUGAL** ▶ The Capela dos Ossos, or Chapel of Bones, in Évora, Portugal,

Floral FEAST

Every year, the streets of Chelsea, England, are flooded with flowers!

Chelsea in Bloom is an annual flower festival with a different theme each year. The theme in 2024 celebrated two things Chelsea is famous for: food and flowers! More than 100 shops, businesses, and restaurants covered their storefronts with "floral feasts." Blooms were arranged to look like cakes, ice cream, fruits, pastries, and more. There was even a roast chicken made of flowers! First held in 2006, the event is free to attend and lasts for about a week each year.

CHICKEN IN BLOOM!

SEEK THE STRANGE

RIPLEY'S Believe It or Not!®

TONGUE EATER

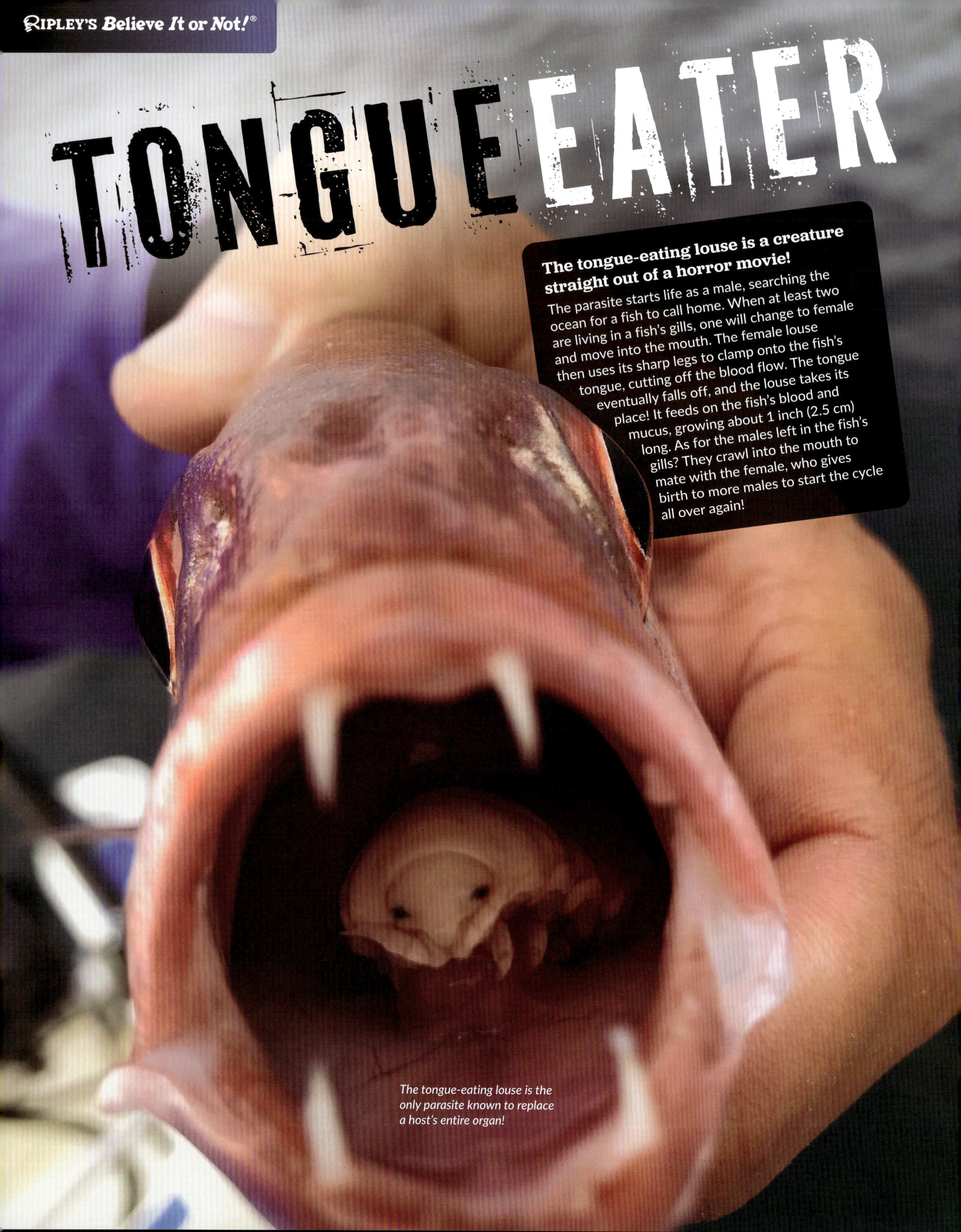

The tongue-eating louse is a creature straight out of a horror movie!

The parasite starts life as a male, searching the ocean for a fish to call home. When at least two are living in a fish's gills, one will change to female and move into the mouth. The female louse then uses its sharp legs to clamp onto the fish's tongue, cutting off the blood flow. The tongue eventually falls off, and the louse takes its place! It feeds on the fish's blood and mucus, growing about 1 inch (2.5 cm) long. As for the males left in the fish's gills? They crawl into the mouth to mate with the female, who gives birth to more males to start the cycle all over again!

The tongue-eating louse is the only parasite known to replace a host's entire organ!

begins with the letter Q. **ROMANIA** ▶ Found near the village of Costesti in Romania, trovants are a type of rock that appears to grow and multiply.

TOUGH STUFF

This bright green blob may look out of place, but it is right at home in this extreme environment! Called the yareta plant, it is native to South America and is only found at high altitudes. To survive in this cold and harsh setting, yareta has a few special tricks. The plant tends to grow on rocks, which absorb heat. To help hold on to that warmth, it grows in tightly packed groups. The yareta's leaves are very tough, making it hard to crush. It also grows very slowly. In fact, it is thought to be one of the oldest growing plants, possibly living over 3,000 years!

COFFIN WINE ▶ For Halloween 2023, English wine brand 19 Crimes launched the world's first coffin-aged wine. They took 100 bottles of red wine, put them in an oak casket, and buried them 6 feet (1.8 m) below ground among the dead in London's Tower Hamlets Cemetery.

DRASTIC DETERRENT ▶ People in South Africa can legally attach flamethrowers to their cars to prevent carjacking. The $655 device, which unleashes 16-foot (5-m) plumes of flame, is placed in the car's trunk and is ignited by the driver flipping a switch.

STUCK SHARK

While scuba diving on sand flats off Jamestown, Rhode Island, Deb and Steve Dauphinais rescued a baby shark that had its head stuck inside a discarded work glove.

CHANGING CAPITAL ▶ The capital of Jammu and Kashmir, a region located between Pakistan and India, is different in summer and winter. Srinagar is the capital from May to October but experiences extreme weather in winter, so the capital moves to Jammu City from November to April.

SNOW SHARK ▶ In January 2024, Carlos Maldonado and his two sons, Oscar and Gael, built a realistic 20-foot-long (6-m) great white shark out of snow in their front yard in Iowa. It took them 4.5 hours to sculpt it and another 1.5 hours to color it.

OH MY WASH

It's the early 1920s, and the latest car-washing innovation is... a giant puddle you drive through? Although that's what it looked like, the Auto Wash Bowl was slightly more complicated than that. (Just slightly.) The large, shallow basin was paved with ridges that vibrated the car as it drove over them. The movement splashed water onto the car and helped shake off the dirt caked onto its tires and underside. In 1924, a few laps around the bowl cost drivers just 25 cents—about $4.50 today.

RUSSIA ▶ Whale Bone Alley on Russia's Yttygran Island is a 600-year-old structure made up of

Marie Antoi-knit

Cosplayer Scarlet Stitch crocheted a full Marie Antoinette costume—complete with a bloody necklace!

Scarlet is a self-taught artist who has been making crochet costumes for more than 10 years. They love the challenge of turning yarn into wearable art. Each project can take from a few days to many months to complete. The "Marie Antoi-knit" gown is one of Scarlet's most detailed works. The costume includes a dress, a wig, undergarments, and a guillotine-shaped purse. It took a whopping 1,200 hours to crochet, sew, and add beads to every part of it!

CUTTING-EDGE FASHION!

16-foot-tall (4.9-m) ribs, jawbones, and vertebrae in parallel rows. **RWANDA** ▶ In Rwanda, it is common for people to go to milk bars to socialize and drink

HEADS WILL ROLL

Marie Antoinette was the **last queen** of **France**.

Her extravagant lifestyle during the **French Revolution** angered her subjects, who **overthrew the monarchy in 1792**.

There is no proof **Marie Antoinette** said, **"Let them eat cake"** after being told her subjects had **no bread and were starving**.

Wax-modeling pioneer **Madame Tussaud** took molds of guillotined heads during the **French Revolution**, including Marie Antoinette's.

Marie Antoinette's **beheading in 1793** marked the beginning of the **Reign of Terror**.

Marie Antoinette's **final words** were an **apology to her executioner** for accidentally stepping on his shoe.

The **guillotine's inventor** meant for it to be a **humane form of execution**.

WIZARD WAND ▸ Armed police officers in Leicestershire, England, were called out to reports of a man wielding a large knife at a hotel, but it turned out to be a Harry Potter fan waving a wand.

CHEWING GUM ▸ American Thomas Adams invented modern mass-produced chewing gum in the 1870s after conducting several unsuccessful experiments to turn it into a cheap alternative to rubber for tires.

SNEEZE HOLE ▸ A man in Scotland accidentally tore a small hole in his windpipe after trying to suppress a sneeze while he was driving. He pinched his nose and pressed his lips shut, but the force of the sneeze ripped a hole in his throat. By the time he reached the hospital emergency room, his neck was swollen and he could barely move his head.

PHONE FOOD ▸ When prison authorities at India's Shivamogga Jail conducted a search, one inmate hid his smuggled-in cell phone by swallowing it. But he later started complaining of stomach pains and was transferred to a hospital in Bengaluru, where doctors found the phone stuck at the entrance of his small intestine. When it was eventually removed, the phone had been inside him for 20 days.

TAILGATE WEDDING ▸ Philadelphia Eagles football fans Rob and Brooke Rittner got married at a tailgate party in the parking lot at Lincoln Financial Field before the November 5, 2023, game against the Dallas Cowboys. As a wedding present, the couple received personalized Eagles jerseys bearing the names "Mr. Rittner" and "Mrs. Rittner."

FAKED ILLNESS ▸ A 50-year-old Lithuanian man was arrested after apparently faking heart attacks at 20 restaurants in Spain to avoid paying the check.

TOY GUILLOTINE

Guillotines were used to kill thousands of people during the French Revolution and Reign of Terror, including King Louis XVI and Marie Antoinette. Mini versions of the gruesome killing contraption were popular toys for children at the time.

CATALOG NO. 12999

a child's toy?

Thousands of people attended the execution of Marie Antoinette.

fresh or fermented milk. **SAINT KITTS & NEVIS** ▸ A popular dish found in Saint Kitts and Nevis

RIPLEY'S Believe It or Not!®

SHRAPNEL SAND ▶ Four percent of the sand on the beaches of Normandy, France, is made up of shrapnel left behind from the 1944 D-Day landings during World War II.

STRANGE STATION ▶ Seiryu Miharashi Station in Japan's Yamaguchi Prefecture has no entrance or exit. No roads or footpaths lead to the station, so it can only be reached by train. The station was built as a viewing platform from where passengers could look out over the Nishiki River.

STEEP SAND ▶ The Duna Federico Kirbus sand dune in northwest Argentina stands 4,035 feet (1,230 m) high—nearly three times the height of the Empire State Building.

ANCIENT MEGALAKE ▶ Paratethys, a megalake that existed around 11.6 million years ago, covered 1.08 million square miles (2.8 million sq km) of eastern Europe and Asia and held 10 times more water than all of today's lakes in the world combined.

POOP PROPERTY ▶ Under the Guano Islands Act of 1856, the United States is legally allowed to seize any unclaimed island that is covered in bird poop.

TOILET TROUBLE ▶ When a woman accidentally dropped her smartwatch into an outhouse toilet in Bagley Township, Michigan, she instinctively climbed in to retrieve it, only to become trapped. First responders were called when she was heard crying for help. They had to remove the toilet and use a strap to haul her out.

CLOWNING AROUND

Clowning around... at church? It happens every December at Mexico City's Basilica of Our Lady of Guadalupe. Hundreds of clowns take part in an annual pilgrimage to the religious site. They come to honor the church's namesake and ask for her protection for the coming year. The tradition is more than 30 years old. Despite their loud and playful nature, the clowns are warmly welcomed.

WHEELY FUN

In unicycle hockey, players zip around on one wheel instead of skates! Players have to pedal, steer, and wield their sticks—all while staying balanced. Teams of five use ice hockey sticks and score goals by shooting a tennis ball into the opposing team's net. Unlike hockey, there's no specific goalkeeper! The ball can only move when a player is actively riding a unicycle, and one hand must stay on the top end of the hockey stick. The sport was first featured in a film in 1925 and is now played all over the world. Germany has more than 70 teams!

BIG BURP ▶ Kimberly Winter of Virginia burped at 107.3 decibels—louder than a blender, an electric handheld drill, and most motorcycles at full throttle. She achieved the deafening belch after consuming an iced coffee, a breakfast sandwich, and a beer. She shares her best burps on social media, where fans ask her to burp their name.

LEGO LOVER ▶ Miloš Křeček, from the Czech Republic, owns over 6,000 different LEGO sets. His collection is too big for his house, so he displays more than 9,000 exhibits, containing a total of about 10 million individual pieces, in five museums across the country. His love for LEGO began at age five when he received a set as a Christmas present, and it grew to the extent that he and his wife gave each other rare LEGO pieces as wedding presents. On vacation, he often visits Denmark, the birthplace of LEGO, to hunt through flea markets for more rarities.

MISLEADING MAPS ▶ For more than 200 years, from 1622 to as late as 1865, many maps showed California as an island.

is a stew known as goat water that is made from goat meat and neck bones. **SAINT LUCIA** ▶ Saint Lucia is the only country named after a real woman.

GRIM Grins

What song would you want your grave to play?

Share your thoughts...

DANCING ON A GRAVE!

At Joseph Grimaldi Park in England, visitors are encouraged to dance on graves!

Joseph Grimaldi was the first-ever pantomime clown. He performed in the 1800s and became known as the "king of clowns." The place where he was buried became Joseph Grimaldi Park. His grave was restored and a black fence was added for protection. To honor him, artist Henry Krokatsis created two coffin-shaped graves made of bronze tiles and installed them near Grimaldi's grave in 2010. The tiles chime musical notes when you stomp on them! Visitors are encouraged to see if they can recreate the song "Hot Codlins," which Grimaldi made famous, by tapping the tune on the tiles!

SAINT VINCENT & THE GRENADINES ▶ Commissioned in 1765, the Botanical Garden of

SEEK THE STRANGE

Glowworms aren't actually worms! They are the larvae of several insect species.

GLOW UP

While most caves exist in total darkness, some light up like the night sky, thanks to thousands of glowworms!

Glowworms are bioluminescent, meaning they create their own light. They use their blue-green glow to attract prey. Glowworms drip spiderweb-like threads of sticky mucus from the cave walls to catch their meals. Small insects follow the light and get trapped in the slimy webs! Most glowworm caves, including the famous Waitomo Cave, are found in New Zealand and Australia.

SEEK THE STRANGE

THE RIPLEY'S COLLECTION

HARD TIMES

A currency shortage during World War I led to many German towns issuing their own *notgeld*, or "emergency money." Prisoners of war were also paid with notgeld made just for use within the prison camps.

CATALOG NO. 8247

Emergency money

TRENCH ART

Much of World War I was fought from trenches dug in the ground. To pass time between battles, many soldiers turned used bullet shells into works of art!

CATALOG NO. 14381

RATIONS BOOK

During World War II, the U.S. government rationed many household items for use in the war effort. Families were provided books of stamps, like these, that could be exchanged for rationed goods.

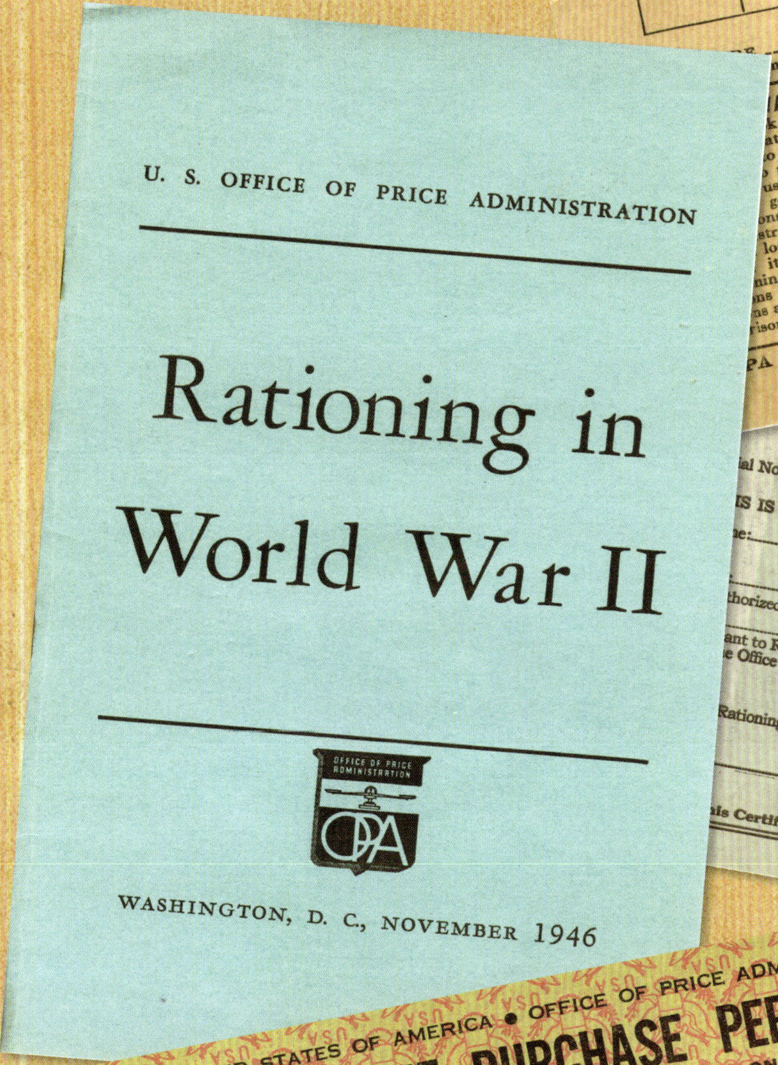

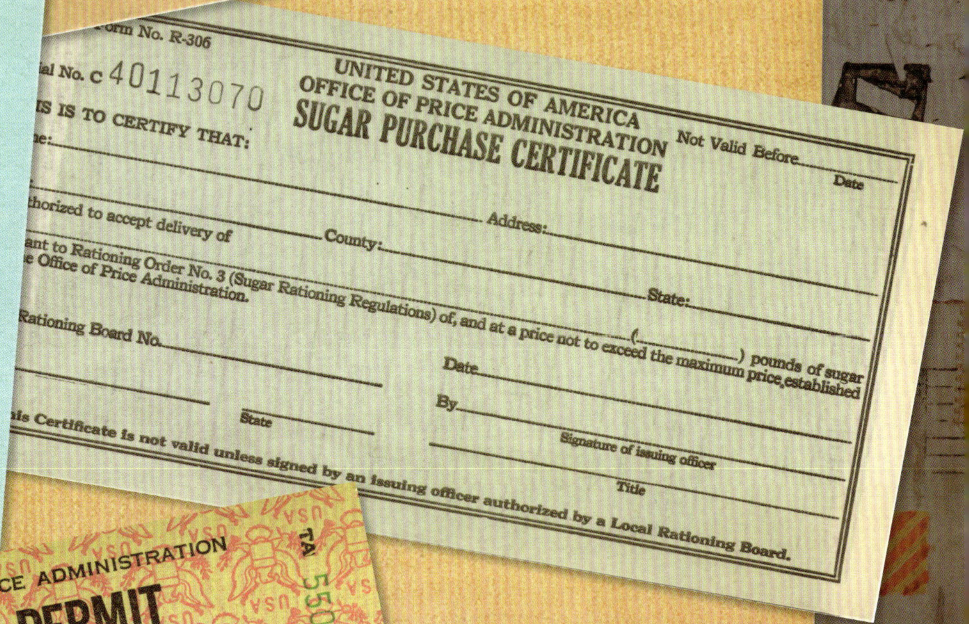

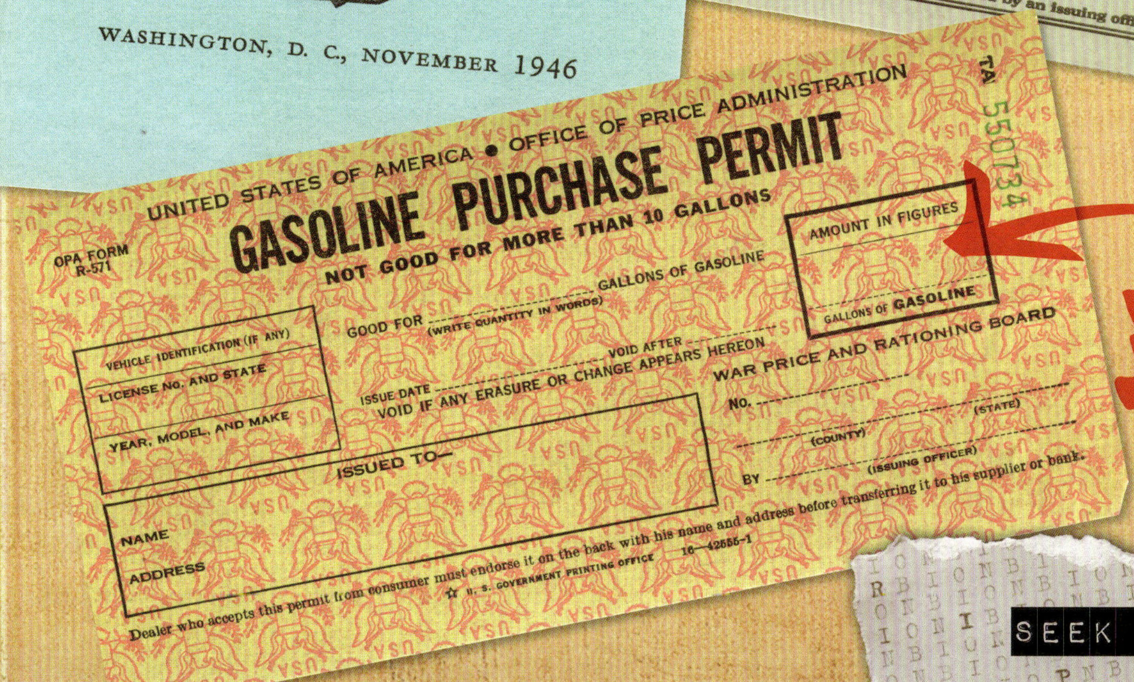

CATALOG NO. 10568

UNITED STATES OF AMERICA
OFFICE OF PRICE ADMINISTRATION

129577 G

Void if altered

NOT VALID WITHOUT STAMP

WAR RATION BOOK No. 3

Identification of person to whom issued: PRINT IN FULL

(First name) (Middle name) (Last name)

Street number or rural route

City or post office State

AGE | SEX | WEIGHT Lbs. | HEIGHT Ft. In. | OCCUPATION

...book is issued. If such person is unable to sign because of age or incapacity, another may sign in his behalf.)

...ARNING
...k is the property of the ...tates Government. It is ...o sell it to any other per... use it or permit anyone ...use it, except to obtain ...goods in accordance with ...ons of the Office of Price ...stration. Any person who ...lost War Ration Book must ...it to the War Price and ...ning Board which issued it. ...ns who violate rationing regu...ns are subject to $10,000 fine or ...risonment, or both.

...PA Form No. R-130

LOCAL BOARD ACTION

Issued by (Local board number) (Date)

Street address State

City

(Signature of issuing officer)

U. S. OFFICE OF PRICE ADMINISTRATION

Rationing in World War II

OFFICE OF PRICE ADMINISTRATION

OPA

WASHINGTON, D. C., NOVEMBER 1946

...orm No. R-306

...ial No. C 40113070

UNITED STATES OF AMERICA
OFFICE OF PRICE ADMINISTRATION
SUGAR PURCHASE CERTIFICATE

Not Valid Before (Date)

...IS IS TO CERTIFY THAT:

...me: Address:

...thorized to accept delivery of County: State:

...ant to Rationing Order No. 3 (Sugar Rationing Regulations) of, and at a price not to exceed the maximum price established ...e Office of Price Administration. (.........) pounds of sugar

Rationing Board No. Date

By

State Signature of issuing officer

Title

...is Certificate is not valid unless signed by an issuing officer authorized by a Local Rationing Board.

UNITED STATES OF AMERICA • OFFICE OF PRICE ADMINISTRATION

TA 550734

OPA FORM R-571

GASOLINE PURCHASE PERMIT

NOT GOOD FOR MORE THAN 10 GALLONS

AMOUNT IN FIGURES

GALLONS OF GASOLINE

VEHICLE IDENTIFICATION (IF ANY)

LICENSE NO. AND STATE

YEAR, MODEL, AND MAKE

GOOD FOR (WRITE QUANTITY IN WORDS) GALLONS OF GASOLINE

ISSUE DATE VOID AFTER

VOID IF ANY ERASURE OR CHANGE APPEARS HEREON

WAR PRICE AND RATIONING BOARD

NO. (COUNTY) (STATE)

BY (ISSUING OFFICER)

ISSUED TO—

NAME

ADDRESS

Dealer who accepts this permit from consumer must endorse it on the back with his name and address before transferring it to his supplier or bank.

U. S. GOVERNMENT PRINTING OFFICE 16—42685-1

Permit to buy gas!

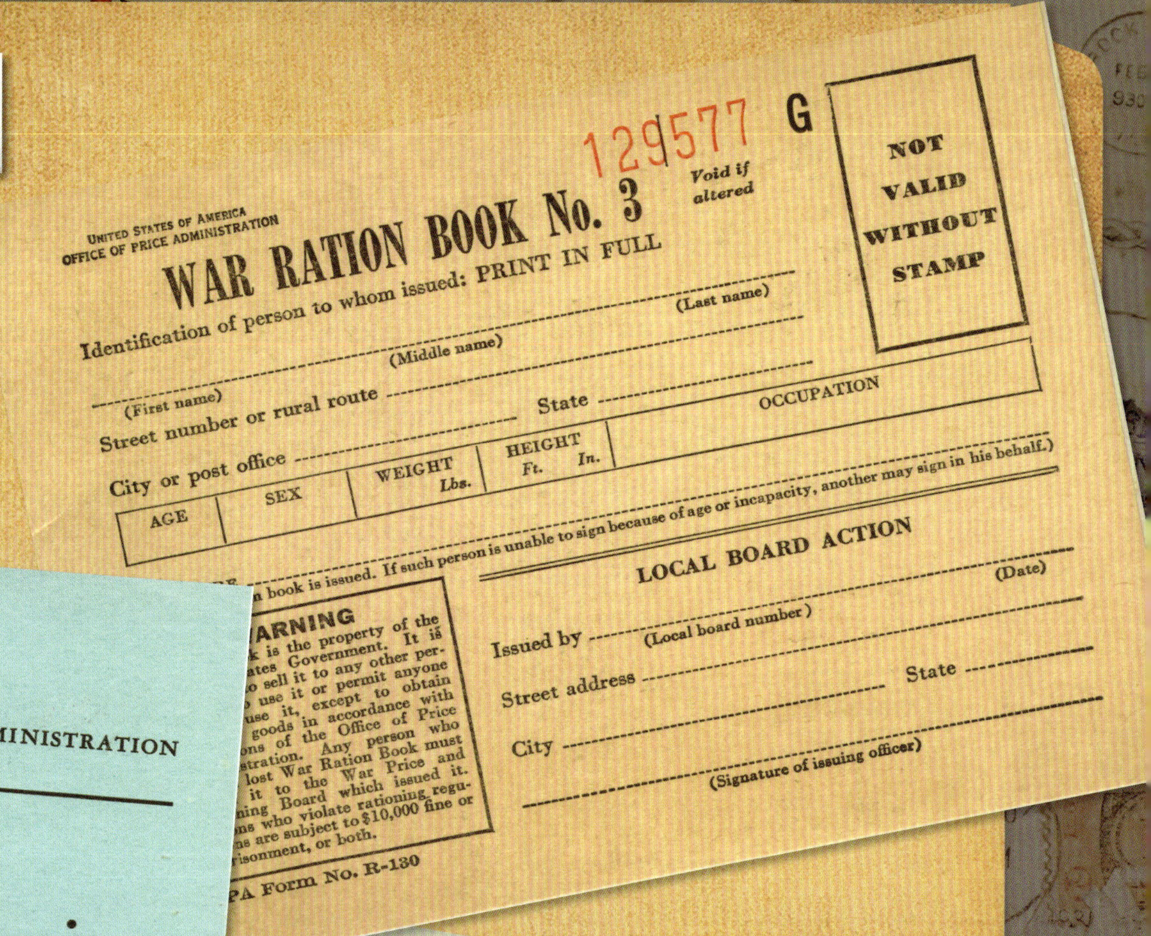

RIPLEY'S Believe It or Not!

Purr-fectly PLANTED

A rice field in Thailand's Chiang Rai province was turned into a sleeping kitty!

Farmer Tanyapong Jaikham led more than 200 helpers to create the work of art. They used rainbow rice to form the desired shapes. The crop changes color over time, so the team used GPS to make sure each seedling was planted in the right spot. After growing for a while, the plants turned into the final desired color at the same time! To give tourists a better view, tall towers were built nearby. Tanyapong hopes to grow more rice artworks in the future!

HOG HEDGEHOG

Hedgehogs made out of raw pork were once a common party food in Germany! Called *mettigel*, the dish was most popular from the 1950s to the '70s. The spines are often made from raw onion or pretzel sticks. But *mett*, or fresh raw pork, is always used to create the body of the hedgehog, or *igel*. To eat mettigel, simply spread the uncooked meat and toppings on a slice of bread and dig in! Mett sandwiches are still enjoyed in Germany to this day, thanks to strict laws around selling meat.

its calendar. **SAN MARINO** ▶ There are more cars registered in San Marino than there are citizens of the country. **SÃO TOMÉ & PRÍNCIPE** ▶ On May 29,

RICE AND SHINE!

COOKIE TUSHY

The Chinese hourglass spider has a bottom that looks like an Oreo cookie! These rare creatures are a type of trapdoor spider, which burrow into the ground and wait for prey to scurry by. But what sets them apart are the detailed markings on their abdomens. When threatened, the hourglass spider will jump headfirst into its burrow and plug the hole with its bottom. That's when you'll see the cool pattern, which some say looks like a coin or cookie!

Spiders in the Cyclocosmia genus go by many names, including Chinese hourglass spider, button spider, happy-bum spider, and, perhaps most disturbingly, Oreo spider.

SEEK THE STRANGE

BOOK TOWN

Hay-on-Wye, Wales, is the dream book nook! Known as the first "book town," this tiny village has 25 bookstores. That's one for every 80 people who live there! There are even outdoor shelves that work on the honor system, where you take a book and drop your money in a box. This town is paradise for book lovers!

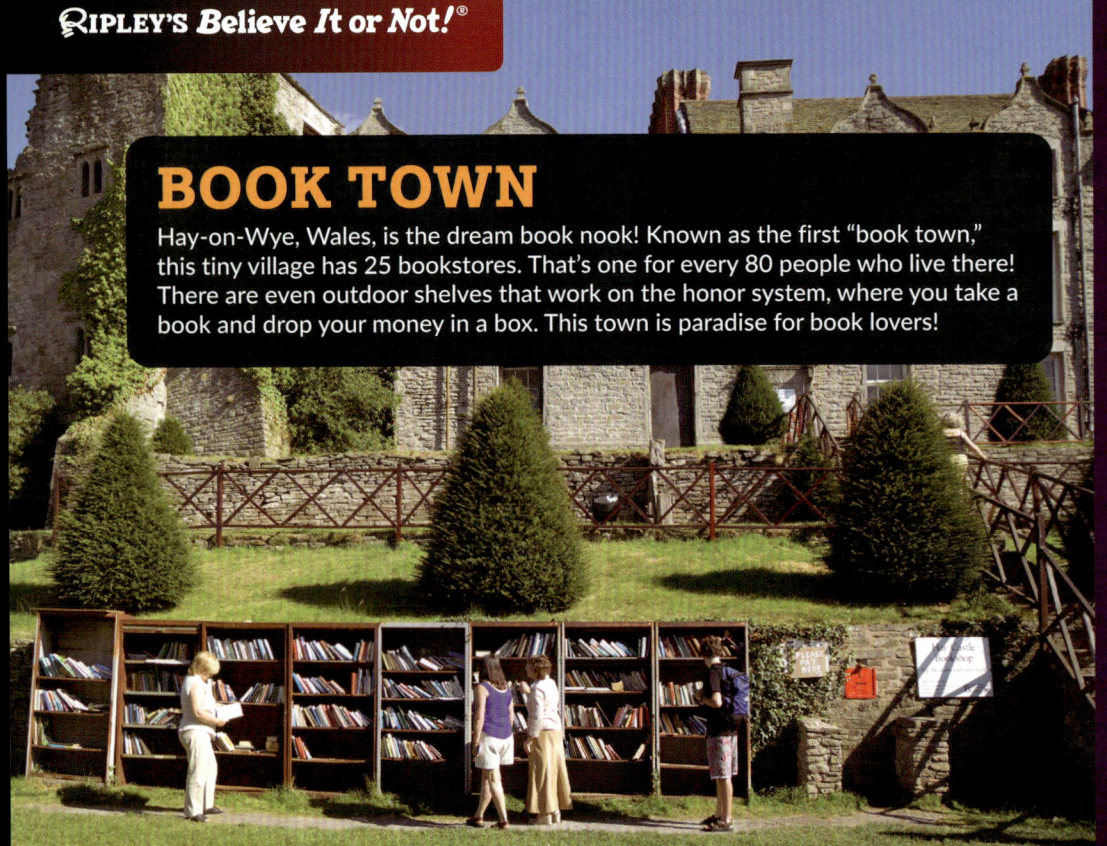

STRAIGHT STRETCH ▶ A 149-mile (240-km) stretch of Saudi Arabia's Highway 10 cuts straight through the Rub' al Khali Desert without a single bend.

MUSTACHE MAYHEM ▶ In 1907, waiters in Paris, France, went on strike for the right to wear mustaches.

UNIQUE COUNTRY ▶ Saint Lucia is the only country in the world named after a real woman—Saint Lucy of Syracuse, who lived from AD 283 to 304.

SHIPPED STATUE ▶ Completed in Paris in 1884, the Statue of Liberty was then dismantled and shipped from France to New York City the following year in 350 individual pieces.

COW CHARGE ▶ As part of an annual post-Diwali celebration, men in Bhidavad village, India, lie face down on the ground and allow dozens of cows to trample over them in the hope that it will make worshippers' dreams come true.

GEOGRAPHICAL ODDITY ▶ New York City, on the east coast of North America, is located further west than Chile's capital Santiago, on the west coast of South America.

HAT MUSEUM ▶ Located in an old chapel, Jerry's Hat Museum in Illinois is home to over 16,000 hats and 32,000 pens and pencils, all collected by Jerry Roth.

MOUNTAIN MASK ▶ The Japanese town of Fujikawaguchiko became so overrun with tourists coming to photograph Mount Fuji that in 2024 it erected a screen to block one of the most popular views of the mountain. The black mesh screen is 8 feet (2.5 m) high and 66 feet (20 m) long.

SURPRISE BIRTH ▶ In 2023, a western lowland gorilla—thought to be male—surprised keepers at the Columbus Zoo in Ohio by giving birth. Sully had been at the zoo since 2019 and was only found to be female when she was seen holding her newborn baby.

RED RIVER ▶ The streets of São Lourenço do Bairro in Portugal ran red in September 2023 after two vats at a local distillery burst and released 580,000 gallons (2.2 million liters) of red wine—the equivalent of nearly three million bottles.

WICKED WATERS

Water may have melted the Wicked Witch of the West, but that doesn't seem to be a concern for this coven! Witch paddles are a new Halloween tradition. Every October, large groups gather at lakes, rivers, and bays dressed up as witches and warlocks. Then, they hop on their paddleboards and float across the water! Witch paddles started in California around 2013. Today, they are held all around the world. Some of the largest events see as many as 500 witches on the water!

Swapping broomsticks for paddles!

the island nation of São Tomé and Príncipe. **SAUDI ARABIA** ▶ Saudi Arabia imports sand from other countries. **SENEGAL** ▶ Chimpanzees in Senegal make

Royal PAIN

Pain is no problem for Casey Severn, a.k.a. Dash Rippington: King of Animal Traps!

Based in Baltimore, Maryland, Dash shocks and awes crowds across the U.S. with his "Dangerously Stupid" show. Name an animal trap, and Dash is itching to snap it on a body part! Ouch! He has spent more than 25 years learning his craft and perfecting his act. The result? A show where audiences laugh, wince, and simply can't look away! From snapping mousetraps on his tongue and sticking his fingers in spring traps to launching nails out of his nose with a crossbow, Dash is fearless!

Step 1: Hammer nail into nose.

Step 2: Attach nail to arrow.

Step 3: Fire!

DASH'S SNOTROCKET BLOCKHEAD TRICK!

sharpened spears to hunt prey! **SERBIA** ▶ Ruzica Church in Belgrade, Serbia, has chandeliers

SEEK THE STRANGE

197

Ripley's *Believe It or Not!*

Silk SHROUD

The haunting look of these trees isn't caused by ghosts—it's thanks to caterpillars!

Ermine moth caterpillars use their webs for defense. There can be thousands of these insects on a single tree. The silk webs protect the caterpillars as they get ready to turn into moths. The webs help keep them safe from predators. Ermine moth caterpillars make a lot of silk and cover their favorite plants with it. The webs start small but grow bigger as the caterpillars do, often covering large parts of the plant or even an entire tree!

TIME TO DYE MY FEATHERS!

RED HEAD

The bearded vulture dyes its feathers red, but scientists aren't sure why! The large bird of prey is born with dark-brown feathers, and as it gets older, the feathers around its head, neck, and chest turn white. Well, they *would* be white if the birds didn't dye them red by rolling in water and mud that's rich in iron oxide! The mineral turns its feathers from white to red. Scientists aren't sure why bearded vultures dye their feathers, but they agree it's not for camouflage. What do you think is the reason?

THE Ripley's COLLECTION

FOSSILIZED STINGRAY

This stingray fossil is around 35 million years old! Complete stingray fossils have been found in just two places in the world: Monte Bolca, Italy, and the Green River Formation in Wyoming—where this fossil came from.

CATALOG NO. 175417

Amazing detail!

SEEK THE STRANGE

Pink EATS

In 2024, more than 42,000 people went to a festival for pink soup!

Pink Soup Fest started in 2023 and takes place in Vilnius, Lithuania. The cold, pink soup is a popular dish in the country. The bright color comes from beets. Other ingredients include cucumber, kefir, and dill. At Pink Soup Fest, you can try different versions of the soup, enter a costume contest, and even glide down a soapy water slide into a giant pink, inflatable soup bowl!

If colors had a flavor, which one do you think would taste best? Share your thoughts...

SOUP-ER TASTY FUN!

the roundest country. **SINGAPORE** ▶ The Changi Airport in Singapore features a 130-foot-tall (40-m) indoor waterfall surrounded by a lush forest.

HAIRY DAIRY

Hair and food are two things most people try to keep far away from each other. But when it comes to making tulum peyniri, the two get very close. Tulum peyniri is a traditional cheese from Turkey that is aged in goat skin! The hairy exterior may be off-putting to some, but the cheesy treat inside has been enjoyed for hundreds of years!

WOULD YOU EAT THIS CHEESE?

SUBZERO SWIM ▶ Canadian underwater explorer Jill Heinerth once swam inside an iceberg. On an expedition to Antarctica, she went cave diving inside an iceberg that was about the size of Jamaica. Down in the depths, she had to deal with extreme cold and powerful currents that threatened to suck her back into the iceberg as she tried to make her way out.

REFLECTION RESCUE ▶ After being pulled into the water by a marlin fish on a solo fishing trip, Will Fransen spent nearly 24 hours in the ocean off the coast of New Zealand's North Island before being rescued. As his boat drifted away, leaving him 35 miles (56 km) from land without a life jacket, he had to fend off the attention of an approaching shark. He tried waving his hat and shouting at passing boats, without success, until he had the idea of shining the Sun's reflection from his watch directly at another boat.

GRENADE GIFT ▶ While Kedrin Simms Brachman was cleaning out the home of her late father, Frank Simms, she discovered a live grenade in a toolbox. He had kept the grenade for about 30 years and it had moved houses with him multiple times.

CANDY COLLECTION ▶ Brian Trauman, from New Jersey, has a collection of more than 5,540 PEZ candy dispensers, including rare likenesses of Prince Harry and Meghan Markle, the Duke and Duchess of Sussex. Some items in his collection are valued at over $10,000. His interest started when he found a bag of about 100 dispensers at his mother's house in 1999.

SOLO SAILING ▶ South African-born Leanne Maiden rowed 3,000 miles (4,800 km) solo across the Atlantic Ocean. She set off from La Gomera in the Canary Islands on December 13, 2023, and, after rowing for up to 14 hours a day, arrived in Antigua 66 days later—despite her boat capsizing at one point. She had originally intended rowing with a partner, but they canceled.

3-INCH-WIDE (7.9-CM) TONGUE!

TONGUE TIED

Brittany Lacayo of Houston, Texas, has a tongue that measures 3.1 inches (7.9 cm) wide—almost as wide as a credit card! When she was a kid, Brittany was teased about her tongue. For a long time, she hid what made her different from others. That is, until she realized she has one of the widest tongues in the world! Now, she embraces what makes her unique.

SLOVAKIA ▶ It's tradition in Slovakia for families to keep a live carp in the bathtub for several days

SEEK THE STRANGE

SPIDEY SNACKS

You might have seen the pipe-like nest of a mud wasp, but did you know that each "pipe" in the nest has several cells filled with spiders? The female wasp paralyzes the spiders with her sting, puts them in the cells, and then lays eggs on them. When the baby wasps hatch, they eat the paralyzed spiders. Yummy!

INSIDE THE NEST!

FOOD DELIVERY!

MONOLITH MYSTERY

A shiny sculpture appeared in a Nevada desert overnight! The 6.5-foot-tall (2-m) pillar showed up near a hiking trail in the Desert National Wildlife Refuge. It had mirrors on all sides. They reflected the desert from every angle. There were no clues as to who left the sculpture there! For safety reasons, it was removed from the hiking trail. Mysterious monoliths like this one have appeared around the world at random since 2020. No one knows where they come from!

NO-NO NAME ▶ In 2023, Spanish aristocrat Fernando Fitz-James Stuart, the seventeenth Duke of Huéscar and a descendant of King James II of England, was informed that the 25-word name he had chosen for his baby daughter was too long to be registered legally.

PERMANENT PROPOSAL ▶ Joe Murray of England proposed to his girlfriend Sara Graham with a 10-inch (25-cm) "marry me then" tattoo on his thigh. She responded by using a tattoo gun to tick the "yes" box on his leg.

DISASTER DOUGH ▶ A woman who stole a delivery truck in Carlingford, Australia, believing that it held cash or valuables, instead discovered that it contained 10,000 Krispy Kreme donuts—not the kind of dough she was hoping for!

WALLET FOUND ▶ In 2023, workers renovating the Plaza Theatre in Atlanta, Georgia, discovered a wallet behind a bathroom wall that had been lost 65 years earlier in 1958. The wallet contained old black-and-white family photos, a library card, and a raffle ticket to win a new 1959 Chevrolet. The wallet's owner died in 2005, so it was given to her daughter.

before eating the fish for Christmas. **SLOVENIA** ▶ The oldest known wooden wheel was found in Slovenia's Ljubljana Marshes and dates back 5,200 years.

SWITCHED SOUNDS ▶ In 1993, a group called the Barbie Liberation Organization switched the voice boxes of more than 100 talking Barbie and G.I. Joe dolls so that Barbie could be heard vowing ultimate vengeance on the enemy, while G.I. Joe praised the virtues of the beach.

CHILD CHAMPION ▶ Twelve-year-old schoolboy Bayleigh Teepa-Tarau won a New Zealand national golf tournament, despite having only played three rounds before in his life. He played with borrowed clubs and wore basketball sneakers on his feet.

FIERY FOOD
Speed eater Mike Jack, from Ontario, Canada, ate 135 fiery Carolina Reaper peppers in one sitting. Carolina Reapers are hundreds of times hotter than jalapeño peppers.

EXTRA TEETH ▶ Kalpana Balan, from India, has 38 teeth—six more than the average adult. She has four extra mandibular teeth on her lower jaw and two extra maxillary teeth on her upper jaw.

BACKWARD BIKER ▶ Alaskan cyclist Will Walker rode a BMX bike 500 miles (800 km) across the entire state of Iowa—while facing backward. Starting in Sioux City and ending in Davenport, he rode for up to 10 hours a day for seven days while sitting on the handlebars of the bike and looking over his shoulder to steer.

FURNITURE FOREST

In Derbyshire, England, there is a special field where trees grow into chairs!

Gavin Munro and his company, Full Grown, make furniture from willow trees. Instead of cutting them down, Gavin uses a custom frame to shape the trees into chairs, lamps, mirrors, and more while the trees grow. Gavin was inspired by bonsai trees. After trying different kinds of wood, Gavin chose willow because the trees grow quickly. Still, it takes at least six years for the trees to grow into shape. Then it takes one more year for the wood to dry. The result is a one-of-a-kind work made from a single piece of wood!

SOLOMON ISLANDS ▶ Dolphin teeth have been used as currency in the Solomon Islands

THE RIPLEY'S COLLECTION

In 1920, more than 50,000 women in Boston registered to vote!

WOMEN'S BALLOT BOX

This box collected the ballots of some of the first women voters in Boston, Massachusetts, in 1920. That year, the Nineteenth Amendment took effect and promised the right to vote could not be denied due to someone's sex.

CATALOG NO. 175890

A unique way to support your candidate!

SOAP BABY

During the 1896 U.S. presidential election, soap companies devised a bizarre product: soap babies! They made babies for both candidates, allowing shoppers to choose who they support. This one was for the eventual winner, William McKinley.

CATALOG NO. 22506

Soap babies did not stick around for future elections. People thought the boxes looked too much like little coffins!

CARTER CARTOON

This Ripley's Believe It or Not! cartoon was signed by former U.S. President Jimmy Carter. It was published on November 14, 1977—the same year Carter became president.

CATALOG NO. 173750

Jimmy Carter was the first U.S. president to reach the age of 100, living more than 40 years after he left office in 1981 and passed in 2024.

SEEK THE STRANGE

RIPLEY'S Believe It or Not!®

CAMO CRITTERS

Many insects use camouflage to hide in plain sight and stay safe from predators. Some bugs pretend to be flowers, while others blend perfectly with twigs and leaves. These unique disguises can help keep these animals hidden from others who might want to eat them. (Or from the prey they want to eat.) It's like a game of hide-and-seek in nature!

CAN YOU FIND THE HIDDEN INSECTS?

SCAN TO SEE WHERE THEY'RE HIDING!

DEAD LEAF MANTIS

The dead leaf mantis lives up to its name by blending in with fallen leaves! Its skin can range in many colors, including dark gray, light green, brown, or tan. Their flat bodies and leaf-patterned wings make it easy to fit in with their surroundings. While it can use camouflage to hide from predators, it's also helpful when hunting prey!

PINK CRAB SPIDER

Next time you stop to smell the flowers, watch out! There might be a pink crab spider hiding. Though they're called the pink crab spider, a female can slowly change between white, pink, and yellow to match a flower's color. They tend to sit in the center of a flower, blending in while they wait for prey, like bees and butterflies.

for centuries. **SOMALIA** ▶ At about 2,070 miles (3,330 km) long, Somalia's coastline is the longest on mainland Africa. **SOUTH AFRICA** ▶ The "Extreme 19th"

BIG-EYED TOAD BUG

The big-eyed toad bug might look and act like a toad, but it's an insect! It gets its name from the big eyes on its back and the way it hops around from place to place. To catch food, it jumps onto smaller insects! Their rough, bumpy skin and mottled brown, tan, and rust colors help them blend in with rocky shorelines, sand, and soil.

PEPPERED MOTH

This black-and-white moth evolved to fit in with its surroundings! The peppered moth is white with many black spots that look like pepper. Before the 1800s, most of these moths were light-colored. They blended in with lichen that grew on tree bark. But during the Industrial Revolution, pollution covered trees in soot. In response, the moth population became darker, too! As pollution decreased, these moths evolved again to the speckled color we often see today.

STICK INSECT

Many stick insects appear smooth and are gray or brown in order to blend in with trees and bushes. But some live in lush forests where trees are covered in fuzzy moss and ferns. To stay hidden in those places, these insects must go the extra mile! Their sticklike bodies are covered in leafy green growths that help them blend in perfectly.

RIPLEY'S Believe It or Not!®

CHISELED CANVAS

Portuguese street artist Vhils turns old walls into art! Vhils uses the sides of buildings that are going to be torn down. To make his art, he scratches, carves, and drills into the wall using chisels, hammers, and explosives. He exposes the layers underneath and uses what he finds, like old paint or bricks, for his art. He creates detailed portraits on walls before the buildings are demolished!

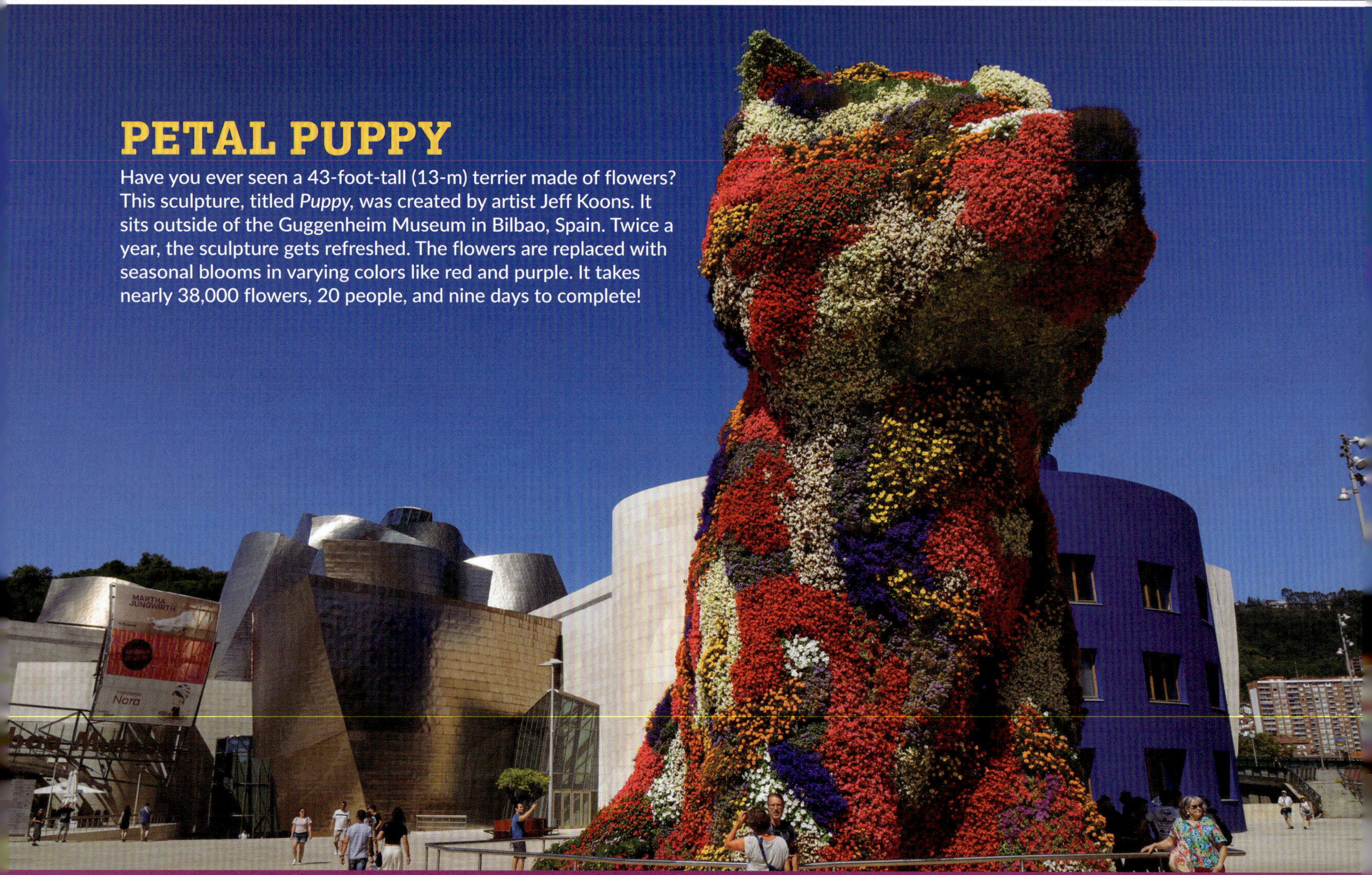

PETAL PUPPY

Have you ever seen a 43-foot-tall (13-m) terrier made of flowers? This sculpture, titled *Puppy*, was created by artist Jeff Koons. It sits outside of the Guggenheim Museum in Bilbao, Spain. Twice a year, the sculpture gets refreshed. The flowers are replaced with seasonal blooms in varying colors like red and purple. It takes nearly 38,000 flowers, 20 people, and nine days to complete!

that is accessible only by helicopter. **SOUTH KOREA** ▶ About 45 percent of South Koreans have one of three surnames: Kim, Lee, or Park (Pak).

Thread Balloon

Irina can even mimic complex embroidery with her balloons!

Artist Irina Gvozdenko makes cross-stitch art out of balloons!

Cross-stitch is a type of sewing that uses X-shaped stitches to form an image. Balloons aren't normally involved in crafts made with needles, but Irina found a way! Instead of fabric, her canvas is a grid of inflated balloons. She threads slightly blown-up balloons through the grid to make her "stitches." Irina's finished pieces are a playful twist on the classic craft. Just be sure to keep sharp objects away—or else you'll end up with "pop" art!

SOUND SUPPORTER ▶ At one of ZZ Top's earliest gigs in Alvin, Texas, the band played to an audience of just one. Nevertheless, they played a full hour-long set for him and even an encore. And that same man was still coming to their concerts 50 years later.

NEW NAME ▶ Actress Sigourney Weaver was born Susan Weaver but began using the name Sigourney at age 14, taking it from a character in the F. Scott Fitzgerald novel *The Great Gatsby*.

SURGERY CELEBRATION ▶ English diarist Samuel Pepys was so pleased with his successful bladder stone surgery in 1658 that he celebrated the event for many years afterward on the anniversary of the operation.

STAIRCASE STOWAWAY ▶ A man secretly lived under the staircase of a shopping mall in Shanghai, China, for more than six months. He had a bed, computer, desk, and chair.

MILLION MISTAKE ▶ UK actor Tom Hollander once mistakenly received a million-dollar paycheck intended for *Spider-Man* actor Tom Holland. They were both with the same agent at the time, and the accounts department mixed up the two names.

BEAR BURGLARY ▶ A full-size stuffed polar bear standing 12 feet (3.6 m) tall and weighing about 500 pounds (227 kg) was stolen in January 2024 from the Lily Lake Resort in Alberta, Canada.

SOUTH SUDAN ▶ Having declared independence in July 2011, South Sudan is the world's

BENNETT BUDDIES

Artist Mike Bennett paints wooden cutouts to look like cartoon characters that have escaped into the real world! He started making his "Bennett Buddies" in 2019. The next year, Mike added cartoon critters to his front lawn for a display he called "A to Zoo." There were 26 animals in all—one for each letter of the alphabet! Locals loved seeing Mike's cute creations! Since then, he has made many more displays and even opened a café featuring the cartoons.

VETERAN BIKER ▶ In 2023, Leslie Harris competed in a motorcycle race in Auckland, New Zealand, just three weeks before his 98th birthday. Riding a historic BSA Bantam 175cc, he finished fourth, beating his oldest son Rod, aged 64, and his 21-year-old granddaughter Olivia. Leslie took part in his first bike race in 1953 and continued to race in his nineties, despite breaking six ribs at an event in 2020.

HAMMER HITS ▶ Known as the "Cuban Ironman," Havana's Lino Tomasén has been hitting his body with a heavy sledgehammer up to 1,000 times a day for more than 17 years. He performs on local streets and beaches, relentlessly hammering himself on his wrists, elbows, and forearms. To the amazement of onlookers, he always appears to survive unscathed.

SOCCER-FREE ▶ As of 2024, the Marshall Islands was the only country in the world without a national soccer team.

COUNTLESS DOORS ▶ There are more than 17,000 doors in the Burj Khalifa, a skyscraper in Dubai, United Arab Emirates. At 2,717 feet (828 m) high, it is the world's tallest building.

LOOK AGAIN

French artist Jacques Monneraud turns clay into cardboard! Kind of. He is really a ceramics artist. His sculptures are masterful illusions. The pieces look like cardboard that has been folded and taped into different shapes. But every last detail is made of clay and the white tape is made of glaze! They are heavy and waterproof, unlike real cardboard. Jacques's art really makes you question your eyes. You can't always believe what you see!

Jacques Monneraud

youngest country. **SPAIN** ▶ In Villar de Corneja, Spain, New Year's is celebrated at noon instead of midnight to accommodate the village's elderly residents.

Mouth *Masterpiece*

Paralyzed from the neck down, artist Sarah Barker from Cornwall, England, paints using her mouth!

When she was 18 months old, Sarah fell and injured her spinal cord. It left her unable to move most of her body, but she didn't let that stop her! Sarah learned to paint by holding a brush with her mouth. She loves painting scenes of nature, from beaches to animals and flowers. Sarah hopes to inspire others with disabilities not to give up and to find creative ways to do what they love. Sarah even plans to open a studio to show her art and host craft fairs.

PERFECTING HER TECHNIQUE SINCE CHILDHOOD!

SOME OF SARAH'S ARTWORK

SRI LANKA ▶ Cinnamon originated in Sri Lanka. **SUDAN** ▶ Twice as many ancient pyramids

ROAD DENT

An unlucky rodent left a lasting impression on a Chicago sidewalk—literally!

The so-called "Chicago rat hole" is said to be more than 20 years old. Back when the neighborhood's sidewalk was being added, a rodent fell into the wet cement. The imprint of its body, tail, and claws has been an honored quirk of the area ever since. People have left coins, candles, and stuffed animals to honor the rat-shaped hole in the sidewalk. One couple even got married next to it! But some think it wasn't a rat at all that left the indent. They say it's more likely that a squirrel fell from a tree into the cement!

What do you think— did a rat or squirrel leave the hole? Share your thoughts...

REST IN PEACE!

Sadly, the Chicago rat hole was removed due to sidewalk damage in April 2024.

TIDY MOUSE ▶ Every night for over two months, a mouse entered Rodney Holbrook's tool shed in Wales and tidied up small items that had been left lying around. The mouse diligently moved objects such as nails, clothespins, and cable ties into a nearby tray.

NOISY FROG ▶ The western bell frog of Australia is also known as the motorbike frog because its mating call sounds like a motorbike changing up through the gears.

NUT CRACKER ▶ The South American agouti—a large rodent with very sharp teeth—is the only species that can open Brazil nuts without the help of tools.

MAGIC TRICKS ▶ Audriana Li, from Toronto, Canada, has taught her labradoodle dog Dobby to respond to *Harry Potter* spells as commands. She uses 15 spells from the *Harry Potter* books and films, including "expelliarmus" (for "drop it"), "wingardium leviosa" (for "jump up"), and "avada kedavra" (for "play dead").

UNIQUE NOSE A mountain gorilla's nose print is as unique as a human fingerprint. No two gorillas have the same nose print, with each animal having a different pattern of wrinkles above its nostrils.

BORDER BANK ▶ The intertwined towns of Baarle-Hertog in Belgium and Baarle-Nassau in the Netherlands have a bank built directly above the border between the two countries. This allowed paperwork to be moved from one side of the building to the other whenever either the Belgian or Dutch tax inspectors called.

can be found in Sudan as in neighboring Egypt! **SURINAME** ▶ Suriname is the only country outside of Europe where the majority of people speak Dutch.

PEE PANTS

These jeans were designed to look as though you've peed yourself! Jordanluca launched a line of "Stain Stonewash" jeans featuring large, dark stains across the front. The stains make it look like the wearer has a wet patch—and not by accident. They debuted in 2023 and made a serious splash. When made available online, the jeans sold out despite costing over $600 a pair!

FASHIONABLY WET!

CATHEDRAL OF JUNK

The Cathedral of Junk in Austin, Texas, is made from more than 60 tons of trash! Vince Hannemann started building the structure in his backyard in the late 1980s. Bike parts, crutches, TVs, toys, tools, signs, and baskets are just some of the items found in the Cathedral. It has multiple levels and rooms, including a special "Throne Room!" Vince often gives tours to visitors and has even hosted weddings in the Cathedral. It may be made of junk, but it is far from trashy!

BRIDGE BUNGEE ▶ Starting at 7 a.m. on October 10, 2023, Mike Heard bungee jumped off New Zealand's Auckland Harbour Bridge an amazing 941 times in 24 hours, averaging more than one jump every two minutes. Apart from an occasional sensation of motion sickness, he said he suffered no ill effects.

HARDY HAIR ▶ Ukrainian strongman Dmytro Hrunskyi pulled a 5,687-pound (2,580-kg) minibus with just his beard. He has also pulled a 17,107-pound (7,760-kg) truck with a rope attached to his neck, as well as a line of six cars and their drivers–a total weight of 16,763 pounds (7,604 kg)–with his teeth.

RESTROOM RAVE ▶ HOP convenience stores in Kentucky have transformed their bathrooms into discos. By pressing a button, customers activate flashing colored lights, a disco ball, and dance music. On Valentine's Day 2024, Tiana Ailstock and Logen Abney got married in the bathroom of the store in Verona.

WORLD WALK ▶ Since 2016, Vinod Bajaj has walked twice around the world without ever leaving Limerick, Ireland. Walking for up to seven hours and covering an average of 23 miles (37 km) per day, he has walked more than 51,500 miles (83,000 km), taking over 105 million steps. During that time, he has worn through 21 pairs of running shoes.

DOUBLY UNLUCKY While sitting outside his home in Zunyi, China, Liu Nan was struck by lightning twice in five minutes. He was knocked out both times but survived with third-degree burns to his waist and feet.

Ripley's Believe It or Not!

Vanishing ACT

With just some paint and a brush, UK-based artist Milly Bampini can make almost anything disappear!

One way she shows off her skills is by painting fruit to blend in seamlessly with her face. First, she attaches the food to a mount so it stays in place. Next, she puts her phone on a tripod with the front camera facing the fruit. Then, she sits behind the food and, using the camera like a mirror, keeps her head still as she paints the fruit to match her face. Milly finds it to be an exciting challenge, different from traditional art. Once, she held a balloon in her mouth for over an hour as she painted it to make it disappear!

It takes Milly about one hour to finish her paintings, but then her neck starts to hurt!

SPOT THE FRUIT!

SEA FOOD

Belgium-based baker Samantha Van de Sompel makes animals out of bread! Using her own recipe, Sam has baked bread spiders, snakes, and fish. Sharks are her favorite animals to bake. But not your typical shark! She's made wobbegong, epaulette, zebra, and basking sharks. To achieve their likeness, Sam must shape, color, and decorate the dough just right. The first bread animal she ever made was a "very flat" frog. Sam eats every loaf or gives it away!

YOU KNEAD TO TRY THIS!

COLOR CONDITION ▶ American singer and actress Olivia Rodrigo has a minor case of a neurological condition called synesthesia, where the sound of certain songs causes her to see different colors.

FOOD PHOBIA ▶ English film director Alfred Hitchcock—the "Master of Suspense," responsible for such horror classics as *Psycho* and *The Birds*—was frightened of eggs, a condition called ovophobia.

DOG ART ▶ In 2023, the Museo Tamayo in Mexico City staged an exhibition of modern art designed to appeal to dogs and their owners.

SUDDEN SPOT ▶ When it was time to come up with a fictional city as a setting for *Batman*, writer Bill Finger decided on a name after spotting "Gotham Jewelers" in a New York City phone book.

PANTS PROOF

A robbery suspect was identified by the brightly colored underpants he was wearing while raiding a New York City tobacco shop. Although he and his two accomplices were masked, his distinctive underwear was clearly visible above his low-slung pants.

SURPRISE BIRTH ▶ A woman from a town called Surprise in Arizona had no idea that she was pregnant until shortly before giving birth. Taylor Dobbins thought she had appendicitis, but it turned out to be labor pains.

BANANA HAMMERS ▶ Iron Factory Ikeda, based in Hiroshima, Japan, launched a range of steel hammers that look just like bananas. For added realism, the curved metal tools even have special banana hammer stickers.

SUSPICIOUS ATHLETE ▶ Daniel Fairbrother trained for the 2024 London Marathon by running through the streets of Stevenage, Hertfordshire, at night with a fridge on his back. On one training run, he was stopped by police officers who thought he was a thief making off with a stolen fridge.

the country's drought and banned the toy! **TAJIKISTAN** ▶ It is illegal to celebrate your birthday

THE Ripley's COLLECTION

TOAST TV

Artist Tadahiko Ogawa made this model television entirely from toasted slices of bread! The picture on the "screen" was made by masking and toasting each slice of bread in a common household toaster.

CATALOG NO. 13846

Toasted to perfection!

KNIFE-FORK COMBO

About 60,000 amputations were performed during the U.S. Civil War. This led to advances in prosthetics and mobility aids like this knife-fork combo, or "knork," made for people with the use of just one arm.

CATALOG NO. 12225

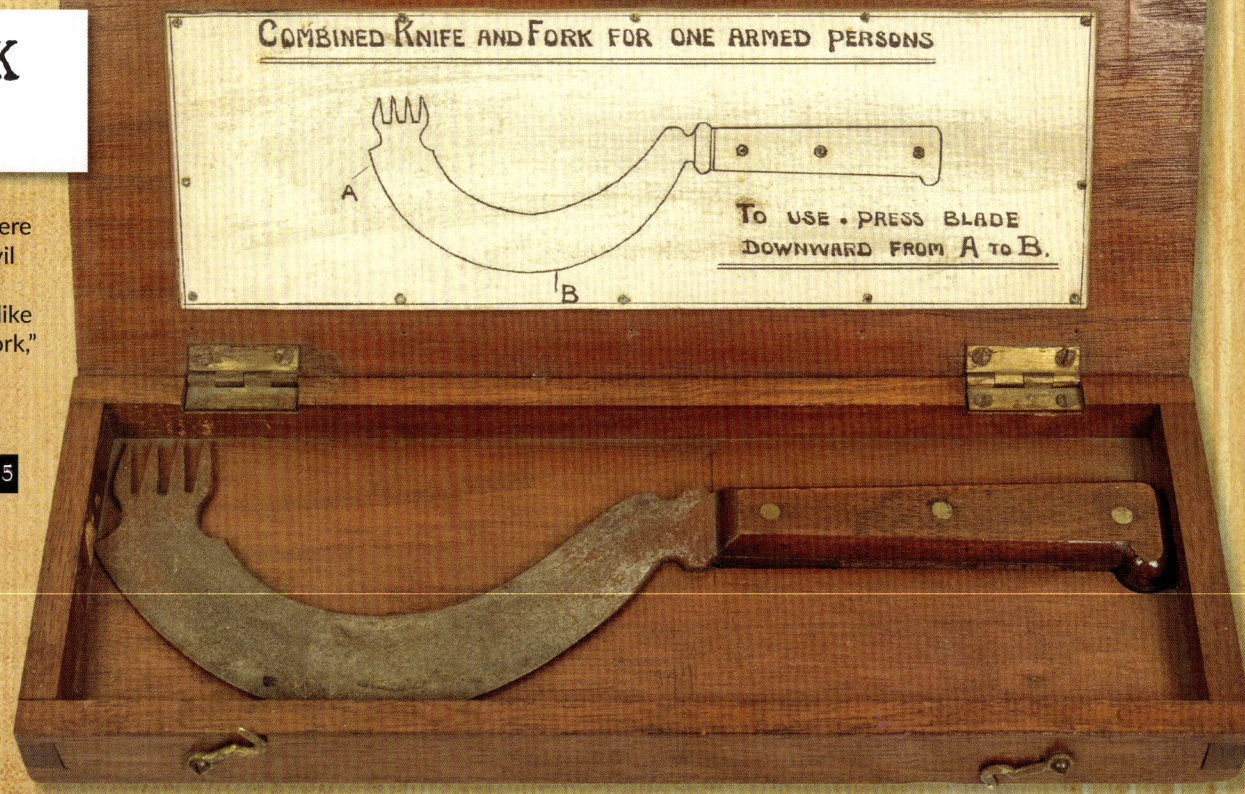

COMBINED KNIFE AND FORK FOR ONE ARMED PERSONS

TO USE · PRESS BLADE DOWNWARD FROM A TO B.

WRAPPER WORK

Created by Lyndon J. Barrois Sr. of New Orleans, Louisiana, each figure in this scene from Super Bowl XI was made from one foil gum wrapper! Lyndon also makes stop-motion films out of his gum wrapper sculptures.

CATALOG NO. 14282

Each player is one wrapper!

"OAKLAND'S GREATEST HITS"
Super Bowl XI
Oakland Raiders 32 · Minnesota Vikings 14
January 9, 1977 · The Rose Bowl · Pasadena, California

SEEK THE STRANGE   217

Ripley's Believe It or Not!

Whipped Up!

BOILED AND COOLED

PULLED AND STRETCHED

Chaku is a sweet treat that's literally whipped into shape!

Eating chaku is a favorite tradition during the Maghe Sankranti festival in Nepal. Chaku is made from a thick, dark syrup called molasses. The molasses is hardened by boiling it and then letting it cool. Once it cools, the molasses is nailed to a wooden post and then pulled back and forth. It's slapped, stretched, and whipped around and around until it's the right color! The sweet treat is popular during the winter festival because it makes your body feel warm after you eat it.

in public in Tajikistan. **TANZANIA** ▶ Lava from the Ol Doinyo Lengai volcano in Tanzania erupts black, then turns white! **THAILAND** ▶ Bird singing contests

SKYDIVER SUCCESS ▸ Sam Sieracki, from Singleton, Western Australia, solved a Rubik's Cube in 28.3 seconds while free-falling at 125 mph (200 kmph), after jumping out of an airplane at a height of 14,000 feet (4,270 m).

SHAVING STOP ▸ Erin Honeycutt, a 38-year-old woman from Michigan, has a 12-inch-long (30-cm) beard. She has been growing it for over two years. She has polycystic ovary syndrome, a condition that can cause hair to grow on women's faces. Before deciding to let her beard grow, she used to shave three times a day.

SERMON SEND-OFF ▸ Dr. Doris Nathaniel Benford Sr. was the pastor at the Rising Star Missionary Baptist Church in Texas City, Texas, for 72 years. He began preaching there in 1950 at age 20 and delivered his final sermon on Easter Sunday 2024.

DURABLE DRESS ▸ To learn more about sustainability, Leah Stamm, from Victoria, Australia, wore the same wool dress for 100 days straight.

BONE APPETIT

At a McDonald's in Rome, Italy, you can eat with 2,000-year-old skeletons! While building the restaurant in 2014, workers found a 150-foot-long (45-m) road underground! The street was built around 200 BC, and it is thought to be one of ancient Rome's busiest roads. The builders preserved the road and the skeletons they found. They made an underground museum for visitors to explore. In the dining area, you can see the old road and skeletons through the floor while you eat!

SENIOR SKIER ▸ In 2023, Katsumi Saeki of Japan competed in two 3.1-mile (5-km) cross-country skiing events at the Masters World Cup in Austria—at age 88. Although she was the only competitor in the over-85 age category, she recorded faster times than some of the skiers in lower age groups, including people 10 years younger.

FUNERAL FUNGI

Dutch company Loop Biotech makes coffins out of mushrooms! Named the Living Cocoon, this special coffin breaks down 45 days after being buried. It's made from hemp and mycelium, the part of mushrooms that grows underground. The coffins are made for people who want a natural, eco-friendly goodbye. They symbolize the endless cycle of life and death.

are common in Thailand. **TIMOR-LESTE** ▸ Around 600,000 people attended a mass led by Pope

BAMBOO BALANCE

Dancers in China perform on floating bamboo poles—without falling into the water!

This tradition is called "bamboo drifting." It started many centuries ago. People used to take bamboo poles that were too long to go on a boat and float them across the water one by one. Over time, the process turned into an art form. Dancers now take part in "water ballet" competitions. One or two dancers work together on a single stick to perform. The trick is to keep your balance while the narrow log moves in the water beneath you!

MUSIC IN THE MUNDANE

OFFBEAT MUSIC

Have you ever seen a broom used to make music? Zic Zazou is a group of nine people from France who make music using everyday things like garden hoses, hammers, and frying pans. Their shows are a mix of music, acting, comedy, and cool inventions. The group has been around for nearly 40 years. They hope to show that music is everywhere and can be found in anything!

SPACE SHOT ▶ French-made Shooting Star Vodka is infused with a meteorite. The addition of the space rock, which was discovered in 1977, gives the drink a special taste and texture, as well as a price tag of $200 a bottle.

DEATH CAVE ▶ Any small creature that enters the tiny Cueva de la Muerte in Costa Rica faces almost instant death because the cave is filled with pure carbon dioxide due to volcanic activity in the area. People are warned against entering the 6.5-foot-deep (2-m) cave, which is located on the edge of the active Poás Volcano, as it contains so little oxygen that not even a flame can burn there.

RAILS RUNAWAY ▶ A driverless, runaway freight train in India traveled 43 miles (70 km) at speeds of over 60 mph (96 kmph) before finally coming to a stop. The 53-car train stopped at Kathua to change crew but when the driver and his assistant left the train, it started to run away downhill. It sped uncontrolled through five stations before officials were able to slow it by placing wooden blocks on the track.

MULTI MURALS ▶ There are more than 4,000 public murals in Philadelphia, Pennsylvania, earning the city the title of the "Mural Capital of the World."

The dancers use poles to help them balance.

BIKE JOUSTING!

BIKE KILL

At Bike Kill in Brooklyn, New York, partygoers ride "mutant" bikes in front of hundreds of people. Some bikes are tall, some are short, and some have special features, such as a disco-ball wheel or a board for people to surf on! Bike Kill is held on the last Saturday in October. The tradition was started in 2003 by the Black Label Bike Club. The club's mechanics build bizarre bikes for the event to this day. The grand finale is a jousting competition on tall bikes—the last rider riding is the winner!

the Batammariba people of Togo always faces west. **TONGA** ▶ In the 1970s, the country of Tonga

SEEK THE STRANGE

RIPLEY'S Believe It or Not!

TOP of CLASS

Freshman year at the U.S. Naval Academy ends with an unusual tradition: climbing a 21-foot-tall (6.4-m), greased-up tower!

The goal is for the first-year students, called plebes, to reach the top of Herndon Monument. There, they must swap the freshman-style hat with an upperclassman's hat. This is no easy task. The tower is covered in about 200 pounds (91 kg) of slippery vegetable shortening. Plus, older students spray the climbers with water! The plebes must work together to succeed. It usually takes over two hours of falling and climbing to swap the hats!

GET A GRIP!

A HUMAN LADDER TO THE TOP!

issued an official stamp shaped like a banana. **TRINIDAD & TOBAGO** ▶ Instead of water, Pitch Lake in Trinidad and Tobago contains up to 10 million tons

HIGHER POWER

This climbing gym is in an old chapel in the heart of Paris, France! The Climbing District has 43-foot-high (13-m) climbing walls and 32 rope-climbing corridors. The 1800s chapel was also once the French National Institute of Intellectual Property library! Climbers can see the chapel's cool ceilings and the old library's bookshelves in a new way. Would you climb here?

COSTUME COMFORT ▸ To make an orphaned fox cub feel at home, staff at the Richmond Wildlife Center in Virginia wore red fox masks at feeding time. They also gave the cub a large stuffed toy fox to sleep with.

POTTY MOUTHED ▸ Lincolnshire Wildlife Park in England added a warning sign to an aviary of African gray parrots because the birds were swearing so much.

GOLFING GOALS ▸ Patrick Koenig, from Washington, played 580 different 18-hole golf courses in 2023. He visited 41 U.S. states and Finland, playing 10,440 holes at an average score of 77 per round.

SOCK PILE ▸ Arlene and Michael Okun began collecting sock monkeys in 2006 and now have more than 2,000 on display at their Sock Monkey Museum in Long Grove, Illinois.

KILLER CATS ▸ Domestic cats kill and eat more than 2,000 different species—mainly birds, insects, and rodents.

SURPRISE VISITOR ▸ Maureen Roberts of Kent, England, was surprised to see an emu peering into the lens of her doorbell camera. After escaping from a nearby home, the giant bird had wandered up to her front door and knocked on it with his beak.

SPRINGY STEP

The klipspringer is a small, hollow-horned antelope that walks on its tiptoes! It has strong back legs and stands about 2 feet (0.6 m) tall. Each hoof is about the size of a dime and gives the klipspringer the ability to jump onto a spot as small as a silver dollar! The rubbery centers of these tiny feet help the klipspringer grip rocky surfaces.

HOOVES OR HEELS?

of liquid asphalt. **TUNISIA** ▸ Star Wars™ creator George Lucas named the fictional planet of

SEEK THE STRANGE

THE RIPLEY'S COLLECTION

BOTTLE MAGIC

Artist Jeff Scanlan of Mesa, Arizona, can bottle up just about anything! He creates objects called "Impossible Bottles." This means he can fit items into glass bottles without changing the bottle or the item! Inspired by magician Harry Eng, Jeff spent over three years learning this tricky skill. He broke a lot of bottles and ruined many decks of cards along the way. Jeff has fit impossible objects into nearly 700 bottles! He's bottled things like golf balls, scissors, and padlocks. Each bottle can take up to 15 hours to finish.

IMPOSSIBLE BOTTLE RULES:
1. The glass must be an ordinary, unaltered bottle.
2. The bottle cannot be heated, cooled, cut, or changed in any way.
3. The item must enter the glass through the bottle's neck.
4. Once inside, the item must still be usable.

DEAL WITH IT

An entire deck of cards hangs from a piece of twine inside this wine bottle. The twine itself is knotted through a wooden ball on top of the bottle's neck. Jeff cut out a square in the deck's case so you can see all of the cards inside!

CATALOG NO. 176128

A full deck of cards!

HIGH-TOP HIJINKS

Somehow, Jeff managed to fit an entire pair of Converse high-top shoes and a tennis ball into this glass gallon jug! The feat was inspired by a piece by impossible bottle master Harry Eng.

CATALOG NO. 176123

How did that get in there?!

What's your unique way to pass the time?

Share your thoughts...

SUPERMAN 3D DECK

Jeff also carves playing cards into 3D art. He cuts each card by hand. He removes different parts from each one. When all the cards are stacked, the layers create a detailed, 3D work of art. This deck is made from a Superman-themed set of cards.

CATALOG NO. 176132

SEEK THE STRANGE

Cookie CANVAS

Baker Lucie Radcliffe Steele turns cookies into realistic portraits!

Her baked goods look like celebrities, TV characters, and cartoons. Some have looked like Dwayne "The Rock" Johnson, Taylor Swift, and Billie Eilish! Lucie decorates the cookies with edible gel and royal icing. To make each face, she shines a photo onto a cookie with a projector. She uses the image as a guide as she paints. Tiny details are added with a fine-tipped paintbrush. It can take Lucie anywhere from a few minutes to a few hours to paint one cookie!

EACH COOKIE IS A WORK OF ART!

Lucie and her children.

CROC CHARGE ▶ Falmira de Jesus, a farm worker in Indonesia, miraculously survived a crocodile attack. She was collecting water from a weed-covered stream when the croc grabbed her by the leg and dragged her into the swamp. Her coworkers extended wooden poles for her to escape, but the croc held on for over an hour and a half. Falmira was treated for deep puncture wounds to her arms and legs.

BACKUP BRAINS ▶ Leeches have 300 teeth, two hearts, 10 stomachs, and 32 brains. The leech's interior body is divided into 32 different segments, each with its own brain.

CHARTWELL CAT ▶ When the Churchill family gave Chartwell, their family home in Kent, England, to the National Trust, they requested that there should always be "in comfortable residence a marmalade cat named Jock, with a white bib and four white socks" in honor of Sir Winston Churchill's cat. The current Chartwell resident is Jock VII.

PORTRAIT PROJECT ▶ In 2013, artist Grahame Hurd-Wood started painting individual portraits of every person living in the UK's smallest city—St. Davids in Pembrokeshire, Wales. There are about 1,750 residents, and by 2023 he had painted more than 1,000 of them.

MEGA MOUTH ▶ An anaconda can open its mouth up to three times bigger than its head. This enables the snake to snatch and swallow wild pigs and deer.

UNDERWATER WONDER ▶ Beavers can hold their breath underwater for 15 minutes—about 30 times longer than the average human. Beavers also have transparent third eyelids that protect their eyes while they are swimming underwater.

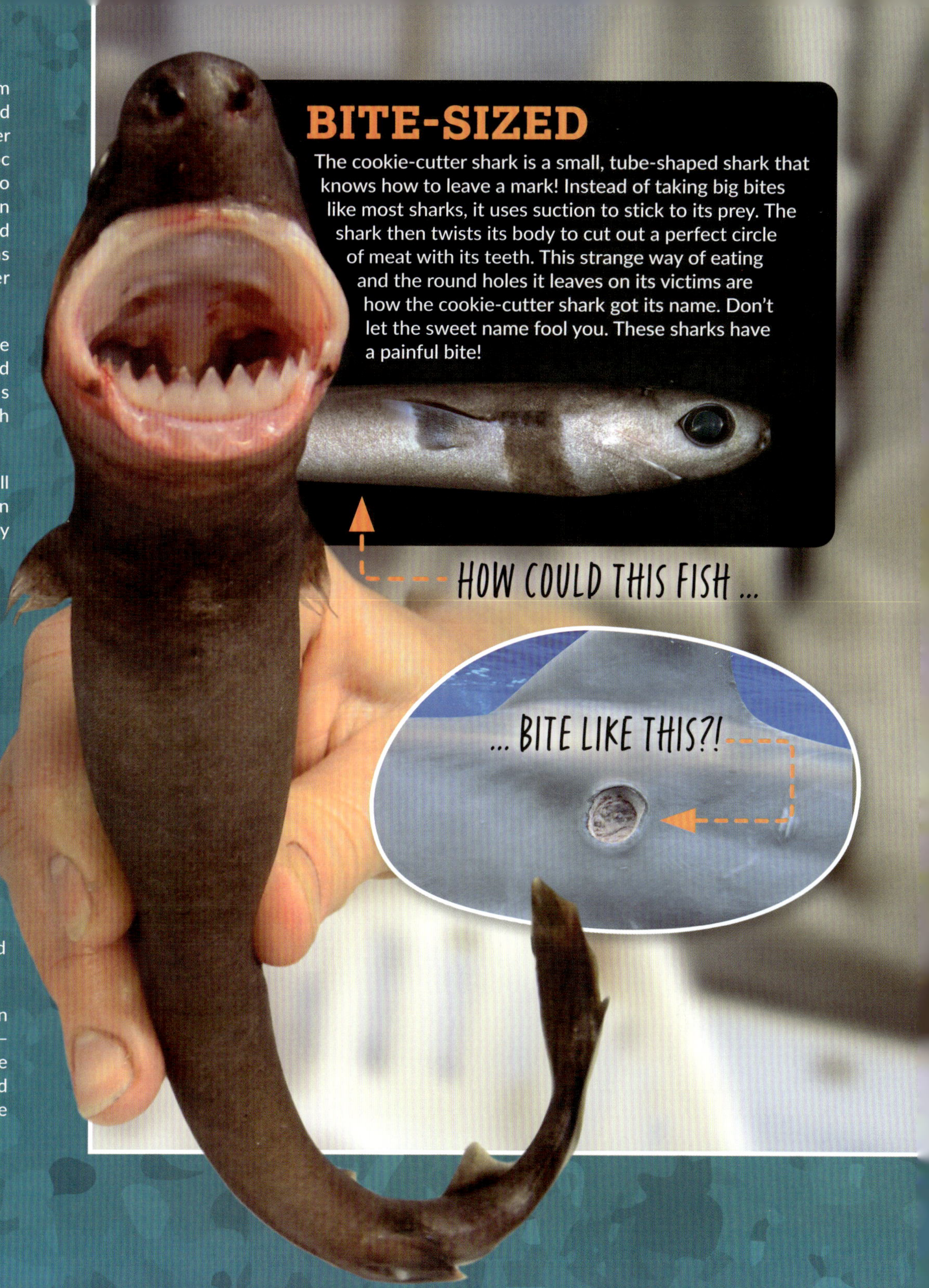

BITE-SIZED

The cookie-cutter shark is a small, tube-shaped shark that knows how to leave a mark! Instead of taking big bites like most sharks, it uses suction to stick to its prey. The shark then twists its body to cut out a perfect circle of meat with its teeth. This strange way of eating and the round holes it leaves on its victims are how the cookie-cutter shark got its name. Don't let the sweet name fool you. These sharks have a painful bite!

HOW COULD THIS FISH ...

... BITE LIKE THIS?!

FIN-TASTIC FACTS

- Sharks can detect the electrical fields of prey—even fish hidden beneath the sand!
- Swell sharks fend off predators by swallowing enough water to swell up to twice their normal size.
- Sharks can move both their bottom and upper jaws, unlike humans, who can only move their bottom jaw!
- Some sharks will force their stomachs out of their mouths to get rid of stuff they can't digest.
- In 2022, scientists witnessed a tiger shark vomit up a whole echidna—a spiky, land-based mammal.
- Frilled sharks can be pregnant for up to 3.5 years before giving birth.
-  Up to 30 percent of a shark's weight can be just its liver.
-  Sharks have been around since before trees, the Atlantic Ocean, and even Saturn's rings ever existed.
- Some shark species must keep swimming to breathe—even while sleeping!

in Turkey. **TURKMENISTAN** ▶ The Darvaza gas crater, a.k.a. the Door to Hell, is a 230-foot-wide

SEEK THE STRANGE

Crystal CAVERN

Painshill Crystal Grotto in Surrey, England, is a man-made cave lined with thousands of crystals!

It was built in the eighteenth century by grotto maker Joseph Lane. He used thousands of crystals to cover the cave! Crystals line the walls and even cover the stalactites hanging from the ceiling. Light bounces off the crystals on sunny days, making the place shimmer and reflect off the water that runs through the middle. The cave has winding paths, so every view is different!

COUNTLESS CARDS ▸ The United States Playing Card Company produces over 100 million decks—more than five billion individual cards—each year. Las Vegas alone uses about 27 million decks of cards in a year.

CHOPPED CHURCH ▸ A private road runs right through the middle of a church in Gmünd, Austria. It is called the Divided Church because it is split in two. On one side is the chancel from where the priest delivers a sermon to the congregation who are seated in a gallery on the other side of the road. If a vehicle is seen approaching during the service, the priest pauses the sermon and waits until it has passed.

BEARD BAN ▸ If they want to grow a beard, male students and faculty members at Brigham Young University in Provo, Utah, must first provide a doctor's note stating that shaving is harmful to them.

DEAD DENTURES

In the early nineteenth century, dentures were usually made from the teeth of dead soldiers. They were known as "Waterloo teeth" because many were from the mouths of soldiers who had fought in the Battle of Waterloo in 1815. The extracted teeth were then crafted into dentures for customers.

FRIED FISH ▸ A large area of Sayreville, New Jersey, was left without power for two hours on August 12, 2023, after a fish landed on a transformer, causing it to explode. Officials believe it was dropped by a bird.

LOW GRAVITY ▸ Possibly due to an ice sheet melting 20,000 years ago, an area in the Hudson Bay region of Canada has less gravity than the rest of the planet. It means that the average person weighs about 0.1 ounces (2.8 g) less there than they would anywhere else in the world.

WRITING ROOM ▸ Room 411 at the Pera Palace Hotel in Istanbul, Turkey, is maintained in the style of the 1930s because it is believed to be where British crime writer Agatha Christie wrote her most famous novel, *Murder on the Orient Express*. The Agatha Christie Room still has furniture from that period and a replica of her old typewriter.

(70-m) hole in the desert of Turkmenistan that has been on fire for over 50 years! **TUVALU** ▸ The small island nation of Tuvalu is one of the world's

STALACTITES COVERED IN CRYSTALS

SEEING CLEARLY

Some jumping spiders, like the magnolia green jumper, are so see-through that you can actually watch their eyes move! Their retinas shift around as they follow things, almost like they've got little googly eyes. It's because they're so transparent that we get to see this rare movement. It might look funny, but these wiggly eyes help them spot prey and avoid danger. Watching them up close gives you a glimpse into how they see the world!

least-visited countries, with just a few flights in and out of its international airport per week.

SEEK THE STRANGE

Picking UP SLACK

LESS THAN 1 INCH (2.5 CM) WIDE!

MORE THAN 330 FEET (100 M) HIGH!

On July 10, 2024, Estonian Jaan Roose walked from mainland Italy to the island of Sicily on a 2.27-mile-long (3.6-km) slackline!

The feat made him the first person to cross the Strait of Messina on foot. Hanging more than 330 feet (100 m) above the water, the line Jaan walked was less than 1 inch (2.5 cm) wide! Winds over 20 mph (32 kmph) threatened to knock him off. He fell only once, near the end, but still finished strong. It took Jaan just under three hours to complete this amazing journey. The breathtaking feat showcased incredible skill, endurance, and courage.

DIG DEEPER
Is this long, scaly creature a snake? A worm? Neither—it's a Mexican mole lizard! This two-legged reptile is found in Mexico and lives underground (that's where the "mole" part of its name comes from). It's also known as a worm lizard thanks to its round, pink body and long tail. But unlike worms, it has two front limbs with claws that help it dig into the soil. An old legend says this lizard attacks people while they are going to the bathroom outside! Luckily, this is totally untrue. It is harmless to humans!

SHARED CELEBRATION ▶ Emma Smith and her partner Dave Mycock of England have three sons who were all born on June 20 in different years, beating odds of 133,000 to 1. Alfie was born in 2016, Jesse in 2019, and Arley in 2023.

SMALL SHOES ▶ When Meesh Davignon adopted Nubz the chicken, who had lost most of his toes due to scaly leg mites, she fitted him with a pair of tiny dog slippers. After she posted a video on TikTok of Nubz learning to walk in the slippers, viewers responded by sending him more than 60 pairs of tiny shoes, including bright-yellow sandals and purple crocs.

SCI-FI SUPERFAN
Mike Kaye from California has more than 10,500 items of Transformers memorabilia. His interest in the robots in disguise began when he was a young boy in 1984 and his collection is now worth over $300,000.

AMAZING ACE ▶ In his 17-year professional career, U.S. tennis player John Isner served 14,470 aces. He averaged almost 19 aces per match.

DONATED DOMINOES ▶ On October 12, 2023, 12,952 cereal boxes were toppled like dominoes on a basketball court in Detroit, Michigan. Afterward the boxes were donated to local food banks.

IMPULSIVE IDEA ▶ Rather than pay for a short taxi ride home, a 43-year-old Australian stowed away beneath a semitruck hauling two trailers and ended up traveling 210 miles (340 km) out of his way from Nambucca Heads, New South Wales, to Coomera, Queensland. He had planned to jump off 30 miles (50 km) into the journey at a red light near Coffs Harbour, but the truck didn't stop. He was lucky to survive after riding for four hours precariously perched on metal racks just 3 feet (0.9 m) above the road.

LUCKY LANDING ▶ Agnus, a 3-foot-long (0.9-m) female corn snake who had been missing for over a year from her home in County Durham, England, was found alive after being dropped onto a nearby garage roof by a crow.

COYOTE CALAMITY ▶ A coyote was rescued near Oconomowoc, Wisconsin, after getting her head stuck inside a hollow statue, probably while chasing a rabbit. The figure was of St. Francis of Assisi, the patron saint of animals!

SEA SEDIMENT ▶ The sea off the coast of Somerset, England, turned bright pink in April 2024. It was caused by severe storm waves that crashed ashore and churned up the sediment from the area's red mudstone cliffs.

DESK DOZE ▶ *Inemuri* is the Japanese art of sleeping at work. Sleeping in the office is commonplace in Japan and is deemed acceptable because it demonstrates how hard the person has been working.

BRANCHING OUT
Does the walking palm tree actually walk? Not quite! Also called the cashapona, the walking palm tree is native to tropical rainforests in Central and South America. For many years, people believed it could "walk" through the forest in search of sunlight. Unlike other plants, the roots of this tree grow several feet above ground level. While old roots can die and new roots grow, the tree doesn't actually move. The new roots grow in different directions for better sunlight or soil, but the trunk stays in one place!

site of the 1986 Chernobyl nuclear disaster in Ukraine because they absorb radioactive material

RIPLEY'S *Believe It or Not!*®

WOVEN WALLS

OVER 2,000 FEET (610 M) OF YARN!

Portuguese street artist Ana Martins creates graffiti out of wool instead of spray paint!

Ana, a.k.a. Aheneah, weaves colorful pieces by wrapping yarn around screws and nails. Her art spans from simple cross-stitches to more complex designs. She was inspired by her grandmother, who taught her embroidery. Ana combines the traditional art form with modern techniques. Before putting her art on the wall, she first plans the design on a computer. To create her piece called Switch-over, Ana used nearly 2,300 feet (700 m) of wool and over 2,300 screws!

COZY CRAFT MEETS STREET ART

through their roots. **UNITED ARAB EMIRATES** ▸ At the 2,717-foot-high (828-m) Burj Khalifa tower in Dubai, United Arab Emirates, visitors can watch the

CAT BURGLAR

Meet Taboo, a real-life cat burglar! This sly feline loves to swipe socks, shoes, and even underwear from her unsuspecting neighbors in West Yorkshire, England. She takes clothes that are hanging out to dry and sneaks into houses. She's even stolen a carton of eggs! Taboo's owner, Sandra, often comes home to find Taboo's prizes in the driveway and inside the house. She tries to return the items to their rightful owners. Taboo is so sneaky that she's rarely caught in the act!

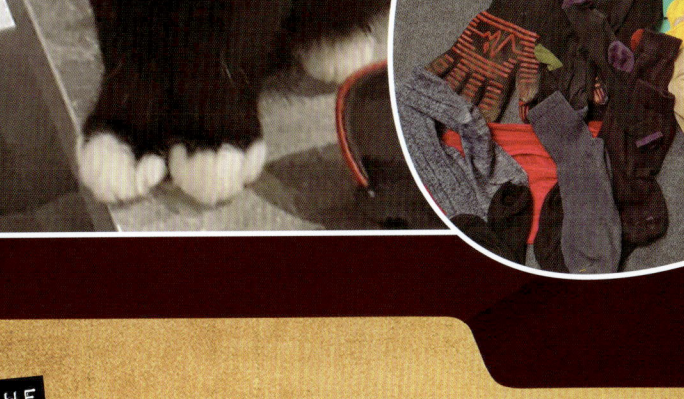

HAUNTED PAINTING ▸ *The Hands Resist Him*, a 1972 painting by American artist Bill Stoneham, is said to be haunted. It depicts a young boy—Stoneham himself—standing next to a lifelike doll in a doorway. People have claimed that just looking at the painting made them feel ill. Others have alleged that the figures move and even leave the artwork at night.

COMICAL CHASE ▸ For safety reasons, actor Steve McQueen's spectacular motorbike jump over a wire fence in the 1963 World War II movie *The Great Escape* had to be performed by a stunt double. But McQueen, who was a keen biker, was allowed to ride as one of the pursuing German soldiers. On screen, he was chasing himself!

COOP CANVAS ▸ In 1889, shortly after cutting off part of his own ear, Vincent van Gogh presented his doctor, Félix Rey, with a portrait as a gift for treating him. Dr. Rey disliked the painting and gave it to his mother, who used it to block a hole in her chicken coop for more than a decade. Today, the painting *Portrait of Doctor Rey* is worth over $50 million.

MISLABELED MASTERPIECE ▸ At an auction in Tahiti, French artist Paul Gauguin's 1894 painting *Breton Village under the Snow* was accidentally showcased upside down and mislabeled as *Niagara Falls*. It was only when Victor Segalen, a friend of the artist, purchased it cheaply and turned it the right way up that it became clear that the picture showed Brittany cottages and not cascading water.

THE RIPLEY'S COLLECTION

HOLY SHOES

Nike Air Max 97 shoes modified by design studio MSCHF. Dubbed the "Jesus Shoes," their soles are filled with water from the Jordan River that was blessed by a priest. MSCHF made the shoes as a statement on "absurd collab culture."

CATALOG NO. 175895

Walking on water?

SEEK THE STRANGE

RIPLEY'S Believe It or Not!®

FLIES HELP SPREAD THE FUNGUS'S SPORES!

BUSTING OUT

The devil's fingers fungus looks like alien tentacles bursting out of an egg!

This mushroom is not only strange-looking but also stinky and slimy. Sometimes called the octopus stinkhorn, it lives underground until it is time to spread its spores. At that point, it "hatches" from an egg-like casing and oozes black goo. The goo smells like rotting flesh! The odor attracts insects like flies, which help spread the fungus's spores.

What would you name this bizarre fungus? Share your thoughts...

the top of the building. **UNITED KINGDOM** ▶ The Great Vine of Hampton Court Palace in the UK's capital of London, England, was planted in 1768 but still

ROCK BLOCK

The people of Setenil de las Bodegas live under a rock—literally! The village was built into the cliffs of Spain's Andalusia region. A giant rock hangs over shops lining the town's main street. In some places, there are buildings both above and below the same stone ledge. In other areas, there are narrow alleys where the view of the sky is blocked by rock.

BUG BEVERAGE ▶ Something Wild, a food company in Adelaide, Australia, created Green Ant Gin, a gin infused with green ants to give it a citrus flavor. A handful of ants float in every bottle.

PILES OF PAINT ▶ About 1.6 million gallons (6 million liters) of white and yellow paint are used every year to paint road markings along the 70,000 miles (112,600 km) of highways in Texas.

ENCIRCLED TOWN ▶ The Italian town of Campione d'Italia is surrounded entirely by Switzerland. When the region of Ticino decided to become part of the Swiss Confederation in 1798, the people of Campione chose to remain part of Lombardy, now a region of modern-day Italy. The town's firefighters and ambulances are provided by Switzerland, but the police are Italian.

BIG BLUEBERRY ▶ In 2023, a farm in Corindi, Australia, grew a blueberry the size of a golf ball. It measured 1.6 inches (4 cm) in diameter and weighed 0.7 ounces (20.4 g), making it about ten times heavier than the average blueberry.

SLIPPERY SHIP ▶ When the cargo ship USS *Cape Lookout* was launched in Beaumont, Texas, in 1941, 3.5 tons of rotting bananas were smeared over the vessel as a lubricant to help it slide out of dry dock and into the Neches River. The fruit was chosen because it was cheaper than the 95 tons of grease that would have been needed to launch the 7,400-ton, 319-foot-long (119-m) ship.

DUMPSTER DIVER ▶ Jennifer Lleras of Baltimore, Maryland, has found $2 million worth of unwanted items by dumpster diving for more than 20 years. Among the discarded items she has recovered have been jewelry, designer handbags, expensive cookware, kitchen gadgets, and a $500 hair dryer.

MUD MAKEOVER

Every spring, the people of Djenné, Mali, gather to cover the world's largest mud-brick building with a fresh coat of mud.

The tradition helps repair and protect the Great Mosque of Djenné from rain and wind damage. Locals collect mud from nearby rivers and mix it with water and rice husks to make a strong plaster called banco. Everyone is split into teams and given a section to replaster. Men, women, and children work together, climbing wooden ladders to spread fresh mud on the 52-foot-tall (16-m) walls. The team that finishes their section first wins a prize!

on the Great Seal of the United States since 1782, the bald eagle didn't become the country's national bird until December 2024—nearly 250 years later.

CLEVER CRIMINAL ▶ A thief in Warsaw, Poland, posed as a shop window mannequin and then waited until the store had closed for the day before stealing jewelry. He had been seen holding a bag in the store window, but staff and passersby failed to notice anything unusual because he stood perfectly still and blended in with the real mannequins.

VINTAGE VACUUM ▶ Mary and Ivor Waite from England clean and polish the floors of their home with a 100-year-old, German-built vacuum cleaner. The multi-purpose Piccolo, which was produced in 1925, was given to the couple by Ivor's aunt as a wedding present in 1976 and has never broken down.

SLAPPY SERVICE ▶ At the Shachihoko-ya izakaya bar in Nagoya, Japan, customers can pay $2 to be slapped around the face by a kimono-dressed waitress before being served. When the bizarre offer of "snacks with smacks" was first introduced, it led to a big boost in business.

TERRIBLE TIMING
A woman tried to flee through the self-checkout at a Walmart store in Genoa Township, Michigan, with more than $700 of merchandise in her coat—at the same time as the store was hosting a "Shop With a Cop" event and 75 police officers were present. She was swiftly arrested in the parking lot where she had parked her vehicle next to a row of police patrol cars.

STOMACH SURGERY ▶ When Kuldeep Singh went to a hospital in Punjab, India, complaining of having suffered stomach pains for two years, doctors performed a three-hour surgery to retrieve 60 household items from his stomach. He had swallowed things such as lockets, chains, nuts and bolts, zippers, shirt buttons, magnets, safety pins, and earphones.

SONG SPARK ▶ Led Zeppelin's rock classic "Black Dog" got its title after a black Labrador retriever wandered into the studio where the band were recording their album.

REAL CYBORG ▶ Anastasia Synn, from California, has over 50 technological implants inside her body. These include a magnetic implant in her ear that allows her to hear inside her head with the help of a Bluetooth receiver. Many of her implants are microchips, enabling her to open locks, turn on computers, and make phone calls remotely. An implant in her left wrist calls her daughter's phone and one in her right wrist calls her husband's phone.

CUTTING THROUGH THE WIND!

GLASS DASH

Dromeas is a giant sculpture in Athens, Greece, made entirely of glass! Also known as "The Runner," the figure is made of thousands of jagged sheets of glass stacked on top of each other to form the blurry shape of a runner. Created by Greek artist Costas Varotsos, it took six years to build and stands nearly 40 feet (12 m) tall! During the day, it reflects sunlight in a dazzling display of an endless dash. As the sun sets and the city lights come on, *Dromeas* turns into a ghostly, glowing beacon that races against time.

URUGUAY ▶ Cattle outnumber humans nearly 4-to-1 in Uruguay! **UZBEKISTAN** ▶ Uzbekistan is

RIPLEY'S Believe It or Not!®

HIGH NOTE

Singer Louis Cardozo played a piano while flying through the air!

The stunt was orchestrated for a music video. Louis removed some of a piano's insides to make it lighter. Connected to a paragliding wing, the piano and Louis were pushed off a windy hill to get them in the air. It took eight tries to film the music video. Some attempts ended in crash landings! But Louis was okay, and the result is jaw-dropping.

IT'S A BIRD! IT'S A PLANE!

IT'S A... PIANO?

"doubly landlocked," meaning it is surrounded by countries that are also landlocked. **VANUATU** ▶ The island nation of Vanuatu has both an underwater

FIT AS A FIDDLE

Fitness trainer Mateo Drottz puts a classical spin on spin classes! The twist? While the people in his Henderson, Nevada, class work up a sweat on indoor bikes, he plays the violin! Most spin classes are set to loud, fast songs. Mateo's violin adds a calm touch to the intense workout. But his mashup of music and fitness isn't just about playing violin or getting six-pack abs. It's about building confidence and community!

THE Ripley's COLLECTION

KITTY CARICATURE

Artist Kevin Champeny made this Taylor Swift portrait out of tiny cat sculptures! He carved the cat shape, then made thousands of copies in different shades of black, white, gray, and silver. He used more than 7,000 to create the image, placing each cat by hand!

CATALOG NO. 175903

Thousands of cats!

post office and a postal outlet near the rim of an active volcano! **VATICAN CITY** ▶ Governed by

SEEK THE STRANGE

RIPLEY'S Believe It or Not!

STRANDED SAILOR ▸ Australian sailor Tim Shaddock and his dog Bella survived for two months at sea by eating raw fish and drinking rainwater. In April 2023, they set off from Mexico on a 3,728-mile (6,000-km) voyage to French Polynesia but their boat was badly damaged in a storm, leaving them drifting in the North Pacific. Eventually, they were spotted by a helicopter whose pilot alerted a trawler to rescue them.

AVALANCHE ACCELERATION ▸ A large avalanche can weigh up to one million tons and can cascade down a mountain at speeds of more than 200 mph (320 kmph).

FALLS SHORT ▸ The Niagara Falls is not even among the top 40 highest waterfalls in Canada. The James Bruce Falls in British Columbia is 2,760 feet (840 m) tall, making it 16 times higher than the Niagara Falls.

PLENTIFUL PRODUCTS Lloyd Groff Copeman, grandfather of American singer Linda Ronstadt, was a prolific inventor. He had nearly 700 patents to his name, including an electric toaster with automatic bread turner, the first heat-regulated stove, and the first flexible rubber ice cube tray. Sales from his ice cube trays earned him about $500,000, equivalent to about $10 million today.

ICE INVASION ▸ Taking advantage of an exceptionally cold winter, Sweden invaded Denmark in 1658 by marching across the frozen sea that separates the two countries. Swedish King Charles X Gustav waited until the end of January when the ice was thick enough to support the weight of his troops. Then, 9,000 cavalry men and their horses, plus 3,000 foot soldiers and their equipment, marched more than 50 miles (80 km) across the ice to surprise the Danes.

LONG-STANDING LETTER ▸ Every day from 1899 to 1918, the Paris Herald newspaper (the Paris edition of the New York Herald) published the same letter from "Old Philadelphia Lady" asking how to convert centigrade (Celsius) to Fahrenheit and vice versa. The newspaper's owner, James Gordon Bennett, ordered the letter to appear in the same place in the paper every day. This went on for 18 years and five months, and it was published 6,718 times in total.

SPEEDY SERVICE

In March 2024, hundreds of servers took to the streets of Paris, France, in a race to reach the finish line—without dropping anything from their trays! Unlike most races, there was no running during the 1.2-mile-long (2-km) Course des Cafés. Balance was more important than speed. Each server had to carry a tray with a glass of water, coffee cup, and croissant on just one hand. No drops or spills allowed! The Course des Cafés dates back to 1914 and was revived ahead of the Paris 2024 Olympic Games to highlight excellent French service.

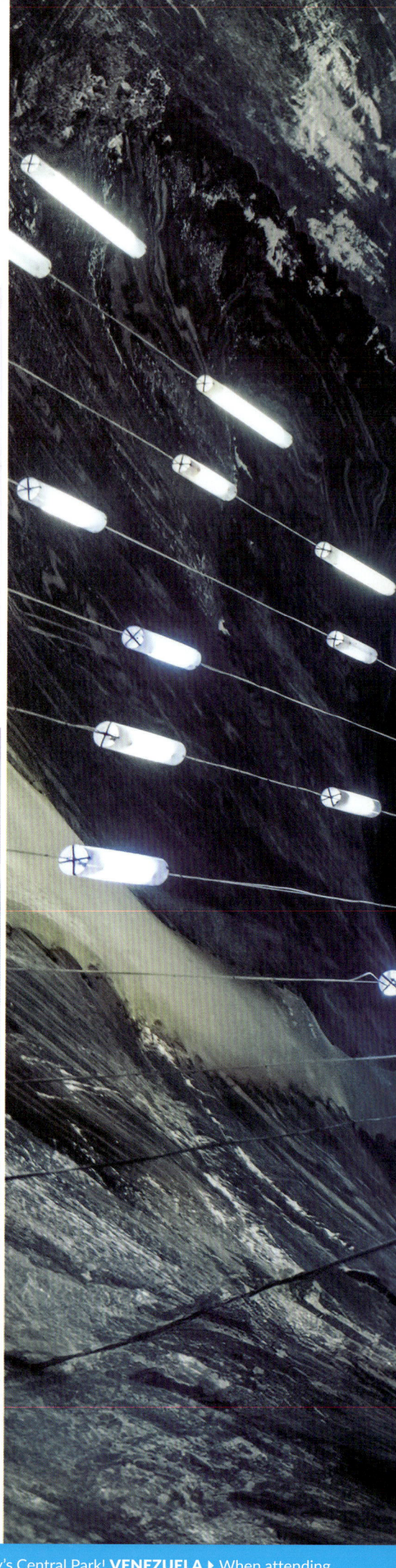

the Holy See and ruled by the Pope, Vatican City is the world's smallest country—smaller than New York City's Central Park! **VENEZUELA** ▸ When attending

LET'S GET DOWN AND HAVE SOME FUN!

UNDERGROUND
playground

Descend 400 feet (122 m) below Earth's surface to Salina Turda, an underground playground!

At more than 2,000 years old, Salina Turda in Romania is one of the earliest known salt mines. Now, it's a theme park! Visitors can ride a full-size Ferris wheel, play mini-golf, bowl, and even row a boat on an underground lake! The huge cavern was made as more than three billion tons of salt were dug out over time. You can ride an elevator to reach the bottom or, if you want a workout, take the stairs!

Christmas mass in December, many residents of Caracas, Venezuela, arrive on roller skates!

SEEK THE STRANGE

Ripley's Believe It or Not!®

Horn to be Wild

From towering spirals to thornlike spikes, the animal kingdom has a wild variety of horns. They are used for things like defense, communication, and even temperature control! Each creature's horns are adapted to fit its lifestyle, resulting in some impressive and quirky designs. Here is some of nature's neatest headgear!

GREATER KUDU

The greater kudu has horns that twist like a curly fry and can grow almost 6 feet (1.8 m) long. This African species has the longest horns of any antelope. They take six years to grow, twisting into perfect spirals. And when it's time for a showdown? Male kudus lock horns and wrestle, using their fancy headgear to see who's boss.

NUBIAN IBEX

The Nubian ibex is a master mountain climber, hopping around the rocky deserts of Africa and the Middle East like it's no big deal. But what really stands out are their horns. The males sport massive, backward-curving horns that can grow up to 4 feet (1.2 m) long! They use these impressive horns to show off for the ladies and to defend their turf.

LONG-NOSED HORNED FROG

The long-nosed horned frog is one sneaky amphibian. With pointed "horns" above its eyes and a body that looks like a dried-up leaf, this frog is a master of camouflage. Found in the rainforests of Southeast Asia, it blends perfectly into the forest floor, making it nearly invisible to predators—and to you, unless you have a really good eye!

VIETNAM ▸ The Hang Son Doong cave in Vietnam is so big a jumbo jet could fly through it. **YEMEN ▸** A popular sport in the Tihama region of Yemen is

JACKSON'S CHAMELEON

With three horns on their head, male Jackson's chameleons are like the triceratops of the modern world—only much smaller. Native to East Africa, these tiny but mighty chameleons use their horns to battle for territory. The males lock horns and try to push each other off branches in a lizard version of a sumo match.

ANKOLE-WATUSI COW

The Ankole-Watusi cow's massive horns aren't just for show—they're for keeping cool. The breed is a mix of two types of cattle from Africa. Blood circulates through the horns, where it is cooled before returning to the body. So, while the cow struts around in the heat, its horns act like built-in air conditioning!

RACKA SHEEP

The Racka sheep from Hungary has corkscrew-shaped horns that spiral straight out from the top of its head. Both males and females sport these impressive horns, which can grow over 2 feet (0.6 m) long! The color of the horns matches the sheep's wool, with light-colored sheep having yellowish horns, while dark-fleeced sheep show off black horns.

THORN BUG

If you're ever in South America and spot a thorn on a tree moving, don't freak out—it might just be a thorn bug! These little guys look exactly like the sharp thorns of a plant, all thanks to the pointy "horn" on their back. This clever disguise keeps birds and other predators from snacking on them.

Ripley's Believe It or Not!

IT'S A SPLASH!

BUMP, SET, SPLASH!

Volleyball is usually played on an indoor court or a sandy beach, but how about on a floating and flooded platform? That's what players do at the International Volleyball on Water tournament! First held in 2023, the games take place on Slovenia's Ljubljanica river. The court sits 6 inches (15 cm) below the surface. Some matches are even played at night! In the dark, the submerged court is lit up with colorful LEDs. Instead of stands, fans cheer from bridges and riverbanks!

Lights OUT!

Cosmic Baseball takes place on a baseball field like any other, but it's played in the dark under black lights!

Once the sun goes down, the black lights come on and everything glows in the dark—including the bats, balls, bases, and uniforms. The new twist on the classic sport debuted in the summer of 2024. The Tri-City Chili Peppers, a college team from Virginia, were the first team to try Cosmic Baseball. The players wore hot pink and neon green uniforms to stand out under the ultraviolet lights. Tickets to the first game sold out in 24 hours!

ZAMBIA ▶ In November, when lured by the ripe fruit of a nearby mango tree, herds of elephants regularly walk through the lobby of Mfuwe Lodge hotel

MOUSE HOUSE

Some of the tennis balls used during the Wimbledon Championships get turned into tiny homes for mice! With a body less than 3 inches (7.6 cm) long, the Eurasian harvest mouse is Europe's smallest rodent. Damage to its natural habitat has left the tiny critter in need of protection. The answer? Tennis balls! A small hole is carved into each ball, which are then mounted up to 5 feet (1.5 m) high on a pole. Mice make their nests inside the tennis balls, keeping them safe from predators like birds or weasels!

More than 50,000 tennis balls are used in the Wimbledon Championships each year!

CUTE AND COZY!

GLOW FOR THE FENCES!

EVEN THE BATS AND BALLS ARE GLOWING!

in Zambia. **ZIMBABWE** ▶ One of Zimbabwe's Premier Soccer League teams is named Chicken Inn.

SEEK THE STRANGE

Index

A
A to Zoo, 210
Abney, Logen, 213
AC/DC, 126
Acton, Pat, 110
Adams, Thomas, 187
age
  1,700-year-old chicken egg, 107
  18-month-old hosts art exhibition, 139
  3,000-year-old yareta plant, 185
  4,000-year-old lipstick, 157
  competing in Masters World Cup skiing aged 88, 219
  driving trucks aged 90, 42
  first U.S. president to reach 100 years old, 205
  French president age requirement, 84
  grannies who rap, 79
  professional gamer aged six, 130
  oldest botanical garden in Western Hemisphere, 189–190
  oldest known wooden wheel, 202
  oldest olive tree, 173–174
  oldest trees in California, 144
  population of Burkina Faso is one of youngest in world, 41–42
  South Sudan is world's youngest country, 209–210
  teenage town crier, 47
  vacuum cleaner still working after 100 years, 237
Agostini, Barbi, 171
Aheneah, 232
Ailstock, Tiana, 213
airplanes and air travel. *See transportation*
aliens, 121, 136, 234
Amazon rainforest, 20, 178
amphibians. *See reptiles and amphibians*
amphitheaters, 160, 161
Anderson, Robert, 147
Anderson, Steve, 136
animals. *See also aquatic life, birds, cats, dogs, insects, reptiles and amphibians, rodents*
  aardwolf termite diet, 18
  adopt-a-goat program, 15
  Ankole-Watusi cow horns, 243
  bat droppings turn crocodiles orange, 84–85
  bats hunt and eat fish, 170
  Bigfoot hair came from deer, 168
  bear sleeping near dog, 143
  bears raid donut van, 123
  bears ride swan boat, 175
  bonobos and chimps recognize friends, 32
  boots for cows, 121
  breathe underwater through butt, 164
  camel shoots owner, 61
  camel jumping sport, 242–243
  chimpanzees make spears, 196–197
  chupacabra resembles coyote, 168
  civet cat anal secretion used for perfume, 23
  cows outnumber humans, 237
  cows trample over men in post-Diwali celebration, 197
  coyote head stuck in statue, 231
  deer won't cross border, 64–66
  donkey library, 54
  donkeys in gold-mining town, 90
  echidna vomited up by shark, 227
  elephant made from toy bricks, 20
  elephant twins born, 154
  elephant-poop paper, 124
  elephants attack car, 37
  elephants evolving without tusks, 157–158
  elephants walk through hotel, 244
  fox orphan mask, 223
  gelada monkey herds, 78
  gerenuk antelope doesn't drink, 82
  giant straw goats for Christmas, 59
  giraffe shoulder blade painted with Big Five, 163
  giraffe moved 1,200 miles (1,930 km) to new zoo, 18
  globular springtail backflips, 107
  goats adopted on island, 15
  gorilla made from toy bricks, 20
  gorilla nose prints, 212
  gorilla presumed male has baby, 502
  greater kudu curly horns, 242
  hedgehog actually pom-pom, 82
  horse earth sculpture, 182
  horse rodeos of *escaramuzas*, 118
  horse toys made from cheese, 47
  horse on train platform, 41
  hyenas as garbage disposal, 41
  klipspringer walks on toes, 223
  koala steals and eats plants, 82
  microscopic animals color beaches, 24–25
  monkey causes blackout, 122
  monkey walks through Miniature Park, 19
  monkeys found mummified in luggage, 97
  Nubian ibex horns, 242
  orange crocodiles, 84–85
  orangutan heals self, 164
  otter found in orca stomach, 82
  otters smuggled onto plane, 137
  panda born brown and white, 123
  panda made from toy bricks, 20
  pig paints artwork, 16
  pigs outnumber people in Denmark, 70
  polar bear sense of smell, 155
  ponies used in mines, 182
  pygmy hippos, 134
  Racka sheep horns, 243
  reindeer chew cud while asleep, 32
  rhinos sink or swim, 137
  ruffed lemurs color vision, 144
  siphonophore colonies, 32
  sloths close noses when eating termites, 90
  slow loris coats teeth in venom, 135
  South American agouti teeth, 212
  tongue-eating louse replaces fish tongue, 184
  worms revived after frozen, 82
Ankrah, Ace-Liam, 139
Antionette, Marie, 186, 187
Appleton, Jack, 73
Aquarium of the Bay, 133
aquatic life
  beavers hold breath underwater, 227
  by-the-wind sailors on beaches, 122
  candy crab, 71
  carp in bathtub, 201
  dolphin teeth used as currency, 203
  dolphins with pink skin, 18
  eel removed from man, 18
  extinct colossal whale, 137
  extinct spike-toothed salmon, 73
  fish drums on swim bladder, 20
  fish fall from sky, 103
  fish causes power outage, 228
  fish delivers venom and electric shock, 51
  fish's tongue replaced by louse, 184
  fish with letters on tails, 164
  fishpond on sidewalk, 164
  Jellyfish Lake, 172–173
  jellyfish lookalike, 32
  Lake Malawi fish species, 138
  mussels to monitor water quality, 179–182
  orca with otters in stomach, 82
  Portuguese man o' war, 32
  pygmy seahorse, 135
  red-lipped batfish, 102
  shark alert in Scotland, 85
  shark baby gets head stuck, 185
  shark bites in circle shape, 227
  shark made from bread, 215
  shark made from snow, 185
  shark sanctuary, 146
  sharks track prey by heartbeat, 123
  shark vomits echidna, 227
  shark with rare coloring, 73
  stingray fossils, 199
  squid covered in tiny lights, 128
  whale shark's eyeball teeth, 164
aqueducts, 91
Archer, Doyle, 42
Arènes d'Arles, 160
Argoland, 147
art
  0.06-inch (1.5-mm) wooden spoon, 130
  abstract artwork using store pens, 16
  ancient Roman female gladiators, 119
  Back to the Future matchstick scene, 110–115
  balloon cross-stitch art, 209
  balloon sculpture of dragon, 116
  bee wing veil, 106
  boat made from ice, 175
  boat painted on fence, 130
  bread looks like sharks, 215
  bread sculptures for festival, 96
  Breton Village under the Snow painting, 233
  Bugkiss device for kissing insects, 120–121
  cake made from yarn, 21
  cars turned into art, 108
  ceramics resemble cardboard, 210
  chalk drawing of Northern Lights, 93
  chandeliers made from bullets, 197–198
  chocolate Colosseum, 160
  clothing made from living plants, 158
  cookie portraits, 226
  crochet costumes, 186
  crochet weapons, 172
  disco-ball sculptures, 74
  dog-fur portraits, 69
  dog sculpture of flowers, 208
  doodles by Charles Darwin's children, 159
  exhibition for dogs and owners, 215
  food painted to blend with face, 214
  food tattooed with ink, 138
  fridgescaping, 130–131
  furniture made from trees, 203
  goat straw statues, 59
  graffiti made from wool, 232
  gummy bear mosaic, 73
  gum wrapper football scene, 217
  hair woven into wearable art, 80
  haunted painting, 233
  heliography, 104
  Hot Dog in the City, 97
  Impossible Bottles, 224–225
  junk-mail mosaics, 68
  knitwork porcelain, 131
  manhole covers, 156
  matchbook Godzilla portrait, 133
  matchstick sculpture of Mozart, 139
  painted in under a minute, 17
  painting using garlic, 17
  pencil sculpture, 125
  Philadelphia murals, 220
  pictures in blankets, 136
  pictures on crumbling walls, 208
  pictures made from hair clippings, 142
  pig creates abstract art, 16
  Polly Pocket toys turned into movie scenes, 50
  Portrait of Doctor Rey, 233
  portraits from sushi, 92
  portraits hammered into glass, 68
  portraits made from emojis, 12
  portraits of city residents, 227
  portraits painted on nails, 23
  President John F. Kennedy portrait, 56
  rice field looks like sleeping cat, 194–195
  sandwich miniature model, 23
  sun burns image into wood, 104
  Superman deck of cards, 225
  sushi roll in acrylic block, 93
  Taylor Swift portrait, 239
  The Hands Resist Him painting, 233
  tie-dye art, 72
  trees turned into sculptures, 65
  TV sculpture made of toast, 216
  underwater sculpture park, 95
  wire-mesh portraits, 69
  wooden cartoon characters, 210
  WWI bullet-shell art, 192
artificial intelligence. *See technology*
Auto Wash Bowl, 185
Avanzi, Jamil, 162
Aylesbury Egg, 107
Ayutthaya Elephant Palace and Royal Kraal, 154

B
Bad Bunny (rapper), 103
Bajaj, Vinod, 213
Baker, Rick, 28
Balan, Kalpana, 203
Bali Aga people, 49
ballet, 31, 116, 220
Balneario El Cóndor, 121
bamboo drifting, 220
Bampini, Milly, 213
BANDALOOP dance group, 52
Bannister, Sir Roger, 152
Barbie Liberation Organization, 203
Bargibant, George, 135
Barker, Sarah, 211
Barnum, P.T., 28
Baron, Amanda, 51
Barrois Sr., Lyndon J., 217
Barstow, Stephanie, 171
Bartholmey, Aaron, 42
Bay Area Rapid Transit (BART), 133
Bed-Stuy Aquarium, 164
Bell, Chanell, 21
Bell, Mike, 133
Benford Sr., Dr. Doris Nathaniel, 219
Bennett Buddies, 210
Bennett, James Gordon, 240
Bennett, Mike, 210
Benson, Benny, 129
Bergen, Edgar, 29
Berlin High Swing, 133
Beska, Dr. Ben, 61
Beyonce, 47
Biblioburro, 54
bicycles. *See cycling and bicycles*
Bike Kill, 221
Birch, Marilyn, 159
birds
  African gray parrot swears, 223
  African jacana hides chicks, 32
  aracari curly head feathers, 103
  bald eagle is national bird of USA, 236
  bearded vulture dyes feathers, 199
  bird singing contests, 218
  Blakiston fish owl, 135
  burrowing parrot colony, 121
  chicken wears tiny slippers, 231
  chicken's egg in Roman dig site, 107
  chinstrap penguins micro sleep, 18
  crow drops missing corn snake, 231
  duck rides roller coaster, 164
  emu spotted on doorbell camera, 223
  Ferruginous pygmy owl, 135
  frigatebird steals regurgitated food, 41
  golden eagle festival, 154
  hawk grabs snake on woman's arm, 21
  kestrels track vole urine, 155
  magpie attacks cyclist, 37
  magpie chick befriended by dogs, 36
  megapode bird buries eggs, 150
  ortolan bunting delicacy, 46
  ostrich has long stride, 41
  owl in Christmas tree, 82
  palm cockatoo taps drumsticks, 41
  parrots accompanied robber, 157
  penguin knighted in Norway, 170
  potty-trained pigeon, 143
  prehistoric bird ate Neanderthal child, 182
  quetzal bird art, 17
  racing pigeon spy, 18
  rooster crowing contest, 116
  swan reflection in school window, 129
  taxidermy turkey, 42
  toucan curly head feathers, 103
  turkey to pub with owner, 137
  vultures drunk on fermented food, 155
  water birds lured by alligators, 121
birthdays
  illegal to celebrate birthday in public, 215–218
  leap-year birthday for 100-year-old, 175
  Malcolm Metcalf celebrates 90th birthday, 31
  motorcycle race before 98th birthday, 210
  Robert Louis Stevenson gave away birthday, 61
  three siblings born on same day in different years, 231
Black Label Bike Club, 221
Blanco, Mateo, 69
Blethen, Clarence, 73
blood
  blood flow when blushing, 75
  blood in Ankole-Watusi horns to keep cool, 243
  leech sucks blood from throat, 157
  mosquito sucks blood from frogs' nostrils, 32
  nure onna mythical creature drinks blood, 66
Blue Angels, 179
Blue Pearl, the, 49
boats and ships. *See transportation*
body modifications
  extreme needle body piercing, 88–89
  prosthetics and mobility aids after war, 216
  sharp hooks to attach altars to skin, 42
  tattoo of marry me then, 202
  tattoos and mods to look like cat, 65
  tattoos of daughter's name, 182
  tattoos of rabbits, 41
  technological implants into body, 237
body parts. *See also blood, bones, eyes, hair, teeth*
  baby born with organs on outside of body, 130
  back brace worn by J.F.K., 57
  bowel preserved in jar, 90
  cardiac arrest of woman and emergency responder, 119
  finger amputation, 175
  fingers in spring traps, 197
  foot-binding, 140
  futakuchi onna mythical creature has two mouths, 66
  gout foot pain, 141
  hands massage cyclist's legs, 49
  hearing amplifiers, 177
  innie or outie belly button, 25
  long second toe, 25
  man has 12 fingers and 12 toes, 62
  mouth holds paintbrush, 211
  neck strengthening for backward climb, 88

neck used to pull truck, 213
nervous system triggers increased blood flow, 75
neurological condition where sound makes person see color, 215
nose nail launch, 197
nose whistle at 44 decibels, 42
palmar creases on hands, 25
palmaris longus muscle in wrist, 25
preauricular pit next to ear, 24
severed head purse, 75
skin of murderer, 44
stomach blushes when face blushes, 75
tongue of Gene Simmons insured, 55
tongue snapped by mousetraps, 84, 197
tongue that's 3.1 inch (7.9 cm) wide, 201
windpipe hole after sneezing, 187
Bohan, Sarah, 20
bombs
  bomb used as garden ornament, 182
  grenade found in father's toolbox, 201
Bond, James, 22, 23
bones
  Bali Aga display skeletons of deceased, 49
  Capela dos Ossos decorated with bones, 182–183
  giraffe shoulder blade, 163
  Neanderthal child bones found, 182
  skeleton on car in Houston Art Car Parade, 108
  skeletons under McDonald's, 219
  whale and seal bones on beach, 78
  Whale Bone Alley, 185
books
  al-Qarawiyyin Library, 156–157
  Cardigan Library, 71
  Dracula, 99
  federal inmates reduce sentences by reading, 38–39
  Finnegans Wake, 55
  Harry Potter, 23, 212
  Hay-on-Wye book town, 196
  Icelandic phone books, 105
  Murder on the Orient Express, 228
  Old Knobbly tree book, 144
  On the Origin of Species, 159
  Peanuts comics, 173
  Robinson Crusoe, 23
  Superman comics, 157
  The Amazing Spider-Man Issue No.1, 167
  The Great Gatsby, 209
  The Wonderful Wizard of Oz, 196
  traveling library—Biblioburro, 54
  Treasure Island, 61
Borzachillo, Steven, 172
Bottle Magic, 224–225
brands and businesses
  19 Crimes, 185
  Amazon, 164
  American Airlines, 47
  BARK Air, 129
  Cadbury, 133, 144
  Converse, 225
  Full Grown, 203
  Goodyear Tire & Rubber Co., 176
  Haribo, 73
  Iron Factory Ikeda, 215
  Jordanluca, 213
  Kentucky Fried Chicken, 119
  Krispy Kreme, 123, 202
  LEGO, 42, 49, 188
  Loewe, 139
  Loop Biotech, 219
  Major League Gaming, 130
  McDonald's, 157, 182, 219
  Mercedes, 13
  Mickey Mouse, 164
  Mountain Dew, 170
  MSCHF, 233
  Nike, 233

Oreo, 195
Poochies Pupsicles, 123
Something Wild, 235
United States Playing Card Company, 228
Walmart, 237
bridges
  Auckland Harbour Bridge bungee jump, 213
  bridge washed out by heavy rain, 42
  Las Vegas pedestrian bridges, 150
  makeshift bridge across alligator-filled river, 100
  Millau Viaduct, 43
  narrow footbridge on Caminito del Rey, 179
  Pontcysyllte Aqueduct, 91
  rope bridges for dormice, 90
Brochet, 172
Bronze Age, 144
Brooker, Dave, 137
Brown, Andrew, 164
Brown, Dr. Emmett, 112
Brown, Tijan and Matthew, 47
BTS (pop band), 93
Buckman, Stephanie, 159
Bugg, Emma, 62
Bugkiss, 120–121
burros (donkeys), 90
Byrne, Peter, 168

C
Cabrales blue cheese, 71
Callawaert, Marcie, 77
Caminito del Rey, 179
camouflage
  candy crab polyps on shell, 71
  frog looks like leaf, 242
  insects using camouflage, 206–207
  jacana hides chicks, 32
  thorn bug looks like plant, 243
candy. *See* food and drink
Caño Cristales, 73
Capaldi, Peter, 144
Cape Spear Lighthouse, 116
carbon-dioxide-filled cave, 220
Cardozo, Louis, 238
Carey, Mariah, 226
cars. *See* transportation
Carter, Jimmy, 205
Cathedral of Junk, 213
Catron, Jen, 97
cats
  9,500-year-old grave of human and kitten, 63–64
  art made from rainbow rice crop, 194
  body modifications to look like a cat, 65
  campus cat honorary doctorate, 164
  Cat Mew machine, 176
  cat sculptures make portraits, 239
  Chartwell house cat, 227
  cross-eyed cat, 61
  domestic cat diet, 223
  mailed in Amazon box, 164
  missing cat found after seven years, 171
  rescued by marathon runner, 20
  Shirley Jackson's black cats, 32
  snake removed from cat's neck, 73
  steals neighbors' things, 233
  strollers for cats, 82
  trapped in taxi, 41
Cavallari, Arnaldo, 150
caves
  Abanda Caves, 84
  Cabrales cheese matured in caves, 71
  cave diving inside iceberg, 201
  Crystal Grotto, 228
  Cueva de la Muerte, 220
  dog trapped in cave with bear, 143
  glowworm caves, 191
  Hang Son Doong size, 242
  Marble Caves, 76

Salina Turda, 241
Waitomo Cave, 191
Cawkwell, Tommy, 175
cemeteries
  Joseph Grimaldi Park, 189
  Okunoin cemetery, 124
  Reilig Odhrain cemetery, 150
  Sad Hill Cemetery, 71
  Tower Hamlets Cemetery, 185
Cemolonskas, Liutauras, 42
Chained Tree of Peshawar, 144
chainsaw carves sculptures, 51
Champeny, Kevin, 239
Champlin, Jacob, 133
charity work, 27, 174, 231
Charles, Charlie, 153
Chartwell, 227
Chase Center, San Francisco, 49
Chernobyl nuclear disaster, 231
Chicago rat hole, 212
Chicago World Fair, 31
children. *See* age
CHiPa, 160
Choon Chiek, Lee, 182
Christie, Agatha, 228
Churchill, Sir Winston, 227
circus, 38–39, 162
Clark, Carrie and Matt, 164
Claypool, Helen, 107
cliffs
  Caminito del Rey cliff trail, 179
  colony of burrowing parrots, 121
  dance performed on cliffs, 52
  mudstone cliffs turn sea red, 231
  tiny store on vertical cliff, 105
  vehicles launched off cliff, 147
  village built into cliffs, 235
Climbing District, 223
cloacal respiration, 164
clothing. *See* fashion
clowns, 188, 189
coffee. *See* food and drink
collections and collectibles
  1,100 hotel key cards, 144
  10,000 items of *Doctor Who* memorabilia, 144
  10,000 vintage American menus, 15
  10,500 items of Transformers memorabilia, 231
  120,000 eyeglasses at Tokyo Spectacles Museum, 15
  15,000 frog-related items, 107
  2,000 items of *Ghostbusters* memorabilia, 93
  2,000 sock monkeys, 223
  5,548 PEZ candy dispensers, 201
  5,600 rubbers ducks, 182
  50,000 colored pencils, 139
  6,000 LEGO sets, 188
  70 coins in alligator's stomach, 20
  70,000 McDonald's toys, 182
  70,000 preserved snakes at museum, 164
  70,000 wooden pencils, 42
  8,200 items of Batman memorabilia, 107
  models of European towns and cities, 49
Concha, Douglas, 116
Connors, Lily, 144
Constable, Etienne, 130
contests and championships
  Alaska's flag design, 129
  Arches of Bread sculpture contest, 96
  autographed Chevrolet Corvette prize, 126–127
  Bike Kill jousting competition, 221
  bird singing contests in Thailand, 218
  Brisbane International tournament, 143
  Celine Dion siren battles, 100
  Condiment Wars wrestling match, 97
  golf tournament in Dubai, 157
  Heavy Metal Knitting World Championship, 85
  hot dog eating contest, 97

International Volleyball on Water tournament, 244
lying down the longest, 155–156
Mali mud-brick building contest, 236
Masters World Cup skiing, 219
mushroom picking tournament, 135
New Zealand national golf tournament, 203
New Zealand's Tree of the Year, 166
robot soccer match, 65
Rock Paper Scissors with robot, 63
rooster crowing contest, 116
run under-4-minute mile, 152
sleep contest in Seoul, 119
solve Rubik's Cube underwater, 105
spring vs. winter festival, 54
Stanley and Stella Shouting Contest, 93
students climb greased tower, 222
TRAM-EM European TramDriver Championship, 48
tug-of-war on beach near Pembrey, 93
U.S. Open, 143
water ballet competitions, 220
Wimbledon Championships, 245
World Dog Surfing Championship, 178
Coors, Adolph, 15
Copeman, Lloyd Groff, 240
coprolites, 159
Cosmic Baseball, 244
cosplaying, 186
Cottle Dock, Maddie, 162
countries, territories, etc.
  Afghanistan, 12
  Albania, 12, 160
  Algeria, 13
  ancient Rome, 119
  Andorra, 14
  Antarctica, 18, 100, 124, 201
  Antigua and Barbuda, 18, 201
  Argentina, 19, 121, 188
  Armenia, 20
  Australia, 21, 32, 36, 37, 41, 42, 61, 73, 77, 82, 88, 107, 116, 123, 124, 133, 135, 143, 147, 155, 171, 191, 202, 212, 219, 231, 235, 240
  Austria, 22, 219, 228
  Azerbaijan, 23
  Bahamas, 24
  Bahrain, 25
  Bangladesh, 26
  Barbados, 27
  Belarus, 30, 175
  Belgium, 30, 212, 215
  Belize, 32
  Benin, 33
  Bhutan, 34
  Bolivia, 35
  Bosnia & Herzegovina, 37
  Botswana, 38
  Brazil, 38, 49, 76, 82, 100, 165
  Brunei, 39
  Bulgaria, 40
  Burkina Faso, 41
  Burundi, 42
  Cambodia, 43
  Cameroon, 46, 151
  Canada, 47, 49, 71, 77, 84, 88, 116, 119, 121, 130, 139, 143, 159, 175, 201, 203, 209, 212, 228, 240
  Cape Verde, 48
  Central African Republic, 49
  Chad, 50
  Chile, 51, 76
  China, 50, 52, 70, 95, 100, 105, 116, 123, 124, 137, 140, 209, 213, 240
  Colombia, 54, 73, 100
  Comoros, 55
  Congo, 58
  Costa Rica, 58, 133, 220
  Côte d'Ivoire, 60
  Croatia, 61, 139, 161
  Cuba, 62, 100, 134, 210

Cyprus, 63
Czech Republic, 64, 188
Democratic Republic of the Congo, 66, 97, 98
Denmark, 70, 85, 188, 240
Djibouti, 70
Dominica, 71
Dominican Republic, 72
Ecuador, 73, 150
Egypt, 15, 74
El Salvador, 76
Equatorial Guinea, 77
Eritrea, 78
Estonia, 71, 78, 130, 230
Eswatini, 80
Ethiopia, 41, 81
Fiji, 82
Finland, 83, 85, 223
France, 34, 35, 43, 44, 46, 49, 64, 84, 96, 97, 102, 146, 160, 187, 188, 210, 220, 223, 233, 240
Gabon, 84
Galápagos Islands, 102
Gambia, 85
Georgia, 88
Germany, 15, 54, 65, 90, 93, 133, 159, 169, 188, 192, 194, 237
Ghana, 91, 139
Greece, 65, 92, 237
Grenada, 95
Guatemala, 95
Guinea-Bissau, 97
Guinea, 97
Guyana, 100
Haiti, 101
Honduras, 102
Hungary, 104, 243
Iceland, 105
India, 18, 90, 94, 95, 105, 130, 175, 185, 187, 203, 220, 237
Indonesia, 49, 50, 106, 135, 147, 164, 227
Iran, 108, 139, 157
Iraq, 108, 142
Ireland, 55, 58, 65, 109, 213
Israel, 117
Italy, 15, 65, 73, 96, 117, 143, 150, 161, 199, 219, 230, 235
Jamaica, 119
Japan, 15, 47, 55, 62, 63, 66, 71, 93, 95, 101, 118, 124, 132, 135, 140, 155, 156, 160, 171, 176, 188, 196, 215, 219, 231, 237
Jordan, 120
Kazakhstan, 121
Kenya, 122
Kiribati, 123
Kuwait, 124
Kyrgyzstan, 124
Laos, 125
Latvia, 128
Lebanon, 130
Lesotho, 131
Liberia, 132
Libya, 133
Liechtenstein, 134
Lithuania, 134, 187, 200
Luxembourg, 136
Madagascar, 137, 144
Malawi, 138
Malaysia, 37, 139, 182
Maldives, 142
Mali, 143, 236
Malta, 144
Marshall Islands, 146, 210
Mauritania, 146
Mauritius, 148
Mexico, 15, 18, 47, 97, 118, 124, 148, 150, 188, 215, 231, 240
Micronesia, 150
Moldova, 150
Monaco, 15, 151
Mongolia, 154
Montenegro, 71, 155
Morocco, 49, 156, 171
Mozambique, 157
Myanmar, 20, 94, 147, 158
Namibia, 78, 160
Naura, 161
Nepal, 26, 161, 218

Netherlands, the, 58, 157, 162, 212, 219
New Zealand, 85, 100, 163, 166, 191, 201, 203, 210, 213
Nicaragua, 165
Niger, 164
Nigeria, 71, 165
North Korea, 166
North Macedonia, 167
Norway, 170
Oman, 170
Pakistan, 144, 171
Palau, 172
Palestine, 173
Panama, 174
Papua New Guinea, 176
Paraguay, 77, 176
Peru, 133, 177
Philippines, 17, 77, 178
Poland, 179, 182, 237
Portugal, 182, 196, 208, 232
Prince Edward Island, 71
Qatar, 183
Romania, 184, 241
Russia, 19, 61, 75, 147, 155, 185
Rwanda, 186
Saint Kitts & Nevis, 187
Saint Lucia, 188
Saint Vincent & the Grenadines, 189
Samoa, 190
San Marino, 194
São Tomé & Príncipe, 194
Saudi Arabia, 196
Senegal, 196
Serbia, 197
Seychelles, 198
Siberia, 82
Sicily, 230
Sierra Leone, 199
Singapore, 15, 105, 200
Slovakia, 201
Slovenia, 202, 244
Soloman Islands, 203
Somalia, 206
South Africa, 16, 132, 201, 206
South Korea, 79, 82, 119, 208
South Sudan, 209
Spain, 51, 55, 71, 85, 160, 161, 179, 187, 201, 202, 208, 210, 235
Sri Lanka, 83, 211
Sudan, 15, 211
Suriname, 212
Sweden, 59, 75, 143, 213, 240
Switzerland, 97, 213, 235
Syria, 214
Tahiti, 233
Tajikistan, 215
Tanzania, 88, 218
Tasmania, 62
Thailand, 58, 124, 134, 137, 154, 194, 218
Timor-Leste, 219
Togo, 220
Tonga, 221
Trinidad & Tobago, 222
Tunisia, 161, 223
Turkey, 31, 201, 226, 228
Turkmenistan, 227
Tuvalu, 228
Uganda, 230
Ukraine, 19, 47, 213, 230
United Arab Emirates, 14, 148, 157, 210, 232
United Kingdom, 20, 22, 27, 31, 37, 42, 44, 47, 49, 51, 52, 58, 61, 65, 71, 78, 82, 85, 88, 90, 91, 93, 100, 107, 119, 123, 129, 130, 137, 141, 144, 147, 150, 152, 155, 157, 159, 167, 171, 174, 175, 181, 182, 183, 185, 187, 189, 196, 202, 203, 211, 212, 214, 215, 223, 227, 228, 231, 233, 235, 237
United States, 49, 73, 124, 143, 187, 188, 193, 233, 235
  Alabama, 144
  Alaska, 123, 129, 147, 154, 203
  Arizona, 90, 159, 215, 224
  California, 32, 41, 42, 49, 52, 55, 77, 85, 110, 124, 130, 133, 144, 145, 164, 172, 178, 188, 196, 231, 237
  Colorado, 45, 74, 119, 129, 157
  Connecticut, 42
  Delaware, 15
  Florida, 72, 73, 134, 143, 159, 164, 168
  Georgia, 202
  Hawaii, 65, 77, 116
  Idaho, 80
  Illinois, 15, 55, 90, 97, 100, 105, 180, 212, 223
  Indiana, 87, 136
  Iowa, 42, 119, 203
  Kentucky, 51, 82, 116, 213
  Louisiana, 93, 152, 217
  Maine, 171
  Maryland, 33, 197, 235
  Massachusetts, 20, 93, 97, 143, 147, 204
  Michigan, 58, 75, 188, 219, 237
  Minnesota, 31, 119, 125, 144
  Missouri, 107
  Nebraska, 20
  Nevada, 88, 150, 153, 202, 228, 239
  New Jersey, 15, 88, 201, 228
  New Mexico, 15, 136
  New York, 12, 15, 52, 97, 102, 105, 116, 130, 133, 143, 164, 171, 173, 175, 215, 221, 240
  Ohio, 164
  Oklahoma, 60, 136, 175
  Oregon, 147, 168
  Pennsylvania, 49, 123, 187, 220
  Rhode Island, 185
  South Carolina, 49
  Tennessee, 26, 73, 143, 147, 167
  Texas, 21, 42, 47, 49, 57, 104, 105, 108, 126, 150, 201, 209, 213, 219, 235
  Utah, 144, 228
  Virginia, 157, 188, 223, 244
  Washington State, 42, 88, 182, 223
  Washington, D.C., 49
  West Virginia, 88
  Wisconsin, 73, 97, 231
  Wyoming, 199
Uruguay, 237
Uzbekistan, 237
Vanuatu, 133, 238
Vatican City, 239
Venezuela, 130, 240
Vietnam, 18, 157, 242
Yemen, 242
Zambia, 244
Zimbabwe, 245
Cousins, Julot, 64
Crassus, Marcus Licinius, 159
crime. *See* law and crime
Crystal Grotto, 228–229
Cuban Ironman, 210
Cueva de la Muerte, 220
Curry, Steph, 49
cycling and bicycles
  around the world in nine months, 116
  BMX ride across Iowa, 203
  handcycling across Canada, 116
  magpie attack when cycling home, 37
  mutant bikes for Bike Kill, 221
  New York City cycle carrying couch, 116
  para-cyclist Silke Pan, 38
  poodle rides bicycle, 164
  Robert Murray cycles without using hands, 49
  spinning class with violin music, 239
  tiny bike ridden through mall, 153
  unicycle hockey, 188
Cyrus, Miley, 92

D

D'Angela, Henry, 119
da Silva, Manoel Marciano, 100
DaCosta, Ameen, 133
Dafydd, Dan, 119
Dalai Lama, 58
Dalí, Salvador, 55

Dallas motorcade of President John F. Kennedy, 57
dance. *See also* ballet
  bamboo drifting, 220
  on horseback, 118
  on side of buildings, 52
Danen, James, 47
Dangerously Stupid show, 197
Darwin, Charles, 159
Dash Rippington, 197
Dassiotis, Spyridon, 65
Dauphinais, Deb and Steve, 185
David, Leh-Boy Gabriel, 116
Davignon, Meesh, 231
Daynes, Rebecca, 73
de Jesus, Falmira, 227
de la Vaulx, Henry, 35
De Leon III, Victor, 130
death and dying
  400,000 workers died building the Great Wall of China, 71
  Anga people mummify dead, 176
  assassination of U.S. President John F. Kennedy, 56
  assassination of U.S. President Abraham Lincoln, 49
  Bali Aga corpses in forest, 49
  borrow dead animals from museum, 42
  carbon dioxide cloud deaths, 46
  carbon-dioxide-filled cave, 220
  coffin escape room, 85
  coffin-aged wine, 185
  coffin-shaped graves, 189
  coffins made from mushrooms, 219
  deceased man dropped as a political candidate, 175
  fantasy coffin to represent person's life, 91–92
  flower from white to black when dead, 78
  grave of human and kitten, 63–64
  guillotine beheads Marie Antoinette, 187
  jewelry made with hair of deceased, 81
  John Dillinger killed by FBI, 180
  John Horrocks shot, 61
  Last Rites kit, 98
  Manoel Marciano da Silva mistakenly declared dead, 100
  Marcus Licinius Crassus killed in battle, 159
  Mount Vesuvius eruption, 73
  mummified monkeys found in luggage, 97
  orca dead with otter in throat, 82
  Shakespeare's will, 55
  soccer team killed by lightning, 66–67
  trip to scatter ashes of dead hamster, 65
  whitemargin stargazer fish can kill human, 51
Defoe, Daniel, 23
Dell'Abate, Chiara, 65
Demin, Felix, 147
Denney, Jim, 119
Desert National Wildlife Refuge, 202
deserts
  Atacama, 52
  Erg Chebbi, 171
  Kalahari, 38
  Nevada, 202
  Sahara, 32
Devane, Daisy, 119
Deveraux, Colin, 123
Devi, Saraswati, 175
Devi, Sheetal, 34
DiCaprio, Leonardo
Dillinger, John, 180
dinosaurs. *See* prehistoric
Dion, Celine, 100
Diquís Delta stone balls, 59
Dirty Pig Festival, 54

discoveries
  anaconda measuring 26 feet (8 m), 20
  ancient coins beneath farmhouse, 90
  Argoland continent, 147
  bones of Neanderthal child, 182
  dinosaur carnivore discovery, 20–21
  frog with mushroom on side, 90
  giant sloth remains, 33
  kyawthuite specimen, 159
  LEGO bricks lost cargo, 42
  new longhorn beetle species, 124
  new moth species, 155
  scuba diver finds Apple watches, 15
  Viking Sword in river, 31
  woolly mammoth bones, 155
Dobbins, Taylor, 215
Doctor of Litter-ature, 164
dogs
  art exhibition for dogs and owners, 215
  BARK Air plane travel for dogs, 129
  befriend magpie chick, 36
  born with green fur, 143
  born with six legs, 155
  clothing like Met Gala fashion, 102
  damages lottery ticket, 137
  detects enemy airplanes in World War II, 171
  detects gas leak, 21
  detects smuggled mummified monkeys, 97
  ear spots like dog face, 143
  eats passport before trip, 143
  fur changed from black to white, 60
  fur portraits, 69
  German shepherd at Metallica concert, 32
  giant dog sculpture made from flowers, 208
  goldendoodle chews cash, 123
  ice cream for dogs, 123
  kitesurfs with owner, 165
  labrador inspires Led Zeppelin, 237
  owl in house undetected by dogs, 82
  poodle rides bike, 164
  rescued by crocodiles, 18
  responds to spells as commands, 212
  Snoopy based on cartoonist's dog, 173
  strollers for dogs, 82
  survives at sea with owner, 240
  trapped in cave with sleeping bear, 143
  waits with body of hiker, 129
  World Dog Surfing Championships, 178
Dominguez, Valentina, 47
Donis, Fernando, 14
Door to Hell, 227
Dorset Plane Pull, 27
Downey Jr., Robert, 92
dragons. *See* myths and legends
drinks. *See* food and drink
Drottz, Mateo, 239
Dubai Frame, 14
Duffy, Daniel, 56
dumpster diving, 235
Duna Federico Kirbus sand dune, 188
Durietz, Paul, 116
Dylan, Bob, 68

E

Earhart, Amelia, 147
earthquakes, 160, 175
Eastwood, Clint, 71
echolocation, 170
Edelstein, Lauren, 12
Edwards, Sian and Jeffrey, 182
Eggins, Charlie, 88
Eilish, Billie, 226
Einstein, Albert, 117, 195

Elephant PooPooPaper Park, 124
elevators in constant loop, 15
Emett, Rowland, 23
Eminem, 78
emoji art, 12
Eng, Harry, 224, 225
English Football League, 58
English, Chris, 42
entertainment and performers
  balance 30 swords on legs, 31
  bamboo drifting, 220
  clowns, 188
  escaramuzas at rodeos, 118
  magic lantern projectors, 86
  radio show by 90-year-old, 31
  stroller with radio loudspeaker, 177
  ventriloquist on radio, 29
  Zic Zazou music using everyday things, 220
environment. *See also* plants and trees
  car fueled by eco-oil, 58
  Cathedral of Junk, 213
  China's sinking cities, 53–54
  pollution, 185, 207
  wear dress for 100 days, 219
  waste in Bahrain, 26
Epic of Manas, The, 124
escapes
  bees escape from truck, 143
  dog bites lottery ticket, 137
  emu on doorbell camera, 223
  horse enters train station, 41
  inmates tunnel out of cells, 130
  John Dillinger jailbreak, 180
  runaway train in India, 220
  tortoise escapes from home, 143
escaramuzas, 118
Evans, Craig, 41
Evans, Mark Owen, 182
Everson, Shana, 173
Exposition Universelle, 35
extinction
  colossal whale, 137
  spike-toothed salmon, 73
eyes
  beaver's transparent eyelids, 227
  black eye on wedding day, 21
  blindfolded baseball, 58
  cross-eyed cat, 61
  hang buckets from eyes, 84
  jumping spider's wiggly eyes, 229
  pull car with eye sockets, 88
  reshaped like cat's, 65
  strawberry squid's lopsided eyes, 128
  whale shark's eyeball teeth, 164

F

Fairbrother, Daniel, 215
Faleh, Hussein, 142
farming
  country's border moved by farmer, 30–32
  cashew farming, 99–100
  crocodile attack, 227
  dung beetles value, 61
  farm grows golf-ball-size blueberry, 235
  grannies rap about farm life, 79
  rainbow rice fields, 194
  rare cacao for chocolate, 150
  rice farme balloon sprayers, 51
  ring lost when feeding cattle, 159
  sheep shearing challenge, 31
fashion
  boots for cows, 121
  brooch made from burger, 62
  clothing made from living plants, 158
  clothing stolen by cat, 233
  coat of Lee Harvey Oswald, 56
  Converse shoes trapped in bottle, 225
  crochet costumes, 186
  dog Met-Gala-inspired clothing, 102
  dresses for *escaramuzas,* 118
  dress socks entry fee to Barkley Marathons, 26

dress worn for 100 days, 219
fox masks, 223
hats made from dried cucumbers, 20
jeans with pee design, 213
jewelry found in dumpsters, 235
jewelry made from golden grass, 76
jewelry made from hair, 80
kimono-dressed waitress, 237
necklace vial containing ashes, 65
Nike Air Max 97 shoes, 233
pearl-studded shoes for coronation, 50
pixelated clothing, 139
purse like severed head, 75
shoes for gout, 141
shoes worn out on 14-month walk, 42
Swarovski crystal Stormtrooper helmet, 75
tie-dye clothing, 72
tiny shoes for chicken, 231
underpants identify robber, 215
uniforms neon for baseball, 244
wigs with braid pictures, 173
fast. *See* speed
fear of eggs, 215
Fedya the cross-eyed cat, 61
festivals and celebrations
  Arches of Bread festival, 96
  asparagus festival, 100
  Bike Kill, 221
  cars off cliff celebration, 147
  Chelsea in Bloom, 183
  clown pilgrimage, 188
  Day of the Dead, 95
  Dirty Pig Festival, 54
  flaming cloth ball throwing, 76–77
  Giant Kite Festival, 101
  Golden Eagle Festival, 154
  Houston Art Car Parade, 108
  Maghe Sankranti festival, 218
  Mushroom Festival, 135
  Pink Soup Fest, 200
  Roswell UFO Festival, 136
  sharpening of giant pencil, 125
  Sheedi Mela festival, 171–172
  Tennessee Williams Festival, 93
  Thaipusam, 42
  witch paddles, 196
Fialka, Gerry, 55
Finger, Bill, 215
fish. *See* aquatic life
Fisher, Avery Emerson, 133
fishing
  boats made from jet fuel tanks, 127–128
  fishermen leave gnomes on island, 37
  fishing for red drum, 164
  fishing caught wallet, 119
  fly-fishing line made from hair, 80
  fly-fishing rod landmark, 77
  magnet fishing finds safe of money, 171
  magnet fishing finds Viking sword, 31
  mammoth bones found, 155
  piebald lemon shark caught, 73
  solo fishing trip rescue, 201
  stilt fishing, 83
Fitzgerald, F. Scott, 209
flags, 129, 162, 177, 178
Fleming, Ian, 22
flowers. *See* plants and trees
food and drink
  asparagus festival, 100
  banana car, 109
  banana-shaped hammers, 215
  banana-shaped stamp, 221–222
  bananas slide ship, 235
  bears raid donut delivery van, 123
  beer drinking before loud burp, 188
  beer drinking in wheelbarrow race, 85
  beer tester job, 78
  blueberry giant grown, 235
  bread animals, 215
  bread church sculptures, 96

burger brooch, 62
Cabrales blue cheese wheel, 71
Cadbury Creme Egg family heirloom, 133
Cadbury Creme Eggs stolen, 144
cake brings good luck, 93
cake made from yarn, 21
candy gummy bear mosaic, 73
candy protest after price increase, 130
Carolina Reaper peppers, 203
cashew producers, 99–100
chaku candy made from molasses, 218
cheese horses, 47
cheese wrapped in goat skin, 201
chewing gum banned, 15
chewing gum wrapper art, 217
chile sauce questions, 15
chocolate bar costs $450, 150
chocolate Colosseum, 160
chocolate from Côte d'Ivoire, 60
chocolate invented in Jamaica, 119
cinnamon from Sri Lanka, 211
coffee caused loud burp, 188
cookies baked on car dashboard, 49
cookies portraits, 226
cucumbers made into hats, 20
donut delivery van stolen, 202
donut-dunking device, 177
fruit as painting canvas, 214
garlic paintings, 17
goat water stew, 187–188
Green Ant Gin, 235
hedgehog party food made of raw pork, 194
hot dog sculpture, 97
hot dog stands, 100
hummus serving of 23,042 pounds (10,542 kg), 131–132
ice cream for dogs, 123
ice cream per day—4,200 gallons (16,000 liters), 100
Italian ciabatta bread invention, 150
KFC eaten on Christmas Day in Japan, 119
lemon aged 285 years, 175
marshmallow weighing 1,429 pounds (648 kg), 15
meals on Estonian New Year's Eve, 78–80
meteorite-infused vodka, 220
mettigel party food, 194
Mountain Dew drink, 170–171
ortolan bunting bird delicacy, 46
petrified peanut shells, 159
picnic above waterfall, 49
pink soup, 200
pork skewers in 60-year-old sauce, 93
rainbow Ramen, 62
rainbow rice fields, 194
rat broth, 124
rationing during war, 193
rice mortar for the Great Wall of China, 71
sandwich miniature model, 23
snacks with smacks, 237
spider resembles Oreo cookie, 195
Starbucks at the Great Wall of China, 71
sushi at baggage claim, 93
sushi portraits, 92
tattooed with squid ink, 138
tea in tanks, 78
toast TV sculpture, 216
tulum peyniri cheese, 201
waiters poison food, 90
wine aged in coffins, 185
wine runs through streets, 196
Fooks, Robert and Betty, 90
foot-binding, 140
Ford, Henry, 182
forensic science, 44
forests
  Adak National Forest, 154
  California's Redwood Forest, 145

Forest of Dean, 90
  Tuskegee National Forest, 144
Forsythe, Mary, 175
fossils. *See* prehistoric
Foster, Judy, 78
Frandsen, George, 159
Fransen, Will, 201
Frattaroli, Donato, 143
Freeman, Morgan, 55
Frog Lady, 107
frogs and toads. *See* reptiles and amphibians
fungi
  coffins made from fungi, 219
  devils' finger fungus, 234
  ghost pipe sucks nutrients, 78
  mushroom growing from frog's side, 90
furniture
  Chitty Chitty Bang Bang rocking chair, 23
  willow tree furniture, 203

G

G., Carmen, 30
games. *See* toys and games
Garland, Mark, 58
gastroschisis, 130
Gates of Hell, The, 78
Gauguin, Paul, 233
gemstones and precious metals
  gold crystals, 124
  gold mining, 90
  meteor crater diamonds, 91
genetics. *See also* medicine and medical procedures
  corn genome, 150
  DNA mutation in pandas, 123
  genetically identical aspen trees, 144
  Ötzi the Iceman, 22–23
  piebald genetic condition, 73
ghosts
  ghost yokai, 66
  haunted painting, 233
giant
  Amphitheatre of El Jem, 161
  anaconda, 20
  animal exhibit of toy bricks, 20
  baobab trees, 48–49
  blueberry, 235
  building for city views, 14
  Burj Khalifa, 210, 232
  car modifications, 108
  caterpillar swarm, 133–134
  colossal whale, 137
  gas crater, 227–228
  Godzilla sculpture, 132
  Hang Son Doong cave, 242
  hot dog sculpture, 97
  hummus serving, 131–132
  iceberg thickness, 100
  kites for Day of the Dead, 95–96
  kite measures 47.6 feet (14.5 m) wide, 101
  marshmallow, 15
  megalake Paratethys, 188
  miniature-model zoo display, 19
  mirrors in Italian village, 117
  mud-brick building, 236
  Palace of the Sultan of Brunei, 39–40
  Pando tree root system, 144
  pencil, 125
  picnic, 96
  picture frame, 14
  popsicle-stick model of *Hindenburg*, 15
  prehistoric bird, 182
  pumpkin, 144
  sinkhole at Gordon Moore Park, 55
  siphonophore group, 32
  spike-toothed salmon, 73
  statue of dog made from flowers, 208
  statue of Gollum from *The Hobbit*, 166
  statue of mirrored spider, 74
  straw goats, 59
  sushi at baggage claim, 93

tongue, 201
  wagon, 78
  wine cellars, 150–151
  zucchini, 119
Gienger, Travis, 144
Glacier View, 147
glow in the dark
  baseball, 244
  glowworm caves, 191
  nail art, 23
  strawberry squid senses, 128
  tires, 176
Gnome Island, 37
Godzilla, 132
Golden State Warriors, 49
Gomez, Selena, 69
Gosling, Ryan, 73
governments and leaders
  1896 presidential election, 204
  Albert Einstein, 116
  candy bar protest, 130
  donkey honorary mayor, 90
  Emperor Bokassa of the Central African Republic, 50
  European female monarchs, 85
  general Marcus Licinius Crassus, 159
  Ghana's First Lady, 139
  Inca Empire, 63
  Kim Jong-un, 166
  King Charles II, 107
  King Charles X Gustav, 240
  King Edward VIII, 107
  King Henry VIII, 141
  King James II, 202
  King Louis XIV, 49
  King Louis XVI, 187
  King Mansa Musa of Mali, 144
  Malaysia rotational monarchy, 139, 142
  Maldives president's underwater meeting, 142–143
  Mao Zedong, 124
  Marie Antoinette, 187
  President Mohamed Nasheed, 142
  Prince Harry, 51, 201
  Queen Margrethe II of Denmark, 85
  Reform UK, 175
  Sardar Vallabhbhai Patel, 95
  Sir Winston Churchill, 227
  Swiss Confederation, 235
  Switzerland council rule, 213–214
  U.S. President Abraham Lincoln, 49
  U.S. President Barack Obama, 167
  U.S. President Jimmy Carter, 205
  U.S. President John F. Kennedy, 56, 57
  voting in Gambia, 85–88
  voting in Canadian federal election, 159
Graham, Sara, 202
gravity. *See* space
Greek toe, 25
Gregory, Patsy, 49
Grubb, Brian, 148
Gundapwar, Preeti, 93
guillotine, 187
Guns N' Roses, 126
Gus the Asparagus Man, 100
Gvozdenko, Irina, 209

H

Hadid, Gigi, 102
Haicha, Bella, 31
hair
  bearded woman, 219
  beard pulls minibus, 213
  beards banned, 228
  braided into jewelry, 80
  double crown spirals, 24
  kamikiri mythical creatures steal hair, 67
Halsa, Connor, 119
Hamel, Félix-Antoine, 159
Handerson, Handy, 85
Hannemann, Vince, 213
Hansen, Zen, 80
Harris, Leslie, 210

Harry Potter, 23, 187, 212
Hathaway, Anne, 55
Hayashi, Hirofumi, 160
Heard, Mike, 213
Heinerth, Jill 201
Heinig, Cameron, 133
heliography, 104
Henley, Georgie, 77
Hernandez Garrido of Baracoa, Yoandri, 62
Hernández, José Remedios, 124
Herndon Monument, 222
Herringer, Michelle, 131
HI-SEAS research station, 77
Higgins, John, 125
high up
  BASE jumping, 148
  Berlin High Swing, 133
  canoeing above ground, 91
  climbing wall in chapel, 223
  dance group performance, 52
  hula hooping on pole, 64
  James Bruce Falls, 240
  picnic above waterfall, 49
  slackline walk, 230
Hill, Julia "Butterfly", 145
Hindenburg, 15
Hinton, Charles, 88
Hitchcock, Alfred, 215
Ho, Kun Lung, 116
hobbies and crafting
  crochet, 172, 186
  cross-stitch art, 209, 232
  embroidery, 21, 232
Holbrook, Rodney, 212
holidays
  Chinese New Year, 116
  Christmas, 59, 61, 82, 119, 154, 171, 188, 203, 241
  Easter, 96, 119, 219
  Halloween, 173, 185, 196
  New Year's, 78, 88–89, 92, 210
  St. George's Day, 85, 100
  Valentine's Day, 213
Holladay, Logan, 73
Holland, Tom, 209
Hollander, Tom, 209
Holloway, Jeff, 136
Honeycutt, Erin, 219
Hoogenraad, Zara, 165
Horrocks, John, 61
Horvat, Tomislav, 139
Horwood, John, 44
hotels and resorts
  Address Beach Resort, 148
  Berlin's Park Inn Hotel, 133
  Elmwood Hotel, 139
  key card collection, 144
  Legend Golf and Safari Resort, 207
  Lily Lake Resort, 209
  luggage left behind, 47
  Mfuwe Lodge, 244
  Pera Palace Hotel, 228
houses and homes
  Chartwell house to National Trust, 227
  doorbells in Paraguay, 77
  farmhouse renovation ancient coin discovery, 90
  home inside supermarket sign, 75
  home under supermarket staircase, 209
  houses in Philippines, 77
  sphere homes, 157
  tornado damage, 147
  village in cliff face, 235
Hrunskyi, Dmytro, 213
Hughes, Neil, 15
Humphrey Herington's nursery, 82
Hunter, Erin, 31
Hurd-Wood, Grahame, 227
Hurtado, Aribeth, 32
Hutchings, Tom, 41
hydroelectric dam, 179

I

Ice Age, 82
icebergs and ice sheets, 100, 201, 228

Ide, Annie, 61
Impossible Bottles, 224–225
Incas, 63
Industrial Revolution, 207
inemuri, 231
Ingvoldstad, Curtis, 125
insects and bugs. *See also* spiders, parasites
  Amazon giant leech, 41
  ant gin, 235
  bee parts art, 106
  bees fall off truck, 143
  beetles, 61, 72
  big-eyed toad bug, 207
  blunthead slug snake, 129
  Bugkiss device, 120, 121
  caterpillars, 89, 133–134, 198
  cuckoo wasp larvae, 41
  dead leaf mantis, 206
  dung beetles, 61
  ermine moth caterpillars, 198
  extinct Tyrannasorus rex beetle, 72
  flies, 41, 234
  giant-headed vampire wasp, 137
  glowworms, 190–191
  hickory horned devil caterpillar, 89
  houseflies taste, 41
  leech brains, 227
  maggots on plane, 58
  mosquito sucks blood, 32
  moths, 89, 155, 198, 207
  mud wasp, 202
  peppered moth, 207
  postman butterfly poison, 107
  regal moth doesn't eat, 89
  slugs and snails, 129
  stick insects blend in with trees, 207
  termites, 18
  thorn bug camouflage, 243
  waspss, 41, 137, 202
instruments. *See* music
interviews. *See* Ripley's Exclusives
inventions
  Auto Wash Bowl, 185
  chewing gum, 187
  chocolate, 119
  ciabatta bread, 150
  donut-dunking device, 177
  ear amplifiers, 177
  electric toaster with automatic bread turner, 240
  flexible rubber ice cube tray, 240
  glowing car tires, 176
  heat-regulated stove, 240
  instruments out of household stuff, 220
  knife-fork combo, 216
  mewing machine, 176
  radio for strollers, 177
  safety scoop on cars, 176
  telescope, 55
Iron Factory Ikeda, 215
islands. *See* countries, territories, etc.
Isner, John, 231

J

Jack, Mike, 203
Jackson, Michael, 28, 69
Jackson, Shirley, 32
Jacobs Field, 97
Jaikham, Tanyapong, 194
Jardine, Abby, 143
jellyfish. *See* aquatic life
Jeom-sun, Park, 79
Jet d'Eau fountain, 97
Jett, Joan, 127
Jockel, Luci, 106
John, Elton, 127
Johnson, Dwayne "The Rock", 226
Jones, Dave, 144
Jones, Peggy, 21
Jones, Ty, 51
journeys
  18-hour round trip to ride train, 65
  7,000 miles (11,200 km) to scatter ashes of hamster, 65
  Amelia Earhart's solo Atlantic flight, 147
  around the world in electric car, 146
  cat mailed in Amazon box, 164
  cat trapped in a taxi, 41
  detour after bridge collapse, 42
  detour to avoid taxi fare, 231
  giraffe travels to new zoo, 18
  handcycle across Canada, 116
  Mexico to French Polynesia by sailor and dog, 240
  Patrick Koenig visited 580 golf courses, 223
  rowing across Atlantic, 201
  rowing across Pacific Ocean, 133
  walked 51,500 miles (83,000 km) around Limerick, 213
Joyce, James, 55
Judish, Lynzi, 130, 131
juggling, 162
Julbocken, 59

K

Kalonov, Kamoljon, 75
Kane, James, 171
Kardashian, Kim, 92
Karpitsky, Ivan, 175
Kasteleiner, Joseph, 138
Katanga cross, 98
Kaye, Mike, 231
Keller, Fred, 78
Kentucky State Fair, 116
Khawaja, Rehana, 105
Khmer alphabet, 43
King of Animal Traps, 197
King of the Monsters, 132
King of the Mountain race, 77
kings. *See* governments and leaders
Klee, Paul, 93
Klopek, Sweet Pepper, 84
Klune, Rob, 88
knots, 47
Koenig, Patrick, 223
Koons, Jeff, 208
Krause, Carol-Ann, 49
Křeček, Miloš, 188
Krokatsis, Henry, 189

L

Lacayo, Brittany, 201
Ladner, Brad, 107
Lakehurst, Naval Air Engineering Station, 15
lakes. *See* oceans, rivers, etc.
landmarks
  Arc de Triomphe, 96
  Basilica of Our Lady of Guadalupe, 188
  Burj Khalifa, 210, 232
  Champs-Élysées, 96
  Colosseum, 160, 161
  Empire State Building, 188
  Great Wall of China, The, 70
Lane, Joseph, 227
Langos, Darick, 15
Laolongtou, 70
law and crime
  arrested tree, 144
  arrested waiters for poisoning customers, 90
  assassination of U.S. President John F. Kennedy, 56, 57
  banned beards, 228
  banned televisions, 35
  banned yo-yos, 214–215
  camel shoots owner with shotgun, 61
  car flamethrowers, 185
  criminal John Dillinger shot by FBI, 180
  cross-section of criminal's head, 44
  damaged Yule goats in Sweden, 59
  dice made for cheating, 180
  employee displays own artwork on museum wall, 93
  fake heart attacks, 187
  federal inmates reduce sentences by reading, 38–39
  fined for driving dirty car, 30
  Guano Islands Act of 1856, 188
  illegal camouflage clothing, 27
  illegal group running, 42
  illegal ortolan bunting bird delicacy, 46
  illegal public birthday celebration, 215–218
  illegal stove selling, 77
  illegal to stop walking on pedestrian bridges, 150
  instructed to erect fence to conceal boat, 130
  Kamoljon Kalonov escapes on release day, 75
  Lee Harvey Oswald assassinated J.F.K., 56, 57
  murderer John Horwood, 44
  Nineteenth Amendment, 204
  rules on broomsticks flying, 80
  smuggle mummified monkeys, 97
  smuggle otters and prairie dog, 137
  stolen Boeing 727, 15
  stolen Cadbury Creme Eggs, 144
  stolen clothes by cat, 233
  stolen getaway vehicle, 157
  stolen polar bear model, 209
  stolen Sir Paul McCartney's bass guitar, 93
  stolen Krispy Kreme donut truck, 202
  suspected cannibalism, 45
  suspected knife attack, 187
  suspected mass killing, 171
  suspected pigeon espionage, 18
  suspected squirrel espionage, 108
  suspected theft of fridge, 215
  thief accompanied by parrots, 157
  thief posed as mannequin, 237
  thief tries to steal merchandise, 237
  thieves raid check-cashing business, 157
  thieves raid tobacco shop, 215
  trespassing koala ate plants, 82
  U.S. seize unclaimed bird-poop land, 188
Laykyun Sekkya, 94
Lee, Charlotte, 182
Lee, Lilian, 152
Lefson, Joanne, 16
Legboot, 120, 121
Li, Audriana, 212
Lieber, Peter, 87
Lil Poison, 130
Limitless, Lexie, 146
Lincoln Financial Field, 187
Lind, Jenny, 28
lists
  body parts, 24–25
  camouflaged insects, 206–207
  coliseums, 160–161
  doomed inventions, 176–177
  horned animals, 242–243
  myths and monsters, 66–67
  pygmy animals, 134–135
  tallest statues in the world, 94–95
Liu, Paul, 133
Living Cocoon, the, 219
Lleras, Jennifer, 235
Lluvia de Peces, 104
Lopez, Adam, 88
lost and found
  Amelia Earhart disappearance, 147
  ancient coins discovered, 90
  Argoland continent discovered, 147
  baby found after tornado, 147
  cash inside safe when magnet fishing, 171
  cat found after seven years, 171
  cell phones on London public transport, 167
  corn snake found after dropped by crow, 231
  cross-eyed kitten found in garden, 61
  engagement ring found by detectorist, 159
  escaped dog found at concert, 32
  escaped tortoise found years later, 143
  forest buried under sand, 144
  goldfish dropped in yard, 61
  left-behind hotel luggage, 47
  LEGO bricks found on beach, 42
  pilot returns doll, 47
  Sir Paul McCartney's bass guitar, 93
  smartwatch in toilet, 188
  wallet behind wall of Plaza Theatre, 202
  wallet fished out of lake, 119
  wallet found on beach, 77
Loti pencil, 125
Lotus, LuLu, 42
Loudfoot, Tina, 90
love and marriage
  dogs befriend magpie, 36
  first date gift of Cadbury Creme Egg, 133
  friendship with turkey, 137
  hair cut off by mythical creature before wedding, 67
  kissing insects, 120, 121
  preserved bowel as reminder of happy marriage, 90
  tattoo marriage proposal, 202
  wedding after dog ate passports, 143
  wedding at Philadelphia Eagles game, 187
  wedding in HOP convenience store, 213
  wedding next to Chicago rat hole, 212
  wedding with celebrity lookalikes, 51
  wedding-present vacuum cleaner, 237
  weddings at Cathedral of Junk, 213
Lucas, George, 223

M

Macarenia clavigera, 73
Mackereth, Austin, 72
Maddox Dock, 162
magic, 93, 133, 162, 212, 224, 225
Maiden, Leanne, 201
Maki Master, The, 92
Maldonado, Carlos, 185
Malone, Post, 68
Mansa Musa, 143
Marie Antoi-knit gown, 186
Marley, Bob, 92
marriage. *See* love and marriage
Martins, Ana, 232
Marylebone Station, 105
Master of Suspense, 215
Mazapán de la Rosa, 15
Mazri, Magda, 143
McCabe, James, 143
McCarthy, Charlie, 29
McCarthy, Cormac, 167
McCartney, Sir Paul, 93
McFly, Marty, 110, 111, 112, 115
McIlroy, Rory, 157
McKinley, William, 204
McQuade, Darren, 93
McQueen, Steve, 233
McWhirter, Norris, 152
medicine and medical procedures. *See also* genetics
  amputations during U.S. Civil War, 216
  baby born with organs outside body, 130
  back brace worn by U.S. President John F. Kennedy, 57
  bee stings, 143
  body integrity identity disorder, 175
  broken ankle led to handboarding, 85
  broken bones of Emma Stone, 21
  broken ribs in motorcycle race, 210
  cardiac arrest of patient and emergency responder, 119
  fake heart attacks, 187
  gout in King Henry VIII, 141
  haunted painting makes people feel ill, 233
  hole in windpipe after suppressing sneeze, 187
  hypothermia death, 129
  injured spinal cord, 211
  injury after crocodile attack, 227
  injury after cycling accidents, 116
  injury after water jet launch, 97
  leech found inside throat, 157
  orangutan treats wounds with plant, 164
  polycystic ovary syndrome, 219
  shaving is harmful for students, 228
  struck by lightning twice, 213
  surgery removes cell phone from intestine, 187
  surgery removes coins from alligator stomach, 20
  surgery removes colon, 90
  surgery removes eel from abdomen, 18
  surgery removes extra dog legs, 155
  surgery removes gear shift knob from snake, 33
  surgery removes household items from stomach, 237
  surgery removes palmaris longus muscle, 25
  surgery removes parasitic roundworm larvae, 107
  surgery removes Pepys' bladder stone, 209
  suspected appendicitis was labor pains, 215
  synesthesia, 215
  toothache led to 32-year hibernation, 143
  toothbrush stuck in woman's throat, 51
  van Gogh cuts off own ear, 233
  vitiligo, 60
Megan Thee Stallion, 130
Mekasha, Fekadu, 69
Met Gala, 102
Metallica, 23
Metcalf, Malcolm, 31
Midway-Frogtown Arborators Band, 144
Millennium Force roller coaster, 164
Mills, Kevin, 31
Minaj, Nicki, 103
miniatures. *See* small
Mirsaitova, Maryam, 155
mistaken identity
  beetle mistaken for bird poop, 124
  bomb mistaken for garden ornament, 182
  cake made of yarn, 21
  California mistaken for an island, 188
  Manoel Marciano da Silva mistakenly declared dead, 100
  painting displayed upside down and mislabeled, 233
  pom-pom mistaken for baby hedgehog, 82
  racing pigeon suspected of espionage, 18
  suspected appendicitis was labor pains, 215
  Tom Hollander mistaken for Tom Holland, 209
  wizard wand mistaken for knife, 187
  yoga class mistaken for mass killing, 171
models and sculptures
  animal exhibit using toy bricks, 20
  boat made from ice, 175
  bread sculptures, 96
  cars turned into art, 108
  cat sculptures, 239
  ceramics resemble cardboard, 210
  charred trees sculptures, 65
  chocolate Colosseum, 160
  Christmas tree made from lobster traps, 171
  dog made from flowers, 208
  dragon balloon sculpture, 116
  Dromeas, 237

European towns and cities models, 49
famous landmarks of Crimea, 19
giant pencil made from tree, 125
Godzilla sculpture, 132
gum wrapper Super Bowl XI figures, 217
Hobbit sculptures in airport, 166
Hot Dog in the City, 97
knights carved with chainsaw, 51
matchstick *Back to the Future* models, 110–115
matchstick Mozart sculpture, 139
matchstick Michelangelo and David sculpture, 139
mirrored pillar in Nevada desert, 202
model TV from toast, 216
popsicle-stick *Hindenburg* model, 15
polar bear model stolen, 209
shark made from snow, 185
Sultan the Pit Pony, 182
toys made from cheese, 47
wooden sculptures carved with chainsaw, 51
money
  ancient coin discovery, 90
  bank built on country border, 212
  Boba Fett action figure sale, 130
  Cabrales blue cheese wheel sale, 71
  candy bar price increase, 130
  coins of British monarchs, 107
  dog chews cash, 123
  dolphin teeth used as currency, 203
  dung beetle worth, 61
  Ed Sheeran makes cheap music video, 73
  Emperor Bokassa's pearl-studded shoes, 50
  Ford's Theatre tickets sale, 49
  Gene Simmons tongue insurance, 55
  giant wagon sale, 78
  jeans cost $600, 213
  Katanga cross used as currency, 98
  King Mansa Musa of Mali riches, 144
  LEGO gold mask auction sale, 49
  lemon auction sale, 175
  Lloyd Groff Copeman's invention earnings, 240
  lottery ticket chosen by dog, 137
  lottery win of millions, 105
  meteorite-infused vodka cost, 220
  Monaco millionaires, 151, 154
  notgeld used as currency, 192
  pay $2 to be slapped by waitress, 237
  paycheck to Tom Hollander by mistake, 209
  PEZ dispenser value, 201
  Portrait of Doctor Rey value, 233
  prize for designing Alaska's flag, 129
  rat broth cost, 124
  resale of dumpster goods, 235
  richest man in Rome: Marcus Licinius Crassus, 159
  safe found when magnet fishing, 171
  Sir Paul McCartney's bass guitar value, 93
  tax avoidance, 212
  The Amazing Spider-Man Issue No.1 auction sale, 167
  Tijan and Matthew Brown concert spending, 47
  Titanic wooden door sale, 133
  To'ak chocolate bar cost, 150
  Transformers memorabilia value, 231
  U.S. banknotes, 71
  waiters poisoned bad tippers, 90
  wallet fished out of lake, 119
Monfet, Olivier, 68
Monneraud, Jacques, 210
Monroe, Marilyn, 13, 29
monsters. *See* myths and legends
Montgomery, Dorothy, 130

Moo Deng, 134
moon. *See* space
Moore, Rich, 129
Moore, Sydney, 147
Morgan, Erin, 47
Mortensen, Reece, 36
Morton's toe, 25
mountains
  Ben Nevis, 88
  Blackhead Peak, 129
  Boggy Peak, 18
  Carpathian Mountains, 47
  Estonian mountains, 71
  Gaizinkalns hill, 128
  Moroccan mountains, 49
  Mount Chimborazo, 74
  Mount Disappointment, 21
  Mount Everest, 26, 73
  Mount Fuji, 156, 196
  Mount Kilimanjaro, 88
  Mount Obama, 18
  Mount Parnitha, 65
  Mount Taranaki, 163
  Mount Wycheproof, 77
  Qinling mountain range, 123
  Rocky Mountains, 116
  Suur Munamägi, 71, 130
  Taranaki Maunga, 163
movies
  Armageddon, 167
  Back to the Future, 110–115
  Batman, 23, 107, 215
  Beetlejuice, 130
  Chitty Chitty Bang Bang, 22, 23
  Coraline, 50
  Elf, 226
  Ghostbusters, 93
  Godzilla, 132, 133
  Home Alone, 226
  Joker, 226
  Lilo & Stitch, 50
  Pirates of the Caribbean, 51
  Psycho, 215
  Puss in Boots: The Last Wish, 49
  Robin Hood: Prince of Thieves, 55
  Schindler's List, 167
  Shrek, 226
  Spider-Man, 209
  Star Wars, 75, 130, 223
  Superman, 157
  The Birds, 215
  The Chronicles of Narnia: The Lion, the Witch and the Wardrobe, 77
  The Fall Guy, 73
  The Godfather, 73
  The Good, the Bad and the Ugly, 71
  The Great Escape, 233
  The Hobbit: The Desolation of Smaug, 166
  The Little Mermaid, 226
  The Lord of the Rings, 166
  The Munsters, 15
  The Nightmare Before Christmas, 50
  The Wizard of Oz, 50
  Titanic, 133
  Transformers, 231
  X-men, 151
Mozart, 139
Mulligan, Barbara, 155
mummified or preserved remains
  bowel preserved in formaldehyde, 90
  mummified Anga people, 176
  mummified head of Alfred Packer
  mummified monkeys found in luggage, 97
  Ötzi the Iceman, 22
  preserved cross-section of criminal's head, 44
  preserved snake collection, 164
Munro, Gavin, 203
Murray-Lang, Lisa, 65
Murray, Joe, 202
Murray, Robery, 49
Murray, Wayne, 105
museums
  AKC Museum of the Dog, 102
  Elephant PooPooPaper Park, 124
  Guggenheim Museum, 208

LEGO museum, 188
McDonald's memorabilia museum, 182
McDonald's underground museum, 219
Musée des Plans-Reliefs, 49
Museo Tamayo, 215
Museum of Science and Technology, 139
Museum of Zoology at University of Michigan, 164
Pinakothek der Moderne, 93
Poozeum, 159
San Diego Natural History Museum, 42
Sock Monkey Museum, 223
mushrooms. *See* fungi
music
  autographed Chevrolet Corvette, 126–127
  bass guitar owned by Sir Paul McCartney, 93
  concerts in one year, 47
  disco in HOP convenience stores, 213
  heavy metal bands in Finland, 83
  Hot Codlins song, 189
  Louis Cardozo plays flying piano for music video, 239
  male palm cockatoos drum to attract female, 41
  matchstick sculpture of Mozart, 139
  rapping grannies, 79
  Road 67 plays song by Republic, 104
  Uganda has short national anthem, 230
  wave-powered organ plays music, 61
Mutianyu Great Wall, 71
Mycock, Dave, 231
myths and legends
  Bigfoot, 168
  chupacabra, 168
  dragons, 70, 116
  vampires, 73, 78, 99, 137, 168
  witches, 80, 196, 150
  Wolpertinger, 169
  yokai mythical creatures, 66–67

N

nail art, 23
names
  Batman's Gotham City name, 215
  Boggy Peak renamed Mount Obama, 18
  Chad's nickname, 51
  change name to Marylebone, 105
  city named Batman, 226–227
  Khaleesi name popularity, 167
  Icelandic phone books, 105
  illegal 25-word baby name, 202
  Saint-Louis-du-Ha! Ha! town name, 47–48
  Sigourney Weaver changed name, 209
  Star Wars' Tatooine name, 226
  surnames in South Korea, 208
  two men named Mark Garland, 58
Nan, Liu, 213
National Trust, UK, 227
National Weather Service, 49
Nature-to-You Loan Library, 42
Noonan, Fred, 147
Northern Lights, 93
Nowakowski, Sammie, 159
Numan, Gary, 105

O

Oakes, Russell E., 177
Obama, Barack, 18
oceans, rivers, etc. *See also* aquatic life
  Amazon river, 18
  Atlantic Ocean, 147, 175, 201, 227
  Atomic Lake, 121
  Bering Sea, 82
  Boiling River, 177
  Caño Cristales, 73
  Cascata da Sepultura, 49

English Channel, 231
Gaira River, 100
Gulf of Mexico, 150
Hudson Bay, 228
Indo-Pacific, 51
James Bruce Falls, 240
Jellyfish Lake, 172
Jordan River, 233
Kaieteur Falls, 100
Kuwait has no natural lakes or rivers, 124
Lake Assal, 71
Lake Chagan, 121
Lake General Carrera, 76
Lake Malawi, 138
Lake Nyos, 46
Lake of the Woods, 119
Lake Ohrid, 170
Ljubljanica, 244
Neches River, 235
Niagara Falls, 233, 240
Nishiki River, 188
North Atlantic, 133
oasis in extinct Waw an Namus volcano, 133–134
Oka River, 155
Pacific Ocean, 73, 133, 147, 175, 240
Paratethys, 188
Pitch Lake, 222
Qiantang River, 100
rainbow swamps, 150
River Cherwell, 31
River Liffey, 58
River Ouse, 174
Strait of Messina, 230
Umi-Jigoku spring, 155
waterfall in Changi Airport, 200
Ogawa, Tadahiko, 216
Oita Airport, 93
Okun, Arlene and Michael, 223
Old Knobbley tree, 144
Old Philadelphia Lady, 240
old. *See* age
Oldman, Gary, 105
Olsson, Karolina, 143
Olympic Games, 34, 35, 58, 240
Ono, Jiro, 92
Oodako matsuri, 101
Orbax, Burnaby Q., 84
Oswald, Lee Harvey, 56, 57
Ötzi the Iceman, 22
Outlaw, Paul, 97
ovophobia, 215

P

Packer, Alfred, 45
Packington, Jemima, 100
Palace of the Sultan of Brunei, the, 39
Pan, Silke, 38–39
Pando tree root system, 144
Pang, Sze Tai, 116
Papadakis, Michael, 104, 105
Paralympics, 34
parasites
  roundworm larvae, 107
  tongue-eating louse, 184
Paris, Jasmin, 26
Parker, Thomas, 147
parking lots, 124, 150, 187, 237
parks
  Chain O'Lakes State Park, 15
  Coppelia Park, 100
  Death Valley National Park, 41
  Frozen Head State Park, 26
  Gordon Moore Park, 55
  Joseph Grimaldi Park, 189
  Molinere Underwater Sculpture Park, 95
  Nijigen no Mori Park, 132
  Park of Souls, 65
  Shiniuzhai National Geological Park, 105
  Steelhead Park, 77
Parton, Dolly, 12, 13
Patel, Sardar Vallabhbhai, 95
paternoster elevators, 15
Penny, Trevor, 31
Pepys, Samuel, 209

Pet Gala, 102
Peters, Ainslie, 133
Peterson, Abby, 51
Petts, Mick, 182
Phillips, Keith, 159
phobias, ovophobia, 215
photophores, 128
Picasso, Pablo, 93
Piedra de Plata valley, 150
piercings. *See* body modifications
Pigcasso, 16
Pinakothek der Moderne, 93
Pink Soup Fest, 200
plants and trees
  akar kuning plant, 164
  Atacama Desert flowers, 52
  Botanical Garden of Saint Vincent and the Grenadines, 189–190
  camouflage, 206, 207, 243
  charred trees into sculptures, 65
  coco de mer palm tree seeds, 198–199
  Congo's rainforests, 58
  flower festival in Chelsea, 183
  fragrant plants on Comoros, 55
  ghost pipe flower, 78
  giant baobab trees, 48–49
  giant pumpkin, 144
  giant zucchini, 119
  Great Vine of Hampton Court Palace, 234
  koala steals plants, 82
  Macarenia clavigera, 73
  northern rātā tree, 166
  oldest olive tree, 174
  passionflower vines 107
  plant clothing, 148
  Soybean car, 182
  sunflowers absorb radioactive material, 230–231
  traveler's tree of Madagascar, 144
  tree covered in webs, 198
  tree turned into pencil sculpture, 125
  tulips grown in the Netherlands, 162
  walking palm tree, 231
  willow-tree furniture, 203
  woman lived in tree for two years, 145
  yareta plant, 185
plays and playwrights. *See* theater
poison and venom
  death adder snake venom, 143
  postman butterfly, 107
  siphonophores, 32
  skin of newt, 32
  slow loris's venomous bite, 135
  spitting spiders, 18
  venomous eastern brown snake, 143
  waiters poison customers, 90
  whitemargin stargazer fish's venom, 51
Pontcysyllte Aqueduct, 91
Poochies Pupsicles, 123
poop
  beetle mistaken for bird poop, 124
  carpet pythons droppings, 107
  dung beetles break down manure, 61
  elephant dung paper, 124
  fossilized poop in museum, 159
  Places I've Pooped app, 93
  Poozeum, 159
  searching dog poop for bills, 123
  U.S. seize unclaimed bird-poop island, 188
Pope Francis, 219–220
Powis Castle, 107
Prajapati, Shashikant, 130
prehistoric
  dinosaurs, 21, 159
  fossilized poop, 159
  fossilized stingray, 199
  giant prehistoric bird, 182
  saber-toothed tiger, 82
  woolly mammoth, 82
presidents. *See* governments and leaders
Price, Edna, 31

Priest, Arthur John, 71
prime ministers. *See* governments and leaders
prisons and jails
  Amphitheatre of Tarragona, 161
  Irkutsk penal colony, 75
  Maracaibo prison, 130
  prisoners of war, 192
  Shivamogga Jail 187
  Strangeways, 181
props
  Chitty Chitty Bang Bang rocking chair, 23
  Doctor Who, 144
  Michael Jackson fangs, 28
  Superman cape, 39
  telescope in *Robin Hood: Prince of Thieves*, 55
  Titanic door, 133
protests
  Barbie Liberation Organization, 203
  candy bar price increase, 130
  vow of silence, 175
  woman lives in tree, 145
Pula Arena, 161
pyramids
  Great Pyramid of Giza, 74
  Mayan Kukulcan, 149
  Sudan pyramids, 15, 211–212

Q

queens. *See* governments and leaders

R

races and marathons
  Barkley Marathons, 26
  Chicago Marathon, 20
  Course des Cafés, 240
  King of the Mountain, 77
  Lewes to Newhaven Raft Race, 174
  London marathon, 215
  Mexico City Marathon, 47
  motorcycle race before 98th birthday, 210
  run 1 mile (1.6 km) in pool, 88
  run under-4-minute mile, 152
  wheelbarrow race, 85
  World Coal Carrying Championships, 27
Radcliffe Steele, Lucie, 226
Rafi, Mohammed, 139
rainforests, 20, 58, 59, 103, 147, 178, 231, 242
rarities
  black-and-white lemon shark, 73
  Boba Fett action figure, 130
  body integrity identity disorder, 175
  Brazilian flea toad, 82
  brown-and-white panda, 123
  dog fur pigmentation, 143
  double crown in human hair, 24
  fish scale tide, 100
  gastroschisis, 130
  LEGO found on beach, 42
  LEGO gold mask, 49
  LEGO wedding presents, 188
  outie belly button, 25
  PEZ candy dispensers, 201
  tickets from Ford's Theatre, 49
  white alligator, 20
Reeve, Christopher, 39
Reign of Terror, 187
religion and spirituality
  Amphitheatre of Tarragona, 161
  Ayodhya temple demolished, 175
  Basilica of Our Lady of Guadalupe, 188
  blessed Nike Air Max 97 shoes, 233
  Buddhism, 94
  Capela dos Ossos, 182
  Catholicism, 98, 105
  chapel climbing wall, 223
  Chapel of Bones, 182
  clown pilgrimage, 188
  Divided Church, 228
  Great Mosque of Djenné, 236
  Hinduism, 42, 94
  Malta churches clocks, 145
  Redeemed Christian Church of God, 71
  Rising Star Missionary Baptist Church pastor, 219
  road runs through church, 228
  Ruzica Church, 197
  Spring Temple Buddha, 95
reptiles and amphibians
  African sulcata tortoise escape, 143
  alligator's stomach coin removal, 20
  anaconda mouth, 227
  Brazilian flea toad size, 82
  breathing through butt, 164
  California newt's poisonous skin, 32
  carpet python droppings, 107
  corn snake dropped on garage, 231
  crocodiles at Sheedi Mela festival, 171–172
  crocodile attacks farm worker, 227
  crocodiles lure water birds, 121
  crocodiles rescue dog, 18
  death adder snake venom, 143
  eastern brown snake removed from cat's neck, 73
  eastern brown snake stops tennis match, 143
  frog made from bread, 215
  frog on Dominica coat of arms, 71–72
  frog with mushroom on side, 90
  giant northern green anaconda discovery, 20
  Jackson's chameleon, 243
  long-nosed horned frog, 242
  Mexican mole lizard, 231
  mosquito sucks frog blood, 32
  Mozambique spitting cobra, 37
  preserved snakes in museum, 164
  purple frog lives underground, 41
  rat snake swallows car part, 33
  saltwater crocodile attacks farmer, 123
  slug snake, 129
  snake eats itself, 18
  snake wraps around woman's arm, 21
  spitting cobra, 37
  western bell frog, 212
  wolverine frog, 151
  yellow-striped dwarf frog, 134
rescues
  baby shark head stuck, 185
  dog detects gas leak, 21
  dog helped by crocodiles, 18
  dog stays with hiker's body, 129
  dog trapped in a cave, 143
  kitten rescued by runner, 20
  magpie chick rehomed, 36
  man overboard by marlin fish, 201
  shipwrecked sailor and his dog, 240
  sinking ships survivor, 71
  tennis-ball homes for mice, 245
  woman lives in tree, 145
  women trapped in toilet, 188
restaurants
  Abe-chan pork skewers, 93
  Gordos ice cream in toilet bowl, 124
  KFC first date, 31
  Kipposhi, 62
  McDonald's, 157, 182, 219
  milk bars, 186–187
  New Mexico chile question, 15
  Shachihoko-ya izakaya bar, 237
Rey, Félix, 233
Ringer, Holden, 42
Rios, Alejandro, 37
Rios, Heather, 21
Ripley, Robert, 152
Ripley's Believe It or Not!, 31, 104, 173, 205
Ripley's Collection
  1900 Olympic Medal, 35
  autographed Chevrolet Corvette, 126–127
  Back to the Future matchstick models, 110–115
  Bob Dylan portrait, 68
  boots for cows, 121
  carved Super-Man deck of cards, 225
  Charlie ventriloquist puppet, 29
  cheating dice, 180
  Chitty Chitty Bang Bang rocking chair, 23
  chupacabra footprint cast, 168
  Conni Gordon fast art, 17
  Converse shoes in a glass jug, 225
  cross-section of criminal's head, 44
  cup survives fire, 63
  deck of cards in bottle, 224
  early washing machine, 87
  eclipse art, 105
  fabric from Amelia Earhart's plane, 147
  FBI letter about Bigfoot, 168
  field mass kit, 98
  foot bath, 140
  fossilized stingray, 199
  garlic painting, 17
  giraffe scapula, 163
  gum wrapper Super Bowl XI figures, 217
  jewelry made with hair of deceased, 81
  John Dillinger wanted poster, 180
  junk-mail mosaic of Bob Dylan, 68
  Katanga Cross, 98
  King Henry VIII's gout footwear, 141
  knife-fork combo, 216
  Lee Harvey Oswald coat, 56
  limelight lamp, 28
  magic lanterns, 86
  matchbook Godzilla 3D portrait, 133
  mechanical calculators, 87
  Michael Jackson fangs, 28
  Michael Jackson portrait, 69
  model TV from toast, 216
  mummified head of cannibal, 45
  murderer skin, 44
  Nike Air Max holy water, 233
  notgeld money, 192
  petrified peanut shells, 159
  Pigcasso painting, 16
  Post Malone portrait, 68
  President Carter cartoon, 205
  President Kennedy, 56–57
  rations book, 192
  sculptures carved with chainsaw, 51
  Selena Gomez portrait, 69
  soap babies, 204
  stopwatch records under-4-minute mile, 152
  Strangeways door, 181
  Superman cape, 39
  sushi roll in acrylic, 93
  Swarovski crystal Stormtrooper helmet, 75
  Taylor Swift portrait, 239
  toy guillotine, 187
  trench art, 192
  urinal slippers, 140
  vampire cabinet, 99
  Wolpertinger, 169
  women's ballot box, 204
Ripley's Exclusives
  Bugkiss device for kissing insects, 120–121
  hairwork and table braiding, 80
  Maddox Dock circus performer, 162
  Silke Pan performer, 38–39
Rittner, Rob and Brooke, 187
rivers. *See* oceans, rivers, etc.
RM (singer), 93
roads
  Highway 10 in Saudi Arabia, 219
  Road 67 in Hungary, 104
  runs through Austrian church, 228
  Texas highways, 235
  U.S. Route 20, 147
Roberts, Maureen, 223
Robinson, Tom, 133
RoboCup, 65
rodents
  beavers hold breath underwater, 227
  hamster's ashes, 65
  mouse deterrent, 176
  mouse tennis ball homes, 245
  mouse tidied shed, 212
  prairie dog smuggled onto plane, 137
  pygmy jerboa size, 134
  rat broth, 124
  squirrel sidewalk impression, 212
  squirrels accused of espionage, 108
Rodrigo, Olivia, 215
Roman artifact, 107
Romero, Cesar, 23
Ronstadt, Linda, 240
Roose, Jaan, 230
Rowling, J.K., 23
Rubio, Anthony, 102
Rudolph, Amelia, 52
running. *See* races and marathons

S

Saeki, Katsumi, 219
Saint George, 100
Salar de Uyuni, 36
Salina Turda, 241
Sanquhar Post Office, 100
Sarajevo Clock Tower, 37
Scanlan, Jeff, 224, 225
Schalkx, Gijs, 58
Schimmel Gold, Sandhi, 68
schools and universities
  Brigham Young University, 228
  Centre d'Art Acrobatique Keita Fodeba acrobatic school, 96–97
  chess lessons, 20–21
  Community Driving School, 119
  exam internet restrictions, 13
  Mountview Middle School, 93
  Princeton University, 88
  Steven Spielberg returns to college, 167
  students climb greased tower, 222
  Telford Park School, 129
  University of California Berkeley, 133
  University of Michigan Museum of Zoology, 164
  University of Tokyo, 63
  University of Wisconsin-Parkside, 73
  Vermont State University, 164
  Woodland Middle School, 116
Schulz, Charles, 173
sculptures. *See* models and sculptures
Segalen, Victor, 233
Seiryu Miharashi Station, 188
Severn, Casey, 197
Shaddock, Tim, 240
Shakespeare, William, 55, 78
sharks. *See* aquatic life
Sheeran, Ed, 51, 73
shipwrecks, 37, 78
Shop with a Cop event, 237
Siddhartha Gautama, 94
Sieracki, Sam, 219
Simmons, Gene, 55
Simms Brachman, Kedrin, 201
Simms, Frank, 201
Sinatra, Frank, 23
Singh, Kuldeep, 237
sinkholes, 32, 55, 150
Sisk, Bryan, 92
skating and skateboarding. *See* sports
Skeleton Coast, 78
skeletons. *See* bones
Skywalker, Luke, 226
sleep
  chinstrap penguins nap, 18
  hibernating animals, 164
  hibernating woman, 143
  inemuri (napping at work), 231
  mythical creature steals breath during sleep, 67
  nightmares about fingers, 175
  reindeer sleep and chew cud, 32
  Salvador Dalí power naps, 55
  sharks swim when asleep, 227
  sleep contest In Seoul, 119
  sleeping black bear, 143
slow. *See* speed
slugs and snails. *See* insects and bugs
small
  bicycle, 153
  Brazilian flea toad, 82
  candy crab, 71
  Cardigan library, 71
  Eurasian harvest mouse, 245
  fish, 20
  Mount Wycheproof, 77
  national forest in America, 154
  Polly Pocket toy movie scenes, 50
  preauricular pit near ear, 24
  pygmy animals, 134–135
  sandwich model, 23
  yellow-striped dwarf frog, 134
Smith, Emma, 231
Smith, Matt, 60
snacks with smacks, 237
snakes. *See* reptiles and amphibians
Snoopy, 173
Snopp Dogg, 12
soap babies, 204
Soerensen, Morten, 144
SoFi Stadium, 32
Soybean car, 182
space
  Artemis I mission, 173
  astronauts, 77, 173
  gravity on Earth, 228
  Mars, 77
  meteor crater diamonds, 90
  meteorite vodka, 220
  Moon, 37, 71, 77, 104, 105, 173
  NASA, 167
  Orion spacecraft, 173
  Sarajevo Clock Tower, 37–38
  Snoopy used in zero-gravity test, 173
  solar eclipse, 104, 105, 195
  Sun, 104, 105, 195
Spears, Britney, 12, 167
speed
  avalanches, 240
  Eminem fast rap, 78
  flic-flac spider cartwheels, 171
  jet stunts, 179
  painting in under a minute, 17
  solve Rubik's Cube underwater, 105
  solve Rubik's Cube while blindfolded, 88
  solved Rubik's Cube while freefalling, 219
  speed eating, 203
  spitting spiders fire silk, 18
  springtail flips, 107
spiders
  bread spiders, 215
  Chinese hourglass spider, 195
  Darwin's bark spider, 137
  diving bell spider, 40
  flic-flac spider, 171
  jumping spider, 229
  pink crab spider, 206
  scorpion-tailed spider, 77
  spiders eaten by mud wasps, 202
  spitting spider, 18
  tarantula causes accident, 41
  yatsukahagi mythical spiders, 67
Spielberg, Steven, 167
sports
  adaptive, 58
  archery, 34
  BASE jumping, 148
  baseball, 58, 73, 88, 97, 175, 244
  basketball, 49, 58
  beep baseball, 58
  bungee jumping, 213
  camel jumping, 242–243
  cave diving, 201
  freefalling, 219
  golf, 88, 97, 157, 203, 207, 223
  handboarding, 85

horseriding, 31, 118
hot-air ballooning, 35
hula hooping, 64
kitesurfing, 165
Olympic track races, 58
paddleboarding, 196
paragliding, 238
plank position, 88
rodeo, 118
roller skating, 162, 241
scuba diving, 133, 143, 185
skateboarding, 85, 164
skiing, 71, 219
soccer, 55, 58, 65, 66, 117, 124, 210, 245
spin class, 239
surfing, 164, 178
table tennis, 117
tennis, 117, 133, 143, 231, 245
teqball, 117
unicycle hockey, 188
volcano surfing, 164
volleyball, 244
wakeskating, 148
walking, 213
Sprinkle, Mel, 88
Stade Louis II 15
Stallone, Sylvester, 73
Stamm, Leah, 219
Stanley Cup, 63
Stanton, Andrew, 88
statues
 Buddha, 95
 Laykyun Sekkya, 94
 Spring Temple Buddha, 95
 St. Francis of Assisi, 231
 Statue of Belief, 94
 Statue of Liberty, 95
 Statue of Unity, 95
 Ushiku Daibutsu, 95
 Whale Bone Alley structure 185–186
Stevens, Emmie, 123
Stevenson, Robert Louis, 61
Stewart, Ben, 88
Stitch, Scarlet, 186
Stocki, Jay, 97
Stoker, Bram, 99
Stone, Emma, 21
Stoneham, Bill, 233
Stormtrooper helmet covered in Swarovski crystals, 75
Stourbridge Shuttle, 65
Stuart, Fernando Fitz-James, 202
Stutzman, Matt, 34
Suni and the Seven Princesses, 79
Sunscribes, 104, 105
Super-Man, 157, 225
surgeries. *See* medicine and medical procedures
 elephants damage car, 37
 ship sinkings, 71
Suur Munamägi, 71
Suvarnabhumi International Airport, 137
Swallow Craig, 37
Swift, Taylor, 226, 239
Swope, Zachariah, 49
sword balancing, 31
sword swallowing, 30, 31, 88
Synn, Anastasia, 237

T

Tahiru, Abubakar, 144
Tan Hong An, Daryl, 105
tattoos. *See* body modifications
taxidermy, 42, 169
teams
 Chicken Inn soccer team, 245
 Cleveland Indians baseball team, 97
 Dallas Cowboys, 187
 Knoxville Smokies baseball team, 73
 Los Angeles Clippers, 49
 New York Yankees, 175
 Philadelphia Eagles, 187
 RoboÉireann team, 65

Tri-City Chili Peppers baseball team, 244
Watford soccer club, 58
technology
 3D printing, 75
 Apple watches, 15
 cell phone emoji art, 12
 cell phone swallowed by inmate, 187
 cell phones lost on London public transport, 167
 cherry pickers trim hedges, 107
 drone drops tennis ball, 133
 drone pulls wakeskater, 148
 early washing machine, 87
 GPS to plant seeds for rainbow rice art, 194
 magic lantern projector, 86
 paternoster elevators, 15
 Places I've Pooped smartphone app, 93
 robot wins Rock Paper Scissors, 63
 robots play soccer, 65
 slide adder calculators, 87
 stopwatch for under 4-minute mile, 152
 technological implants in body, 237
 vacuum cleaner, 237
Teepa-Tarau, Bayleigh, 203
teeth
 dentures from dead soldiers' teeth, 228
 extra teeth, 203
 false teeth butt bite, 73
 Michael Jackson fangs, 28
 pull cars with teeth, 213
 teeth turned green, 124
theater and plays
 A Streetcar Named Desire, 93
 Peter Pan, 23
 Plaza Theatre, 202
 tickets from Ford's Theatre, 49
 William Shakespeare, 55, 78
Thiem, Dominic, 143
Tomasén, Lino, 210
Tottori Sand Dunes, 55
toys and games. *See also* video games
 Barbie voice box changed, 203
 Boba Fett action figure, 130
 cheese toys, 47
 chess lessons, 20–21
 chess possibilities, 63
 dice for cheating, 180
 G.I. Joe voice box changed, 203
 giant festival kites, 101
 LEGO gold mask, 49
 LEGO octopus found, 42
 LEGO collection, 188
 playing cards made in U.S., 228
 Polly Pocket transformations, 50
 rubber duck collection, 182
 rubber duck found after years, 58
 Rubik's Cube records, 88, 105, 219
 sock monkey collection, 223
 stuffed toy fox, 223
 toy brick animals, 20
 toy guillotines, 187
 ventriloquist puppet, 29
 yo-yo ban, 214–215
TRAM-EM European TramDriver Championship, 48
transportation. *See also* cycling and bicycles
 Alcantara ship, 71
 Amelia Earhart's Lockheed Vega 5B, 147
 banana car, 109
 BARK Air, 129
 Blue Angels stunt planes, 179
 boat for bears, 175
 boat made of ice, 175
 boat damaged in storm, 240
 Boeing 737 plane stolen, 15
 Boeing 737 plane villa, 147
 Britannic ship, 71
 canoe along aqueduct, 91
 car art parade, 108–109
 car autographed by musicians, 126
 car Auto Wash Bowl, 185
 car fueled by eco-oil, 58

car loudspeaker Celine Dion battles, 100
car pulled with eye sockets, 88
car quantity in San Marino, 194
car scoop invention, 176
cars pulled with teeth, 213
car turned into UFO, 136
car-rolling stunt for *The Fall Guy*, 73
cargo ship lost load, 42
coffin-shaped dragster car, 15
DeLorean, 111
Donegal ship, 71
Dorest Plane Pull, 27
electric car round-the-world trip, 146
first electric car, 147
flight halted due to maggots, 58
flight of two Mark Garlands, 58
free public transportation in Luxembourg, 136
Hindenburg, 15
homemade rafts in race, 174
homemade wooden boat, 133
hot-air ballooning at Olympics, 35
Mercedes popularity, 12
minibus pulled with beard, 213
mobility scooter becomes movie replica, 22
motorbike jump in *The Great Escape*, 233
motorcade of U.S. President John F. Kennedy, 57
motorcycle race for 98 year old, 210
pickup truck turned into wagon, 78
plane causes hole in clouds, 37
plane travel for dogs, 129
plane sounds detected by dog, 171
rowing across Atlantic, 201
ship sinking survival, 71
Soybean car, 182
tanks fitted with water-heating devices, 78
Titanic ship, 71
train runaway in India, 220
train station with no entrance or exit, 188
train transporting asparagus, 100
train transporting iron ore, 147
tram driving championships, 48
truck delivering Krispy Kremes, 202
truck driving at 90 years old, 42
truck pulled with neck, 213
truck stowaway, 231
USS *Cape Lookout*, 235
Trauman, Brian, 201
travel and tourism
 Berlin High Swing, 133
 Cathedral of Junk, 213
 coffin escape room, 85
 Godzilla zipline, 132
 Great Wall of China visitors, 71
 Mount Fuji problem, 196
 Sad Hill Cemetery attraction, 71
 Umi-Jigoku spring, 155
 visit Bay Area Rapid Transit (BART) stations, 133
 visit Britain's shortest branch line, 65
 visit UK train stations, 144
Trinh, Garry, 116
Trouble Version Two, 137
trovant rocks, 184
trucks. *See* transportation
Turner, Danielle, 63
turtles. *See* reptiles and amphibians
Tussaud, Madame, 187
TV
 Bridgerton, 131
 Doctor Who, 144
 Friends, 93
 Game of Thrones, 167
 Ripley's Believe It or Not!, 153
 Superman, 157
 The Brady Bunch, 23
 Wednesday, 226
Tweed, James, 124
twins, 154, 159
typewriters, 167, 228

U

U.S. Marines, 56, 179
U.S. Navy, 179, 222
Udiljak, Janina, 75
Umi-Jigoku, 155
unicycles. *See* cycling and bicycles
universities. *See* schools
Ushiku Daibutsu, 95

V

vampires. *See* myths and legends
Van de Sompel, Samantha, 215
van Gogh, Vincent, 233
Varotsos, Costas, 237
vel kavadi, 42
Vhils, 208
video games
 clothes look pixelated, 139
 Sonic the Hedgehog, 107
 World of Warcraft, 15
 youngest pro gamer, 130
Vikings, 31
Villa, Kathy, 32
Vishwas Swaroopam, 94
vitiligo, 60
Voigt, Henry, 15
volcanoes
 Cerro Negro, 164
 Mauna Loa, 77
 Mount Erebus, 124
 Mount Vesuvius, 73
 mud volcanoes, 23
 Ol Doinyo Lengai, 218
 Poás Volcano, 220
 Teoca volcano, 124
 Waw an Namus, 133
voting rights, 204
Vujity-Zsolnay, Barnabás, 15

W

Waite, Mary and Ivor, 237
WakeBASE, 148
Walker, Will, 203
Walt Disney Concert Hall, 85
Wanderwell, Aloha, 146
Wardman, Vin, 22
Warhol, Andy, 93
wars
 Battle of Normandy, 78
 Battle of Waterloo, 228
 civil war, 133, 216
 Cold War, 67
 D-Day landings, 188
 field mass kit, 98
 French Revolution, 187
 gladiators, 119, 161
 Mexican Revolution, 118
 Parthian army, 159
 Pastry War, 97
 peace treaties, 71
 Russo-Japanese War, 71
 U.S. Civil War, 216
 Vietnam War, 128
 World War I, 192, 198
 World War II, 78, 83, 154, 171, 182, 188, 193, 233
Warwick Farm train station, 41
water ballet, 220
waterfalls. *See* oceans, rivers, etc.
Waterloo Teeth, 228
weather
 avalanches, 240
 clouds, 37
 heat wave spontaneous combustion, 106
 high temperatures in Paraguay, 77
 high tempertaures in Texas, 49
 high temperatures at Walt Disney Concert Hall, 85
 lightning strike twice, 213
 mist at Millau Viaduct, 43
 National Weather Service, 49
 rainstorm fish from sky, 103
 rain washed out bridge, 42
 rainwater creates sinkhole, 55
 snow on Tottori Sand Dunes, 55
 snow shark, 185
 storm revealed a 4,500-year-old forest, 144

storm leaves stranded sailor, 240
storm waves turn sea pink, 231
tornado sweeps away baby, 147
Weaver, Sigourney, 209
weddings. *See* age
Wellington International Airport, 166
Wells, Jim, 121
Wells, Juliette, 36
Westcott, Percy, 171
Whale Bone Alley, 185
WhatHoWhy, Laurence of, 93
White, Michelle, 82
Wilde, DonnaJean, 88
William, Jeremy, 119
Williams, Beth, 158
Williams, Tennessee, 93
Winslet, Kate, 133
Winter, Kimberly, 188
witches. *See* myths and legends
World Coal Carrying Championships, 27
World Dog Surfing Championship, 178
world's first writing system, 108

X

X-rays, 31
Xandiloquence "Xandi" Bizarre, 20
Xu Laifu, 164
Xue Rahey, Vivian, 23

Y

yokai. *See* myths and legends
Young, Lauren, 74
young. *See* age
Yule goats, 59

Z

Zedong, Mao, 124
Zeglen, Casimir, 105
Zeppelin, Led, 237
Zhuang, Winnie, 133
Ziqing, Liu, 31
zoos and wildlife parks
 Ayutthaya Elephant Palace and Royal Kraal, 154
 Edinburgh Zoo, 20
 Henry Doorly Zoo, 20
 Khanzir at Kabul Zoo, 12
 Khao Kheow Open Zoo, 134
 Lincolnshire Wildlife Park, 223
 Miniature Park zoo, 19
 Richmond Wildlife Center, 223
 Second Chance Wildlife Center, 33
 Woburn Safari Park, 175
ZZ Top, 209

ACKNOWLEDGMENTS

Cover Rose Audette/Shutterstock AI Generator Template/background graphics BTC Studio/Shutterstock, Natthapon Chinon/Shutterstock, hero mujahid/Shutterstock, Guki/Shutterstock, Miloje/Shutterstock, killykoon/Adobe Stock, klyaksun/Shutterstock, ESB Professional/Shutterstock, swavo/Shutterstock, javarman/Shutterstock, David Smart/Shutterstock, Heather Bridge/Shutterstock, Siam SK/Shutterstock, Juksy/Shutterstock, photolinc/Shutterstock, Wachiwit/Shutterstock, FocusStocker/Shutterstock, pics five/Shutterstock 5 (cl) Courtesy of Steven Borzachillo (@Brochetcroxet - IG, @the.cro.bro - TT), (br) Jam Press/@fedja_kot 6–7 (bkg) Triff/Shutterstock 9 (b) Randall Hill/AP Content Services for Ripley Entertainment Inc. 12–13 (dp) Lauren Edelstein 14 (c) Tavarius/Shutterstock, (bl) Captured Blinks/Shutterstock 15 (bl) Johannes Jansson/norden.org (CC BY-NC-SA 4.0), (br) dpa picture alliance archive/Alamy 16 (tl) IS MODE/Shutterstock, (br) REUTERS/Sumaya Hisham 17 (bl) Porstocker/Shutterstock, (br) Alessio Orru/Shutterstock 18 (t) imageBROKER.com/Alamy, (b) Martin Harvey/Getty, (c) Picture by Tambako the Jaguar/Getty 19 (sp, bl) REUTERS/Alexey Pavlishak 20 (tl) RZSS/Cover Images, (cl, bl, br) Courtesy of Xandiloquence Bizarre the ab3rd 20–21 (bkg) Anna Minkina/Shutterstock 21 (t) Courtesy of Heather Rios, (b, bc, br) Courtesy of Xandiloquence Bizarre the ab3rd 22 (b) Atlaspix/Alamy, (t) Anita Maric/SWNS 23 (t) Courtesy of Vivian Xue Rahey 24–25 (dp) Good Studio/Adobe 24 (t) JLMcAnally/Stockimo/Alamy, (b) Salman Arif Farooqi/Shutterstock 25 (tl) K.K.T Madhusanka/Shutterstock, (tr) Rawpixel.com/Shutterstock, (bl) Susan Edmondson/Shutterstock, (br) Galih Yoga/Adobe Stock 26 (t, cl, cr) Courtesy of Jacob Zocherman, (c) Preston Keres/The Washington Post/Getty, (bl, br) ArnaPhoto/Shutterstock 26 (bc) Nazarii M/Shutterstock, (b cl) Abimanyu hs/Shutterstock, (b c) KaterinaDesignShop/Shutterstock, (b cr) Earth_spikes/Shutterstock 27 (t) REUTERS/Lee Smith, (b) Finnbarr Webster/Getty 28 (tr) Francis Bicknell Carpenter/National Portrait Gallery via Wikimedia Commons. Public Domain., (bl) Optimum Productions/Album/Alamy 29 (cr) Glasshouse Images/Alamy, (bl) Everett Collection Inc/Alamy 31 (bl) Keystone Press/Alamy, (b) Keystone/Getty 32 (t) Wolfgang Pölzer/Alamy, (b, bl) JMx Images/Shutterstock 33 Second Chance Wildlife Center/Cover Images 34 (sp) Alex Slitz/Getty, (br) dpa picture alliance/Alamy 35 (tl, tr) World History Archive/Alamy, (br) History and Art Collection/Alamy 36 Courtesy Juliette Wells 37 (t) HASPhotos/Shutterstock, (c) Katielee Arrowsmith/SWNS, (b) dpa picture alliance/Alamy 38 (sp) Alexander Yip, (bl) Anthony Demierre, (br) Gravity Circus/SWNS 39 (cl, cr) Erica Poggianti, (br) PictureLux/The Hollywood Archive/Alamy 40 (sp) blickwinkel/Alamy, (br) Teemu Heinonen/Alamy 41 (t) Kanyshev Andrey/Shutterstock, (b) Nature Picture Library/Alamy 42–43 (t) Chris Jung/NurPhoto SRL/Alamy 43 (tr, cr) nedla/Shutterstock, (b) Iakov Filimonov/Alamy 46 Jacques Lange/Paris Match/Getty 47 (t) Joann Randles/Cover Images, (bl) Ukrinform/Alamy, (br) Ukrinform/Shutterstock 48 dpa picture alliance/Alamy 49 (c) Storm Is Me/Shutterstock, (cr) Yavuz Sariyildiz/Shutterstock 50 (sp) Courtesy of Theria Sofa 51 (t) Cynthia Lee/Alamy 52–53 (dp) Sipa USA/Alamy 52 (t) lev radin/Shutterstock 53 (t) Paul Quezada-Neiman/Alamy, (b) Imaginechina Limited/Alamy 54 Matthias Bein/dpa picture alliance/Alamy 55 (tr) REUTERS/Lawrence Bryant, (b) The Asahi Shimbun/Getty 56 (tl) PNG BOARD/Shutterstock, (bl) ARCHIVIO GBB/Alamy 57 (tl) CBW/Alamy 58 (tl, tr) Gijs Schalkx/Cover Images, (b, br) ZUMA Press, Inc./Alamy 59 (sp) Anders Tukler/Alamy, (t) Alona_S/Shutterstock, (bl) TT News Agency/Alamy 60 Matthew A. Smith - Yukon, Oklahoma 61 (t) Dr. Ben Beska, (b) Jam Press/@fedja_kot 62–63 (dp) Photo credit for Big Mac Brooch image: Jesse Hunniford, Other images: Courtesy of Artist (Emma Bugg), (b) Courtesy Kipposhi 64 Hannes Magerstaedt/Getty 65 (t) Aerial-motion/Shutterstock, (tr) Bill Anastasiou/Shutterstock, (b) Tong Yu/China News Service/VCG via Getty 66–67 (bkg) Aloshin Evgeniy/Adobe Stock, (frames) pvl0707/Adobe Stock 66 (tr) Historic Collection/Alamy, (bl) Katsushika Hokusai, artist. Clarence Buckingham Collection. Public Domain., (br) Historic Collection/Alamy 67 (tl) Historic Collection/Alamy, (tr) Sawaki Suushi, artist. Via Wikimedia Commons. Public Domain., (cr) LMA/AW/Alamy, (bl) Tsukioka Yoshitoshi, artist. Los Angeles County Museum of Art, Herbert R. Cole Collection (M.84.31.123). Public Domain. 70–71 (dp) Mirko Kuzmanovic/Shutterstock.com 70 (b) ABCDstock/Shutterstock 71 (l tr) janista/Shutterstock, (l tl) Blan-k/Shutterstock, (l cr) Erifqi Zetiawan/Freepik, (l cl) Firman santri/Shutterstock, (l br) SAMDesigning/Adobe Stock, (l bl) Freepik, (tr) Oksana Maksymova/Shutterstock 72 (sp) Courtesy of Austin Mackereth 73 (t) Jorge Ivan Vasquez C/Shutterstock, (b) Jack Appleton (@huntingforjaws) 74 Courtesy of Abstruse Art/Lauren Young 75 (t) Janina Udiljak 76–77 (t) Kareen Broodryk/Shutterstock 76 (cl) amingdesign/Shutterstock, (bl) Caio Pederneiras/Shutterstock, (br) BrazilPhotos/Alamy 77 (tr) Papilio/Alamy 78 (t) AP Photo/Michael Dinneen, (b) Michael J Stanley/Alamy 79 REUTERS/Kim Soo-hyeon 80–81 (dp) Zen Hansen @hairanthropology 80 (t bkg) ag1100/Shutterstock 82 Martin Pelanek/Shutterstock 82–83 Lukasz Pawel Szczepanski/Shutterstock 84 (sp) Austin Gibson Photography, Big Boys Photography 85 (t) Stephen Chung/Alamy, (b) Handy Handerson (Handboarder), Dan Pouliot (Photographer), James Holak (Filmer) 86 (tr) 914 collection/Alamy, (cr) Glasshouse Images/Alamy 88–89 (t) Mel Sprinkle 89 (bl) Albert Beukhof/Shutterstock, (br) Chase D'animulls/Shutterstock 90 (t) Jon Chica/Shutterstock, (b) Courtesy of Lohit Y.T./WWF-India. Credit: Chimnay. C Maliye, Naveen Iyer, Nisha BG, Asha S, Afran, Lohit Y.T 91 (sp) Clive Wells/Alamy, (cl) Pavlo Kikot/Shutterstock, (cr) MH Canals/Alamy 92 (tl) Natalllenka.m/Shutterstock, (sp) Courtesy of Bryan Sisk, The Maki Master 93 (t) REUTERS/Edgar Su 94 (t) Kadagan/Shutterstock, (b) Bambam Kumar Jha/Alamy 95 (tl) Mahi.freefly/Shutterstock, (tr) Vgbingi/Shutterstock, (c) Stacia020/Shutterstock, (bl, br) Joaquin Ossorio Castillo/Shutterstock 96 (t, tr) JULIEN DE ROSA/AFP/Getty, (bl, br) Di Caccamo A./Adobe Stock 97 (b) Erik Pendzich/Alamy, (bl) Abaca Press/Alamy 98 (tr bkg, bl bkg) Greentellect Studio/Shutterstock 100 (t) PA Images/Alamy, (c) Ian Crowder/GWSR/Cover Images 101 (sp) Reuters/Kim Kyung-Hoon, (b) Damon Coulter/SOPA Images/Sipa USA/Alamy 102–103 (t bkg) Shutterstock AI 102 (t, tr) John Angelillo/UPI/Alamy, (bl) Images & Stories/Alamy 103 (tl) Theo Wargo/Getty, (tr) Doug Peters/Alamy, (cl) Matt Crossick/Alamy, (cr) Justjojo/TheNEWS2/ZUMA Press, Inc./Alamy, (b) topseller/Shutterstock 104 (t, c) Sam Hodde/AP Images for Ripley Entertainment Inc., (c) Sam Hodde/AP Images for Ripley Entertainment Inc., (br) NASA/GRC/Jordan Salkin 105 (t l) SAMDesigningAdobe Stock, (t c) vika_k/Adobe Stock, (t r) JSalasberryAdobe Stock, (b) Sam Hodde/AP Images for Ripley Entertainment Inc. 106 Courtesy of Vivian Marie Doering www.vivianmariephoto.com 107 (t) Adrian Smith/SWNS, (bl, br) PA Images/Alamy 108 (tr, bl) Brian Cahn/ZUMA Wire/Alamy Live News 108–109 (b) Brian Cahn/ZUMA Wire/Alamy Live News 109 (t, br) Brian Cahn/ZUMA Wire/Alamy Live News, (cl, cr) Teresa Otto/Shutterstock 110 (bl) BFA/Alamy, (br) TCD/Prod.DB/Alamy 111 (cr) TCD/Prod.DB/Alamy 112 (cr, bl) TCD/Prod.DB/Alamy 113 (tl) Photo 12/Alamy, (br) TCD/Prod.DB/Alamy 115 (tr) Cinematic/Alamy, (br) AMBLIN/UNIVERSAL/Album/Alamy 116 John Nacion/Getty 117 Rachen Sageamsak/Xinhua/Alamy 118 (sp) Cris_mh/Shutterstock, (c, b) Jason Pemberton/Alamy 119 (t) Universal History Archive/Getty, (b, br) REUTERS/Kim Soo-hyeon 120 (t) JamPress/Legboot, (bl) Legboot 121 (tl, tr, cl) Legboot, (cr) JamPress/Legboot 122 (sp) Oli_of_the_valley/Shutterstock, (b) boulham/Shutterstock 123 (t) Xinhua/Alamy, (b, c) James Linsell Clark/SWNS 124 (t) saiko3p/Shutterstock, (c tl) LeaGuTravels/Shutterstock, (c tr) Hemis/Alamy, (c bl) Joshua Hawley/Shutterstock, (c br) E Pasqualli/Shutterstock, (bl) eFesenko/Alamy, (br) saiko3p/Shutterstock 125 Courtesy of Amy and John Higgins 126 (bc) KC Alfred/ZUMA Press, Inc./Alamy, (br) Trinity Mirror/Mirrorpix/Alamy 127 (bl) Gunter W Kienitz/Shutterstock, (br) jeremy sutton-hibbert/Alamy 128 David Shale/naturepl.com 129 (t) Chien Lee/Minden Pictures, (c, b) REUTERS/Eduardo Munoz 130–131 (t) Courtesy of Lynzi Judish - @lynziliving 131 (b) Courtesy of Michelle Herringer 132 (t) Yomiuri Shimbun/Associated Press, (b) Buddhika Weerasinghe/Getty 133 (t) REUTERS/Nadja Wohlleben 134 (t) Sipa USA/Alamy, (cr) Lauren DeCicca/Getty, (cl) Raphael Sane/Biosphoto/Minden, (b) Juan Aceituno/Shutterstock 135 (tl) nickeverett1981/Shutterstock, (tr) Divelvanov/Shutterstock, (c) Chien Lee/Minden, (b) Arvidas Saladauskas/Alamy 136 (t) Courtesy of Alaska Rayne Holloway, (b) Crawford County Sheriff's Office/Cover Images 137 SWNS 138 (sp) Courtesy of Joseph Kasteleiner 139 (tl) ATTA KENARE/AFP/Getty, (tr) Zunnie Kanittika/Shutterstock, (bl, bc, br) Jam Press/LOEWE, (b bkg) vveronka/Shutterstock 140 (tr) Aflo/Shutterstock, (br) CPA Media PTE Ltd/Alamy 141 (r) Hans Eworth, after Hans Holbein the Younger/Walker Art Gallery via Wikimedia Commons. Public Domain 142 REUTERS/Ahmed Saad 143 Jam Press/@selfie_pup 144 (t) Iolo ap Gwynn/Shutterstock, (cl) camera lucida environment/Alamy, (bl) PackagingMonster/Shutterstock, (br) USER/Shutterstock 145 (sp) Shaun Walker/Times-Standard via AP, (b) Acey Harper/Getty 146 (sp) Courtesy Lexie Alford, @lexielimitless 147 (t) Motoring Picture Library/Alamy, (c) Sueddeutsche Zeitung Photo/Alamy, (br) Eric Long/Smithsonian National Air and Space Museum 148–149 (dp) Pedrag Vuckovic/Red Bull Content Pool 149 (tr) Joerg Mitter/Red Bull Content Pool, (b) Naim Chidiac/Red Bull Content Pool 150 (t) Nature's Charm/Shutterstock, (b) Sailingstone Travel/Alamy, (br) Judy Waytiuk/Alamy 151 (tl, tr) Courtesy of David C. Blackburn, (b) Paul Starosta/Getty 152 (tl) Smith Archive/Alamy 153 (bl) Trinity Mirror/Mirrorpix/Alamy, (br) Daily Mirror/Mirrorpix/Getty 154 (t) AP Photo/Nathathaida Adireksara, (b) Daniel Briem/Shutterstock 155 (t) Valeria Mongelli/Anadolu/Getty, (bl) TOMO/Shutterstock, (br) toomtamgeo/Shutterstock 156 (tl) Jose Miguel Sanchez/Shutterstock, (tc) jummie/Adobe Stock, (tr, c tl) b-hide the scene/Shutterstock, (c) BGStock72/Adobe Stock, (c tr) Kitinut Jinapuck/Shutterstock, (c bl) Ummi Hassian/Shutterstock, (c br) Mystic Stock Photography/Shutterstock, (bl) Aldelo Piomica/Shutterstock, (bc) ahmad.faizal/Shutterstock, (br) Morumotto/Shutterstock 157 (tl) Kurka Geza Corey/Shutterstock, (tr) PixelBiss/Shutterstock, (b) Adriana Iacob/Shutterstock 158 (bkg) GOLDMAN99/Shutterstock, (sp) Courtesy of Beth Williams and Mattia Truppi 159 (t) Poozeum 160–161 (t) CHiPa @CHIPA.INSTA 160 (bl) Nicola Pulham/Shutterstock, (br) Alexey Fedorenko/Shutterstock 161 (tr) TIZIANA FABI/AFP/Getty, (cr) Only Fabrizio/Shutterstock, (bl) trabantos/Shutterstock, (bc) Takashi Images/Shutterstock, (br) Andy Soloman/Shutterstock 162–163 (dp) Linda Dunham Photography 163 (tl) Michael Palmer Photography - www.michaelpalmer.com, (tr) John Young/YoungMedia.co.uk, courtesy of Maddox Cottle Dock, (c) Linda Dunham Photography 164 (t) Andrew Lichtenstein//Corbis/Getty, (c) Jeff Bachner/New York Daily News/Tribune News Service/Getty, (b) drumspots.com, @drumspots 165 Courtesy Zara Hoogenraad 166–167 (t) Stephen Barker/Shutterstock 166 (c) Wirestock Creators/Shutterstock, (b) Gareth Andrews/SWNS 167 (cr) jon lyall/Shutterstock 168 (bl) Nataly23/Shutterstock 170 Christian Ziegler/Minden Pictures 171 (t) Courtesy of Barbi Agostini, James Kane, Let's Get Magnetic, (b) Stan Tess/Alamy, (bl) Rachel Rose/Alamy 172 (tr) Studio ART/Shutterstock, (sp) Courtesy of Steven Borzachillo (@Brochetcroxet - IG, @the.cro.bro - TT) 173 (t) Shana Everson, (bl) NASA, (bc) NASA/Kim Shiflett, (br) Helga_creates/Shutterstock 174 (sp) James McCauley/Alamy, (bl, br) Grant Rooney/Alamy 175 (t) Woburn Safari Park, UK, (b) Jam Press/@Ivan_Karpitski 176 (t) History and Art Collection/Alamy, (bl) Douglas Miller/Getty, (br) Keystone/Getty 177 (t) BNA Photographic/Alamy, (c) Evans/Getty, (b) Evans/Three Lions/Getty 178 (c) AP Photo/Eakin Howard, (bl) San Francisco Chronicle via AP, (br) Photo by Liu Guanguan/China News Service/VCG via AP 179 (t) Alamy, (tr) Operation 2023/Alamy, (b) Giulio Ercolani/Alamy, (bl) SiposM/Shutterstock 180 (tr) ShutterstockProfessional/Shutterstock, (bl) Everett Collection/Shutterstock 182 (t) Richard Whitecombe/Shutterstock, (c) Chronicle/Alamy 183 (r) Brian Minkoff/Shutterstock, (b) ANL/Shutterstock, (c) BBA Photography/Shutterstock 184 Media Drum World/Alamy 185 (t) Lynne2509/Shutterstock, (tc) imageBROKER.com/Alamy, (b) Underwood Archives, Inc/Alamy 186 (sp) Courtesy of Monica Patten, (tr) Heritage Image Partnership Ltd /Alamy, (bkg br) walter_g/Shutterstock 187 (tl) Margaret Jone Wollman/Shutterstock, (t cl) ORLY Design/Shutterstock, (t cr) Martial Red/Shutterstock, (tr) Margaret Jone Wollman/Shutterstock, (cr) Musée Carnavalet via Look and Learn History Picture Archive. Public Domain. 188 (t) REUTERS/Luis Cortes, (c) Isaac Esquivel/EPA-EFE/Shutterstock, (b) GARI GARAIALDE/AFP/Getty 189 (sp, b) Guy Corbishley/Alamy, (bl) Marina/Adobe Stock 190–191 (dp) Marcel Strelow/Alamy 190 (t) Marcel_Strelow/Shutterstock, (c) Nature Picture Library/Alamy 194–195 (dp) REUTERS/Napat Wesshasartar 194 (bl) Panther Media GmbH/Alamy 195 (tr) Wang Teng/Xinhua/Alamy, (b) Benny Trapp/Adobe Stock 196 (t) P A Thompson/Getty, (b) Shae Fischer/Shutterstock, (cr) Jon Osumi/Shutterstock 197 (sp) Courtesy of Casey M. Severn, (b bkg) Inga Linder/Shutterstock 198 (sp) Michel Seelen/Shutterstock, (tr) Milton Cogheil/Alamy, (c) Tomasz Klejdysz/Shutterstock 199 (tl) Antoni Margalida/Ivan Almirall, (tr) Wirestock Creators/Shutterstock 200 (tr, cl, br) AP Photo/Mindaugas Kulbis, (bl) Svetlana Monyakova/Shutterstock 201 (tl) Mehmet Cetin/Shutterstock, (br) Jam Press Vid/Brittany Lacayo 202 (t) blickwinkel/Alamy, (cl) Ernst Haider/Alamy, (cr) Premaphotos/naturepl.com, (b) Las Vegas Metropolitan Police Department via AP 203 (cl, cr) OLI SCARFF/AFP/Getty, (b) Fabio de Paola/Shutterstock 204 (tl) LC-B2- 2772-9 [P&P], Library of Congress. Public Domain. 205 (tl) UPI/Alamy 206 (l) Nature Picture Library/Alamy, (r) Adrian Davies/naturepl.com 207 (t) Katja Schulz via Flickr (CC BY 2.0), (c) Robert Thompson/naturepl.com, (b) Alen thien/Shutterstock 208 (t) Anthony Shaw/Alamy, (cl) PATRICIA DE MELO MOREIRA/AFP/Getty, (b) Joaquin Gomez Sastre/NurPhoto via AP 209 Courtesy of Irina Gvozdenko 210 (t) Mike Bennett, (b) Courtesy of Jacques Monneraud 211 Daniel Dayment/SWNS 212 (t) Scott Olson/Getty, (cr) Tyler Pasciak LaRiviere/Chicago Sun-Times via AP 213 (tl, cl) Marta Kuzniar/Alamy, (cr) JORDANLUCA/Cover Images 214 Courtesy of Milly Bampini 215 Courtesy of Samantha Van de Sompel (Anxious Fish Club) 218 (t, cr, b) Narayan Maharjan/NurPhoto SRL/Alamy, (cl) Narayan Maharjan/Pacific Press Media Production Corp./Alamy 219 (t, c) Cristiano Minichiello/Agf/Shutterstock, (br) AP Photo/Aleksandar Furtula 220 (tl) Onix_Art/Shutterstock, (tr) Qin Gang/Xinhua/Alamy, (b) Sally Anderson News/Alamy 221 (tl) Tao Liang/Xinhua/Alamy, (tr) Xinhua/Shutterstock, (cl) Andrew Lichtenstein/Corbis/Getty, (bl) SOPA Images Limited/Alamy, (bl) Stephanie Keith 100584/Getty 222 (sp) Imago/Alamy, (t) PJF Military Collection/Alamy, (c) UPI/Alamy 223 (t) REUTERS/Sarah Meyssonnier, (b) nwdph/Shutterstock, (bc) MONGO Via Wikimedia Commons (CC BY-SA 3.0) 226 (sp) Courtesy of Lucie Radcliffe, (tl) OLEG525/Shutterstock 227 (tl) Personnel of NOAA Ship PISCES, (tr) Blue Planet Archive LLC/Alamy, (cr) YUNOSUKE/Shutterstock, (b tl) OLIVEIA/Shutterstock, (b tr) Dashikka/Shutterstock, (bc) Prachova Nataliia/Shutterstock, (b bl) AVA AVA/Shutterstock, (b bc) 4LUCK/Shutterstock, (b br) NadzeyaShanchuk/Shutterstock 228–229 (t) Nathaniel Noir/Alamy 229 (tc, tr) PA Images/Alamy, (bl) Avalon.red/Alamy, (br) piemags/nature/Alamy 230 Matteo Mocellin/Red Bull Content Pool 231 (t) Chris Mattison/Alamy, (b) GaiBru_Photo/Alamy 232 SWNS 233 (tl, c) Sandra Deskins/SWNS 234–235 (dp) Phoscar/Shutterstock 234 (t) Eileen Kumpf/Shutterstock 235 (t) Avillfoto/Shutterstock, (c) Georgios Tsichlis/Shutterstock 236 (t, bl, br) Yadid Levy/Alamy, (cl) doidam10/Adobe Stock 237 (l) claudia beretta/Alamy, (r) Jana Janina/Shutterstock 238 (sp) Louis Cardozo, (tc) Meda01/Shutterstock 239 (t) Courtesy of Matthew Drottz 240 (b) Nasser Berzane/Abaca Press/Alamy, (bc) MAXPP/Alamy 240–241 (dp) Ievgen Skrypko/Alamy 241 (t) omihay/Shutterstock 242 (tl) Abrastack Stu Design/Adobe Stock, (cl) NSP-RF/Alamy, (bl) Eng Wah Teo/Alamy, (br) MaximKreiderman/Shutterstock 243 (t) Jan Bures/Shutterstock, (c) Wildnerdpix/Shutterstock, (bl) Levente Vajó/Alamy, (br) Salparadis/Shutterstock 244 (t, cl) REUTERS/Borut Zivulovic, (cr) Ryan M. Kelly/Getty 244–245 (dp) Ryan M. Kelly/Getty 245 (tl) 2001 Shutterstock, (tr) David Tipling Photo Library/Alamy, (br) Ryan M. Kelly/Getty

Key: t = top, b = bottom, c = center, l = left, r = right, sp = single page, dp = double page

All other photos are from Ripley Entertainment, Inc. Every attempt has been made to acknowledge correctly and contact copyright holders and we apologize in advance for any unintentional errors or omissions, which will be corrected in future editions.

SEEK THE STRANGE & FIND THE FUN!

Discover the world of Ripley's at more than 100 exciting attractions in 9 countries!

Amsterdam The Netherlands
Blackpool England
Branson Missouri
Cancún Mexico
Cavendish Beach Canada
Copenhagen Denmark
Gatlinburg Tennessee
Genting Highlands Malaysia
Grand Prairie Texas
Guadalajara Mexico
Hollywood California
Mexico City Mexico
Myrtle Beach South Carolina
Newport Oregon
Niagara Falls Canada
Ocean City Maryland
Orlando Florida
Panama City Beach Florida
Pattaya Thailand
Playa Del Carmen Mexico
San Antonio Texas
San Francisco California
St. Augustine Florida
Surfers Paradise Australia
Veracruz Mexico
Wildwood New Jersey
Williamsburg Virginia
Wisconsin Dells Wisconsin

Follow your curiosity and open your mind with weird and wonderful stories at Ripleys.com or connect with us on social media!

@ripleysbelieveitornot @ripleysbelieveitornot @ripleysbelieveitornot @ripleysbelieveitornot @ripleys @ripleys

SCAN to Plan Your Adventure!